Smart Tax Tips

Grant Thornton

Smart Tax Tips

Winning Strategies to Reduce Your Taxes

Updated for 2010, over 180 tax and RRSP tips

KEY PORTER BOOKS

We have made every effort to ensure the information included in this text is accurate, but no publication should be used as a substitute for competent professional advice in implementing tax-planning decisions. We invite our readers to contact any Grant Thornton office across Canada to meet with a tax adviser to discuss their specific tax situation.

Readers should be aware that the commentary in this book is based on the Income Tax Act *and all pending draft legislation and regulations issued by the Department of Finance as of June 30, 2009. Post-publication changes may have a material effect on the recommendations in this book. Please consult your tax adviser to learn of relevant changes to the legislation.*

Key Porter Books Limited
Six Adelaide Street East, Tenth Floor
Toronto, Ontario
Canada, M5C 1H6

Grant Thornton LLP
50 Bay Street, twelfth Floor
Toronto, Ontario
Canada, M5J 2S8

www.keyporter.com

Electronic formatting: Alison Carr

Printed and bound in Canada

09 10 11 12 13 5 4 3 2 1

CONTENTS

Top 10 Smart Tax Tips 6

Acknowledgements 8

Introduction 9

Reader's Guide 11

SECTION 1: Businesses 13

SECTION 2: Individuals 95

SECTION 3: Investors 219

SECTION 4: Everyone 259

Tax Calendar 279

Tables 282

Grant Thornton LLP Offices 300

Abbreviations 304

Glossary 305

Index 311

TOP 10 SMART TAX TIPS

1. **Maximize your RRSP contributions.** Amounts contributed to your RRSP (or a spousal RRSP) are deductible from your income. As well, tax is deferred on all amounts earned inside the RRSP until amounts are withdrawn from the plan (see articles 64 and 65). Also, after age 71, you can still make contributions to a spousal RRSP if you've earned income and your spouse or common-law partner is not yet 71 years old (see article 63).
2. **Split pension income with your spouse or common-law partner.** If you're receiving income that qualifies for the pension income tax credit (see article 100) and you're in a higher tax bracket than your spouse or common-law partner, consider allocating to them up to half your pension income (see article 79).
3. **Consider an income-splitting loan.** With current interest rates at fairly low levels, you might want to consider an income-splitting loan to your spouse. The current low rate will remain in effect for as long as the loan is outstanding—even if rates increase in the future (see article 119).
4. **Establish a Registered Disability Savings Plan.** If you are disabled or have a disabled dependant, consider setting up a registered disability savings plan. One of the benefits is that the government will also make contributions to the plan (see article 121). To qualify, the beneficiary of the plan must be entitled to the disability tax credit (see article 90).
5. **Implement a freeze or refreeze of your capital property.** Has the value of your company or investments declined in value? If so, an estate freeze or refreeze is a popular method of reducing your tax liability. If you've already undertaken an estate freeze, now may be the time to implement a refreeze (see article 140).
6. **Split income with your spouse or common-law partner and children.** There are many advantages to paying reasonable wages to family members for actual services rendered. Also, when incorporating a business, consider income splitting by including your spouse or common-law partner and adult children as shareholders. Benefits can also be obtained by

including a family trust as a corporate shareholder (see articles 5, 123 and 124).

7. **Save your receipts for your children's physical activity programs.** If you have children who were under the age of 16 at the beginning of 2008, and who were involved in physical activity programs, you may be eligible to claim a tax credit on your tax return (see article 107).
8. **Realize losses to offset gains.** If you have capital gains in the year and have accrued losses on other investments, consider selling your losing investments before year-end. Make sure the settlement date is before December 31, 2009 (see article 151).
9. **Consider the optimal compensation from your company.** If you are the owner-manager of a Canadian-controlled private corporation (CCPC), you need to determine the optimal amount of salary or dividends to receive from your company (see article 32). Consult with your tax adviser to consider the various factors, including whether the dividend should be designated as an eligible dividend (see article 153).
10. **Contribute to a Tax-Free Savings Account (TFSA).** If you have money available for saving, you can contribute up to $5,000 per year (indexed to the nearest $500) to a TFSA. You will not obtain a tax deduction for the contributions, but the income earned in your TFSA is tax-free and all withdrawals are tax-free (see article 78).

ACKNOWLEDGEMENTS

Karen would like to acknowledge her colleagues—chartered accountants and tax specialists across Canada—for their invaluable contributions to this edition. For more information on how to contact our offices, visit our website at **www.GrantThornton.ca**.

Contributions have been made by:
Gary Dent, National Tax Partner
Karen Yull, National
Patricia Allain, Saint John
Nathalie Amirault, Halifax
Zora Booker, Vancouver
Bill Budgell, St. John's
Kathleen Comeau, Montreal
Brett Crawford, Markham
Robin Cyna, National
Marilyn Hayre, Moncton
Renee Higginbotham, Charlottetown
Ellen Kim, Edmonton
Kyle McMurtry, Winnipeg
Janet Newcombe, National
Alan Roth, National

INTRODUCTION

Most of us are not sure where to start when it comes to tax planning. It requires an understanding of Canada's Income Tax Act, tax court rulings, and the bulletins, circulars and rulings put out by the Canada Revenue Agency (CRA).

That's why Grant Thornton LLP, a leading Canadian firm of chartered accountants, management consultants and business advisers, developed *Smart Tax Tips*. This insightful, easy-to-understand book cuts through the confusion to provide helpful advice on taxes and Canada's tax rules. It presents the information you need for your personal or business tax planning in a quick and easy-to-find format. Our smart tips will save you time, money and worry—at tax time and throughout the year.

Smart Tax Tips is a product of the knowledge and experience of the tax experts at Grant Thornton LLP. Whether you are a business owner, an employee, an investor, a retiree or anyone else who needs tax help, *Smart Tax Tips* will help you understand the tax environment in Canada and give you the knowledge to discuss with your tax adviser the "how" and "why" of your tax situation.

This edition includes some new tax tips and a few new topics, including a section on the new Tax-Free Savings Account (TFSA). It also comments on many of the new measures introduced in the 2009 federal budget, including the new temporary Home Renovation Tax Credit.

And last but not least, if you want some quick guidance in developing your tax strategy for the upcoming year, check the Grant Thornton **Top 10 Smart Tax Tips** at the beginning of this book.

READER'S GUIDE

At more than 2,000 pages, the Income Tax Act presents a daunting challenge even to those familiar with Canada's tax system. Few people have hours—let alone days—to pore over its contents in search of information that relates to their circumstances. That's why we designed *Smart Tax Tips* to help you get to the heart of the matter and provide you with sound, useful information. Here's how to get the most out of this publication.

The book is set up in such as way that whatever your situation and your questions might be, you can easily find an answer and appropriate guidance. It is not primarily intended as a beginning-to-end read.

First, there is a comprehensive index that allows you to quickly find the items relevant to your search. It will point you to whichever of the 183 articles that may be of interest to you.

Second, many of the articles include examples—a sample calculation or a typical scenario—to help you better understand how the rules work.

Third, we feature a **Top 10 Smart Tax Tips** list that highlights some of the more important aspects of strategic tax planning—each one cross-referenced to the relevant articles.

And finally, we offer this book's reason for being—the tax tips themselves. They can help you reduce your taxes and also avoid costly tax pitfalls that can arise through inadequate tax planning.

Of course, with a publication this size, it is impossible to include every tax rule in Canada. What we have attempted to do is to cover the most common situations and the everyday rules that have implications for most people's business and/or personal finances. However, *Smart Tax Tips* should not be seen as a substitute for competent professional tax advice. Tax planning is a complex process that must be related to your particular circumstances.

What this book *can* do is familiarize you with the Canadian tax landscape to furnish you with an important resource: the knowledge to confidently discuss your tax status with your professional tax adviser.

There is no need to be intimidated when it comes to tax rules. Understanding them is the first step. To that end, we trust you will find this book beneficial. To keep up with ever-changing tax regulations and rates year-round, visit the Grant Thornton website at **www.GrantThornton.ca**.

SECTION 1

Businesses

IN THIS SECTION

1 Are You Self-Employed?
2 Your Year-End
3 Taxing Partnership Income
4 Which Province Gets Your Tax?
5 Paying Your Spouse or Common-Law Partner and/or Children
6 Employment Insurance and Family Members
7 Calculating Depreciation
8 Amortization and Sale of Eligible Capital Property
9 The Home Office
10 Paying Your Dues
11 Meals and Entertainment Expenses
12 Convention Expenses
13 Canada Pension Plan Contributions
14 Deduction of Health/Dental Insurance Premiums
15 Wage-Loss Replacement Plans
16 Deduction of Life Insurance Premiums
17 Deduction of Fines and Penalties
18 Valuation of Inventory
19 Instalment Sales
20 Tax Treatment of Lease-Option Arrangements
21 Operating Losses and Prior Years' Taxes
22 Apprenticeship Job Creation Tax Credit
23 Investment Tax Credit for Childcare Spaces
24 To Incorporate or Not to Incorporate
25 Incorporating Your Professional Practice
26 Integration
27 The Small-Business Deduction
28 Capital Dividend Account
29 Federal Capital Tax
30 Associated-Company Rules
31 Salaries and Bonuses to Shareholders
32 Salary versus Dividends
33 Salary Deferral Arrangements
34 Directors' Fees
35 Loans from Your Corporation
36 Corporate Losses and Change of Control
37 Taxable Benefits
38 Employee Loans
39 Personal Use of a Company-Owned Automobile
40 Automobile Expenses
41 Tax-Free Travel Allowances
42 The Score on Stock Options
43 Qualified Scientific Research Expenditures
44 Shareholder Agreements
45 Reporting System for Contractors
46 Farming Businesses
47 Fishing Businesses
48 Transfer Pricing
49 Thin Capitalization Rules
50 Interest Deduction for Investments in Foreign Affiliates
51 Withholding Tax on Interest Payments
52 Withholding Tax for Non-Resident Actors
53 Payments to Non-Residents for Services Rendered in Canada

IN THIS SECTION

54 The Goods on the GST/HST

55 GST/HST Registration, Collection and Remittance

56 Input Tax Credits

57 GST/HST and Automobiles

58 GST/HST and Real Property Sales

59 GST/HST and Buying and Selling a Business

Every business owner—from a sole proprietor to the owner of a multimillion-dollar business—knows that sound tax planning is vital to a healthy bottom line. As every successful business owner also knows, expert professional tax advice is essential to ensure tax strategies are on track.

Understanding how the tax rules work and how they might apply to your particular business circumstance will go a long way toward helping you work more effectively with your tax adviser to develop both short- and long-term planning strategies.

This section contains a number of tax tips that address the most common tax situations likely to affect your business operations. Many of the items pertain to all businesses—from sole proprietorships to corporations—whereas others are specific to corporations.

This section includes information about the various deductions allowed, and also what you need to know about the Goods and Services Tax (GST) and the Harmonized Sales Tax (HST).

As well, this section covers the rules on eligible expenses—what you can and cannot deduct, whether it's the cost of business entertainment or operating a vehicle. Other features include taxable benefits, depreciation, home office expenses, inventory issues, business losses, farm businesses and much more.

1 Are You Self-Employed?

If you are self-employed, you have many more options for tax planning than if you are an employee. Therefore, it makes a lot of economic sense to clearly establish whether you are an employee or self-employed. Determining whether you are self-employed or employed is not always cut and dried. It depends on your particular circumstances, and often comes down to how much control the person paying for your services exercises over your work.

For example, if a person (or a company) controls your work hours and where you perform the work, and provides all the equipment, supplies and office help you need, you are likely an employee. On the other hand, if you provide services to a number of different parties and are in a position to prioritize their demands, you will likely be considered self-employed.

The Canada Revenue Agency (CRA) has published a guide to assist in determining employed versus self-employed status. A copy of this guide (RC4110—Employee or Self-Employed?) can be found on the CRA's website at **www.cra-arc.gc.ca** (see Forms and Publications).

2 Your Year-End

Current rules

Since 1995, all sole proprietors, certain partnerships and all professional corporations that are members of affected partnerships must have a December 31 year-end.

Partnerships affected by this rule include those in which at least one member is an individual, a professional corporation or another partnership subject to this rule. (A professional corporation is any corporation that carries on the professional practice of an accountant, dentist, lawyer, medical doctor, veterinarian or chiropractor.)

You may be able to opt out

There is an option that allows you to use a non-calendar year-end. Under this "alternative method," your self-employed business income is determined using a pro-rata formula that adjusts to a calendar-year basis any income earned during the fiscal period. However, be aware that this method may result in greater swings of income from year to year. The way the formula works, income will often be higher in a good year and lower in a poor year. This can result in moving income from a low-tax-bracket year to a higher-tax-bracket year.

If you are starting a new business and would like to use a non–December 31 year-end, you are strongly urged to contact your tax adviser to determine your eligibility and whether this strategy is of any advantage to you. However, once a December 31 fiscal year-end has been adopted, you cannot revert to the alternative method.

3 Taxing Partnership Income

As a member of a partnership, you must report your share of the partnership's profit or loss for the fiscal period ending in 2009. While you can normally claim your share of partnership losses against your other sources of income, this may not always be the case if you are a member of a limited partnership (see article 163).

The allocation of partnership income or losses is normally left up to the partners to resolve. However, if the tax department determines that the allocation is unreasonable, it may disallow your allocation and substitute what it considers to be a more reasonable one. For example, if you provide the capital and do most of the work in your business, while your spouse contributes significantly less, you could be reassessed to disallow a 50:50 allocation of the business's income between the two of you.

Deductible expenses

Certain expenses incurred outside the partnership may also be deductible.

If you borrowed money to invest in the partnership, the interest on that loan is generally deductible. In a significant court case, *The Queen v. Singleton*, the taxpayer was a partner in a law firm and withdrew funds from his capital account in the firm to finance the purchase of a house. The same day, he borrowed money to replace the funds in his partnership's capital account. The Minister of National Revenue attempted to deny the interest deduction on the grounds that the borrowed money was used to finance the purchase of the house and was not a business investment. Significantly, the Supreme Court determined that the interest on the borrowed funds should be deductible.

As long as a direct link can be drawn between the borrowed money and an eligible use, a taxpayer should be entitled to deduct the relevant interest payments from his income. The CRA has since accepted this position (see Interpretation Bulletin IT-533, paragraph 15, which specifically accepts the result in *Singleton* and states that "a taxpayer may restructure borrowings and the ownership of assets to meet the direct use test").

A recent Supreme Court of Canada decision, *Lipson v. The Queen*, has also confirmed that taxpayers can arrange or rearrange their affairs such that capital is used to purchase personal assets and borrowed funds are used to purchase income-producing assets, thereby preserving the deductibility of interest (also see article 160). You should contact your tax adviser to review your situation and determine the best strategy to make your interest tax deductible.

Any expenses that you personally incur in the course of carrying on the partnership business (e.g., promotional and automobile expenses) are also deductible. However, meal and entertainment expenses are only partially deductible (see article 11), and some automobile expenses may be limited (see article 40).

Requirement to file an information return

The Income Tax Act and Regulations provide that all Canadian partnerships, or partnerships carrying on business in Canada, are required to file a partnership information return. However, the CRA administratively exempts certain partnerships from this filing requirement. Specifically, a partnership with up to five partners is not required to file the prescribed information return (T5013) unless one of the partners is another partnership. In September 2008, the CRA stated that it is considering a change to its administrative policy to also require a T5013 for each fiscal period of a partnership that has one or more partners that is a corporation or trust. Given this potential change, you should check the CRA's current administrative position before completing any filings for the 2009 or subsequent years.

TAX TIP

The penalties for not filing a return can be considerable. If you have never filed a partnership return in the past, you should check with your tax adviser to determine if you are now subject to this filing requirement.

Even though T5013 filing may not administratively be required, it's still a good idea to file the Partnership Information Return. This will start the clock running on the limitation period for reassessments.

4 Which Province Gets Your Tax?

Employment and investment income are both taxed by the province in which you reside on December 31. This is the case even if the income was earned in another province. Business income, on the other hand, is taxed in the province where the business was conducted. If you carry on the same business through a permanent establishment in more than one province, a complicated formula is used to determine what portion of your business income is taxable in each province. This is best left to your tax adviser's expertise.

EXAMPLE/**Income allocation**

In general, business income is allocated to each province based on the pro-rata share of the total revenue earned and salaries and wages paid to employees in the province. Assume you have net business income of $200,000. Your head office is in Ontario, and there is a sales office in Alberta. Each office has one employee earning $40,000 per year. If $200,000 in revenue was generated in Ontario and $300,000 in Alberta, the business income would be allocated as follows:

	Revenue ($)	(%)	Wages ($)	(%)
Ontario	200,000	40	40,000	50
Alberta	300,000	60	40,000	50
Total	500,000	100	80,000	100

Therefore, the business income taxable in Ontario would be \$90,000 [200,000 × (40% + 50%) ÷ 2] and \$110,000 [200,000 × (60% + 50%) ÷ 2] would be taxable in Alberta.

TAX TIP

Unless you earn self-employed business income (see above), provincial tax is based on your province of residence on December 31. If you are transferring to a province with a lower tax rate, you should consider accelerating your departure to arrive before the end-of-year deadline. Conversely, if a move to a province with a higher tax rate is in your future, consider postponing your relocation until after the year-end.

5 Paying Your Spouse or Common-Law Partner and/or Children

Salaries paid to your spouse or common-law partner and/or children are tax deductible to your business as long as the wages are reasonable in relation to the services they have provided. As a rule, salaries are considered reasonable if they are representative of an amount that would be paid to an arm's-length party for similar services—in other words, comparable to what you would pay an unrelated employee to do the same job.

TAX TIP

There are many advantages to paying reasonable wages to family members for actual services rendered. A key benefit is that salaries will be taxed in their hands, and probably at rates lower than your marginal tax rate. This arrangement will also allow them to make their own RRSP and CPP contributions.

6 Employment Insurance and Family Members

For family businesses, Employment Insurance (EI) premiums can constitute a considerable expense. There are various exemptions from having to remit EI premiums. For example, if you own more than

40% of the voting shares of a corporation, your employment is not subject to EI premiums. There is another exemption for employees who deal at "non-arm's length" with their employer. The problem with this rule is that there is another rule stating that two related persons are deemed to deal with each other at "arm's length" if the circumstances of the employment are substantially similar to what they would be if an unrelated person were to perform the same job. In other words, if a person not related to you would have been offered the same pay and work arrangements as those provided to your family member for the same services, you generally must withhold EI premiums from the salary paid to your relative.

Consult your professional adviser to determine if there is any way you can structure the employment to justify EI-exempt status.

TAX TIP

If your spouse or common-law partner or other family members are currently employed by you (or your company), review the conditions surrounding their employment to determine if Employment Insurance premiums are required—you could be eligible for a refund.

7 Calculating Depreciation

The cost of a capital asset is generally not deductible as an expense. However, you can depreciate certain business assets for tax purposes. The tax term for such depreciation is "capital cost allowance" (CCA).

Depreciable assets are grouped into classes according to their type and use. There are more than 40 different classes, each with its own rate of depreciation. For example, office equipment and furniture are depreciated at a rate of 20% per annum, automobiles are depreciated at 30%, and any building acquired after 1987 is generally depreciated at 4%.

In some circumstances, due to rapid technological change, the CCA system does not adequately reflect the actual reduction in an asset's value. Nowadays, it is not uncommon for some equipment to become obsolete before being fully depreciated for income tax purposes. Recent federal budgets have introduced several changes to CCA rates to better reflect the useful life of assets. The following are some of the more significant examples:

(1) Manufacturing and processing (M&P) machinery and equipment that would otherwise qualify for a 30% CCA rate under Class 43 will, for a limited time, qualify for an accelerated write-off. Eligible purchases acquired after March 18, 2007, and before 2012 will qualify for a 50% straight-line accelerated CCA rate and will be placed in Class 29.

(2) Buildings acquired after March 18, 2007, and used for M&P in Canada, qualify for a CCA rate of 10% as opposed to 4%. To claim the 10% rate, at least 90% of the floor space must be used in manufacturing or processing in Canada. Other non-residential buildings acquired after March 18, 2007, that are not used 90% for M&P may qualify for a CCA rate of 6% as opposed to 4%. To claim the higher CCA rate, the taxpayer must elect to include the building in a separate prescribed class (Class 1). This election is made by attaching a letter to the taxpayer's income tax return for the tax year in which the building is acquired.

(3) For purchases after March 18, 2007, the CCA rate for computer hardware and systems software increased from 45% to 55%. Such purchases are placed in new Class 50. However, for computer hardware and systems software purchases after January 27, 2009, and before February 1, 2011, there is a temporary CCA rate of 100%. The equipment will not be subject to the half-year rule (see below) in the year of acquisition, thereby permitting a full write-off of the equipment in the year of acquisition. These purchases are included in Class 52.

Most classes of assets are depreciated on a declining-balance basis. The following chart depicts some of the more common CCA classes and their applicable CCA rates.

Class	Rate	Description
1	4%/6%/10%	Buildings acquired after 1987, including component parts (see above for CCA rate)
3	5%	Buildings acquired before 1988 and alterations thereto, subject to a limit
6	10%	Fences, greenhouses, wood buildings without footings below ground level
8	20%	Property not included in any other class, such as accessories, equipment, furniture, photocopiers, telephones, tools costing more than $500, outdoor advertising panels
10	30%	Automobiles, panel trucks, trucks, tractors, trailers; computer equipment and related operating systems software acquired before March 23, 2004
10.1	30%	Passenger vehicles, the cost of which to the taxpayer is equal to or exceeds a prescribed amount ($30,000 + GST/HST + PST since 2001)
12	100%	Computer software (but not including systems software), small tools costing less than $500, cutlery, linen, uniforms, moulds, medical instruments costing less than $500, videos for rental
16	40%	Taxi cabs, automobiles acquired for the purpose of short-term rental, coin-operated video games
17	8%	Parking areas or similar surface construction
29 or 43	50% straight line or 30%	Equipment used for manufacturing and processing (see above for applicable Class and CCA rate)
50	55%	Computer equipment and related operating systems software acquired after March 18, 2007
52	100% (no half-year rule)	Computer equipment and related operating systems acquired after January 27, 2009 and before February 1, 2010

How to calculate

The amount of depreciation you can claim for a year is determined by multiplying the remaining balance in the asset class by the specified percentage rate for that specific class. The remaining balance, referred to as the undepreciated capital cost (UCC), is calculated on a continuous basis.

Each year (subject to the available-for-use rules—see below), you add the cost of assets acquired in the year to the previous year's closing balance. If you have disposed of an asset, you subtract the proceeds up to the original cost of the asset.

The half-year rule

Most depreciable assets are subject to a rule that reduces the maximum depreciation claim in the year of purchase to half the net additions made to the specified class. This "half-year" rule does not apply to the acquisition of certain capital property, such as tools costing less than $500 each and computer equipment and related systems software acquired after January 27, 2009 and before February 1, 2010. Such assets can be written off 100% in the year of purchase.

EXAMPLE/**Sample depreciation**

Assume that you purchased some equipment in November 2009 for use in your consulting business. Its total cost was $8,000. The equipment would be placed in Class 8 and depreciated at a rate of 20% per year, subject to the half-year rule. The CCA claim in 2009 and following years would be as follows:

Year	Opening UCC	CCA (20%)	Closing UCC
2009	8,000*	800**	7,200
2010	7,200	1,440	5,760
2011	5,760	1,152	4,608

*This is the cost of additions for the year 2009.
**CCA rate for 2009 is 10% (20% × 1/2). The half-year rule applies in the year of purchase.

In calculating your business income for 2009, you may claim any amount up to $800 as CCA. You may claim a lesser amount if you want, in which case your opening UCC balance for 2010 would increase accordingly.

Available-for-use rules

The available-for-use rules determine the taxation year in which an amount can first be claimed for depreciation and whether the half-year rule will apply. Rules with respect to the acquisition, construction and/or renovation of a building are especially complex. It's best to ask your tax adviser about this before making a decision. However, the general rule is that property may be depreciated for tax purposes at the date it is first used to earn income, or the second taxation year following the year of acquisition, whichever is earlier.

The maximum depreciation claim may also be reduced for short taxation years. Generally, if the fiscal period of your business is less than 12 months, the depreciation you are entitled to claim is prorated based on the number of days in your fiscal period. However, a few classes of assets are excluded from this rule. Again, it's best to let your tax adviser assess whether it applies.

TAX TIP

You should be aware that the CCA rate, multiplied by the UCC of a particular class of assets, represents the maximum amount of depreciation that can be claimed. You do not have to claim the maximum depreciation in any particular year. For example, if your business is in a loss position, you may decide that you do not want to claim depreciation for that particular year.

Special rules and restrictions

Some depreciation restrictions apply to rental property (see article 143). Others apply to depreciation claims arising from certain "tax shelters" in which the investor is not active in the day-to-day operations of the business. Depreciation claims by taxpayers who lease certain types of property are also subject to certain rules. Since the rules do not apply to all leasing properties, your tax adviser is in the best position to determine if you are affected by these rules.

8 Amortization and Sale of Eligible Capital Property

Eligible capital property can be broadly described as intangible capital property. This includes such things as goodwill and other "nothings," the cost of which neither qualifies for capital cost allowance (see article 7) nor is deductible in the year of its acquisition as a current expense.

For example, if you purchase goodwill (the intangible value of a business, such as a recognized name and reputation), you are permitted to depreciate (or amortize) three-quarters of its cost on a declining-balance basis at the rate of 7%. When the goodwill is sold, three-quarters of the proceeds are credited to the unamortized pool at the time of sale and, if the balance of the pool becomes negative, an amount has to be reported as business income. This amount is split between the recapture of amounts previously claimed as amortization and, if the proceeds exceed the original cost, an amount that represents the equivalent of a capital gain.

When there is only one asset in the cumulative eligible capital (CEC) pool, any gain on the disposition of eligible capital property—after the recapture of amounts previously deducted—is taxed like a capital gain: The amount by which the proceeds exceed the original cost is taxed at 50%. When there are other assets in the pool, the rules are more complicated.

EXAMPLE/**Gain on sale of eligible capital property**

Your business has an unamortized balance in its eligible capital property "pool" of $750,000 for the year ended December 31, 2008. This pool balance reflects $100,000 of previously claimed amortization. In November 2009, you dispose of eligible capital property for proceeds of $1.5 million. For the year ended December 31, 2009, your business will report the following:

Opening balance:	$750,000
Less 3/4 × $1,500,000:	(1,125,000)
Negative balance:	(375,000)
Amount attributable to previous amortization (reported as income):	$100,000
Balance:	$275,000
	× 2/3*
Income inclusion: (this is the amount that is taxed similar to a capital gain)	$183,333

*50% × 4/3 (an adjustment to account for the fact that only 3/4 of costs are added to the pool)

There are further adjustments when the taxpayer previously claimed the capital gains deduction with respect to the property disposed of (see article 145).

Also, if the disposition relates to the sale of qualified farm or fishing property, such as the sale of a quota, all or a portion of the negative balance may qualify for the capital gains deduction (see articles 147 and 148).

TAX TIP

Certain expenditures incurred in relation to a business may not be deductible from income since they are capital in nature but still not eligible for CCA treatment (see article 7). One such item could be legal expenses incurred in connection with the reorganization of a business. If this is the case, you should review the amounts paid with your tax adviser to determine whether they might qualify for amortization as an eligible capital expenditure.

9 The Home Office

Many Canadians now work out of their homes. If you are among this rapidly increasing population, you may be able to deduct a portion of your home office expenses. However, specific rules must be followed. Also, the rules differ depending on whether you are self-employed or an employee.

You are self-employed

If you are self-employed, expenses must relate to workspace that is either your principal place of business, or used exclusively for the purpose of earning income from the business. "Principal" is generally interpreted as more than 50% of the time. For the second criterion to apply, the space must also be used on a regular and continuous basis for meeting clients, customers or patients. If you qualify to claim home office expenses, you can deduct a portion of the operating costs of your home. For example, assume your home office takes up 10% of the total square footage of your home. You can claim as a deduction from your business income 10% of your mortgage interest (not principal), property taxes, heat, hydro, water, home insurance and maintenance costs. Any expenses directly related to the home office can be deducted in full.

Home office expenses can be deducted only from the business

carried on in the home and cannot be used to create a business loss. Eligible expenses you are unable to use in the year they are incurred can be carried forward to subsequent years and deducted from income generated by the business at that time, as long as the business-use criteria discussed above are still met.

EXAMPLE/**Deduction limits for home office expenses**

> Suppose you started a business in 2009. It generated revenues of $40,000 in 2009 and expenses, other than home office expenses, of $36,000. The portion of eligible home expenses attributable to your office space amounts to $5,200. In 2009, you will be able to claim only $4,000 of the home office expenses (i.e., $40,000 – $36,000). The remaining $1,200 of home office expenses can be carried forward and claimed against income generated by the business in a subsequent year.

TAX TIP

Keep a well-organized file of all receipts and a record of payments and go over them with your tax adviser to see if they are eligible deductions for your at-home business. You may be able to deduct a portion of your house expenses, such as property taxes, insurance, electricity, heat and mortgage interest.

TAX TIP

In general, it's not a good idea to claim depreciation on the portion of your home used for business purposes, since there may be negative tax implications if you ever sell your home. If you do not claim depreciation, your entire house may be regarded as your principal residence (see article 117). This way, any gain realized on the eventual sale of your house may be tax-free.

The GST/HST element

If you are registered for the GST/HST and you qualify to claim home office expenses, input tax credits can be claimed for the portion of your home expenses attributable to the business activity. However, an input tax credit can be claimed only for those expenses that are subject to GST/HST—for example, heat, hydro, etc. Mortgage interest, insurance and property taxes are not subject to the tax.

TAX TIP

If you are a GST/HST registrant, you can claim an input tax credit for GST/HST paid on home office expenses even if you are not able to deduct them in a given year because of the limitation on creating or increasing losses.

EXAMPLE/**GST and home office costs**

You are a GST/HST registrant, and your only office is located in your home. You regularly meet with clients and conduct all your business from this location. The office space occupies 10% of the total area of the house. As such, you are entitled to claim a deduction for 10% of the eligible home expenses incurred and input tax credits for 10% of the GST/HST paid on those expenses.

You are an employee

The rules for deducting home office expenses are somewhat different for employees. In this case, you will be permitted to deduct only costs related to a home office if your workspace is either the place where you principally perform your employment duties, or the space is used exclusively on a regular and continuous basis for meeting people while performing your employment duties.

Also, as an employee, the home office expenses you can claim are restricted. If you own your home, your deductions are limited to the maintenance of the premises, such as a portion of fuel, electricity, cleaning materials and minor repairs. You cannot deduct mortgage interest or any depreciation on your home. If you pay rent, a proportionate amount of the rent is deductible. If you are a salesperson on commission, your deductions may include property taxes and insurance. However, other employees are not entitled to claim a deduction for these expenditures.

Like self-employed persons, you cannot create a loss from employment when claiming home office expenses. However, any eligible expenses that you cannot use in one year can be carried forward to subsequent years.

TAX TIP

Your employer must certify on Form T2200 that you are required, under your contract of employment, to use a portion of your home as an office. You must keep this form in the event the CRA requests a copy of it.

If you claim home office expenses, you may also be able to claim a GST/HST rebate for the portion of your home expenses attributable to the employment activity. To qualify, your employer must be a GST/HST registrant other than a listed financial institution such as a bank, insurance company or brokerage firm.

This rebate is calculated as 5/105 of eligible expenses if you live outside the harmonized tax provinces. In the harmonized provinces, the rebate is generally 13/113 of the eligible expenses. Although the rebate claim is generally filed with your income tax return, you have up to four years to file a claim.

10 Paying Your Dues

Many professionals and business people belong to recreational or dining clubs (e.g., golf or tennis clubs). It often comes as a surprise to them, however, that annual dues payable to such facilities are not deductible expenses, even if there is an argument that the expense has been incurred for business purposes.

If you pay annual membership dues for an employee, the dues will not be regarded as a taxable benefit to the employee if it can be demonstrated that it is to your advantage for your employee to belong to the club. Similarly, amounts you pay for your employees' use of the facilities for promotional purposes would not be regarded as a taxable benefit.

TAX TIP

Based on the facts, it should be considered whether a club membership is principally for the benefit of the employee or the employer. In a recent Tax Court of Canada case, the court ruled that a golf membership was not a taxable benefit for an employee because the membership was principally for the employer's advantage. The employee did not want a golf membership because he did not like to play golf; however, the employer insisted that he take the golf membership. Regardless of whether the employee has to report a taxable benefit, the employer is not able to claim a deduction for the amount paid.

What's allowed and what's not

As noted above, an employee's use of a recreational club for promotional purposes may not be viewed as a taxable benefit. At the same time, the Income Tax Act also specifically denies the employer a deduction for such expenses. The CRA's position with respect to expenses incurred at a lodge, golf course or similar facility is as follows: If property such as a lodge or golf course is used for business purposes, and those purposes do not include the entertainment or recreation of clients, suppliers, shareholders or employees, it will allow a deduction for the related expenses. For instance, if you hold a business meeting at a golf club and it does not involve playing golf or use of the other recreational facilities, any reasonable expenses related to that meeting will be deductible.

As for meals and beverages consumed at such facilities, deductibility restrictions are the same as for those consumed at other establishments (see article 11). You must ensure that the costs are clearly itemized and, of course, incurred for the purpose of earning income. If your records show an all-inclusive charge that does not itemize specific costs, the deduction will not be allowed.

TAX TIP

To reduce the risk of being denied a legitimate deduction, keep accurate, timely and detailed documentation of the business purpose of such expenses. It also helps if the costs are clearly itemized on the invoice.

11 Meals and Entertainment Expenses

There are specific limitations on the amount you can deduct for meals and entertainment. In most cases, only 50% of business meals and entertainment expenses are deductible. This includes gift certificates to restaurants or places of entertainment. This rule applies to everyone—sole proprietors, corporations and partnerships.

A few exceptions

The 50% rule does not apply in certain cases, such as the cost of providing meals and recreation for all the employees working at a particular place of business. However, this exception applies only to up to six special events a year. Meals and entertainment expenses incurred for an event intended primarily to benefit a registered charity also escape the 50% limit. However, the cost of executive dining rooms and similar facilities is subject to the 50% limit. There are also exceptions from the 50% rule for meals provided for employment at a special work site or to employees lodged at a construction work camp.

Finally, if you invoice a client for reasonable meal expenses and you specifically identify such expenses in the accounts submitted to your client, you will be entitled to a full deduction for the expenses, while your client would be subject to the 50% restriction.

Rules for long-haul truck drivers

As noted above, the deduction for most meal and entertainment expenses is limited to 50% of the amount otherwise allowed as a deduction. However, in 2007, rules were introduced to increase the deductible portion of the cost of food and beverages consumed by long-haul truck drivers. This measure will also apply to employers that pay, or reimburse, such costs incurred by long-haul truck drivers that they employ.

The deductible amount will increase from 50% to 80% as follows:

- to 60% for expenses incurred after May 18, 2007;
- to 65% for expenses incurred in 2008;
- to 70% for expenses incurred in 2009;
- to 75% for expenses incurred in 2010; and
- to 80% for expenses incurred after 2010.

For this purpose, a long-haul truck driver is either an employee whose principal duty of employment is to drive long-haul trucks for the purpose of transporting goods or a self-employed person whose principal business is to drive long-haul trucks for the purpose of transporting goods. In both cases, the driver must be away for at least 24 continuous hours and the destination for the goods must be at least 160 kilometres away.

How GST/HST fits in

The ability to claim an input tax credit for meals and entertainment expenses is subject to a similar restriction—generally, only 50% is creditable. As an alternative, you can claim all the GST/HST paid on such expenses as they are incurred and then make an annual adjustment to your remittance to add back half the amount claimed in the year.

For food and beverage costs incurred by long-haul truck drivers, the amount of the GST/HST input tax credit that is disallowed will decrease from 50% to 20% over the period from 2007 to 2011.

TAX TIP

To simplify the calculation, it's a good idea to make sure your accounting system keeps such costs segregated from other expenses.

TAX TIP

Meal and entertainment expenses specifically identified on your invoice and billed directly back to your clients are not subject to this limitation. Your client, however, is subject to the limitation.

12 Convention Expenses

If you are carrying on a business or practising a profession, you can deduct expenses for attending up to two conventions per year. These conventions must relate to your business and must be held within the territory in which the sponsoring organization conducts its affairs. You can also deduct 50% of the actual cost of meals and entertainment incurred at conventions (see article 11). If you attend a convention at which meals and/or entertainment are provided, but the cost of the meals and entertainment is not noted separately from other convention fees, $50 per day will be subject to the 50% rule.

Expenses must be reasonable, and you should be in a position to prove your attendance and to support your expenses with vouchers.

EXAMPLE/**Conventions and meal expenses**

You pay a fee of $2,000 to attend a three-day business conference in Banff, Alberta. Meals and entertainment are provided, but no amount of the fee is allocated or identified for those services. In this case, $50 per day (or $150) is deemed to be the amount paid for food, beverages and entertainment and is subject to the 50% limitation. Therefore, the maximum deduction for the conference is $1,925 ($1,850 plus 50% of $150).

TAX TIP

When your spouse attends a convention with you, the associated cost is generally viewed as a personal non-deductible expense. But if there are good business reasons for your spouse to accompany you, these expenses may also be deductible

13 Canada Pension Plan Contributions

Did you earn income from a business as a sole proprietor or partner in 2009? If so, you may be liable for contributions under the Canada Pension Plan (CPP). If you did not earn any employment income in the year, your contribution for 2009 is 9.9% of the difference between your net business income and a $3,500 standard exemption, subject to a maximum contribution of $4,237.20 (the maximum is reached at a net business income amount of $46,300).

If you earned employment income, the amount of CPP premiums that have been withheld from this income is a factor in determining the amount you have to pay. Suppose your 2009 net business income was $50,000. Your CPP contribution for 2009 would be capped at the maximum of $4,237.20. However, if you also had $15,000 in employment income, your required CPP contributions with respect to your business income would be adjusted to take into account the CPP already paid in regard to your employment income.

Let's assume you and your employer have already contributed $1,138.50 [9.9% × ($15,000 – $3,500)] in respect of your employment income; your CPP contribution in respect of your business income would be $3,098.70 [($46,300 – $3,500) × 9.9% – $1,138.50].

Contributions commence the month after you reach the age of 18 and can be made until age 70. You can collect CPP benefits beginning as early as age 60 and as late as age 70, depending on when you retire. The pension amount is reduced before age 65 or increased after age 65 by 0.5% (or 6% per year) for each month between your 65th birthday and the month the pension becomes payable (see Table 4, page 293). Note that the government is proposing to change the way these adjustments are calculated. It's proposed that the reduction for CPP benefits taken between the ages of 60 and 65 will eventually be reduced by 0.6% per month (or 7.2% per year) and that the enhancement for benefits taken after an individual's 65th birthday (to age 70) will be increased by 0.7% per month (or 8.4% per year).

If you are self-employed, you can claim a tax deduction for half the CPP contribution that relates to your self-employment income. The remaining half qualifies for a non-refundable tax credit (see article 87).

Employer CPP remittances

Employers are required to match employee CPP contributions. For example, if your employee is required to remit $1,100 for CPP, you have to remit the same amount for the employer's CPP contribution. The amount an employer must contribute in a year for a given employee is not adjusted for any other amounts remitted for that person by other employers.

EXAMPLE/**Employer remittances**

John Smith was employed by Widget Co. until June 30, 2009. His employment income from this company was $30,000. He commenced employment with Digit Co. on September 1, 2009, and earned employment income of $20,000 for the balance of the year. John's required CPP contribution for 2009 is $2,118.60 [($46,300 – $3,500) × 4.95%]. It's likely that Widgit Co. and Digit Co. (combined) will have remitted more than this amount for CPP premiums on John's behalf. The same amount would have been paid for the employer's portion of the premiums. When John files his 2009 tax return, he will be able to claim a CPP refund to the extent the amount paid on his behalf exceeds $2,118.60. The companies, however, will not be able to claim a similar refund for the employer's portion of CPP.

In situations where a company has been restructured—such as in a wind-up or an amalgamation, employees with uninterrupted employment with the old and new employer will be deemed to have continuous employment with the new employer for purposes of the CPP rules. Similar rules apply to EI premiums.

EXAMPLE/**Wind-up of company**

John Smith was employed by Widget Co. and earned employment income of $30,000 to June 30, 2009. At this time, the company was wound up into Digit Co. John earned another $30,000 from Digit Co. for the balance of the year. Digit Co. can continue to calculate the required CPP premiums for John's employment as if he had been employed by Digit Co. for the whole year.

14 Deduction of Health/Dental Insurance Premiums

If you are self-employed, you can claim as a deduction from your business income premiums paid for coverage under a private health services plan. However, there are certain limitations.

For the premiums to be deductible, you must be actively engaged in a business as a sole proprietor or partner. Also, self-employment must be either your primary source of income in the current year or your income from other sources must not exceed $10,000.

In addition, equivalent coverage must be extended to all permanent full-time arm's-length employees. When a deduction is claimed, no amount paid for coverage will be eligible for the medical expense tax credit (see article 93).

If you have no other full-time employees, the deduction is restricted to an annual maximum of $1,500 for each of you, your spouse or common-law partner and other family members 18 years of age or older, and to $750 for other members of your household.

15 Wage-Loss Replacement Plans

If you are self-employed, you may also pay premiums under a disability insurance policy that will provide you with benefits if you lose your income-earning capacity. The premium on this type of policy is considered a personal expense and is not deductible from income. However, any benefits you may receive under this type of policy will also not be subject to tax.

16 Deduction of Life Insurance Premiums

If you are required to purchase life insurance as part of a package when borrowing money for business purposes, you can deduct the cost of the premiums, provided certain criteria are met. To claim a deduction, the policy must be assigned to the lender as security for the loan, and the lender must require this assignment. In addition, the lender's principal business must be the lending of money, and the interest payable on the loan must be deductible for income tax purposes (or would be deductible, except in the case of special overriding rules).

The amount that can be claimed is restricted to the premium paid or the net cost of pure insurance, whichever is less. The portion of the premium that is deductible could be reduced if the outstanding balance of the loan is less than the amount of insurance coverage.

17 Deduction of Fines and Penalties

Are fines and penalties deductible from business income? A noteworthy Supreme Court of Canada case allowed a taxpayer to claim an income tax deduction for a levy imposed for violating an egg-producing quota. In this case, the court decided that fines, penalties or levies should be deductible, provided the expense is incurred for the purpose of earning business income and the deduction is not specifically denied by the Income Tax Act.

The Department of Finance did not like that outcome. As a result, effective for fines and penalties imposed after March 22, 2004, you cannot claim a deduction for any fine or penalty imposed by a government agency, regulatory body, court or other tribunal or by any other person having the statutory authority to levy fines and penalties.

18 Valuation of Inventory

Two methods are generally used to establish the value of business inventory for tax purposes. All items may be valued at fair market value (as at the end of the particular year), or each item may be valued at whichever is lower—its cost or its fair market value.

There are special rules for property that is held as an "adventure or concern in the nature of trade." This designation usually refers to a one-time transaction, often conducted by an individual. Property held in inventory as an adventure in the nature of trade must be valued at the cost at which the taxpayer acquired it, although certain additions to this cost are permitted. This means that a loss on such a property cannot be recognized until the property is disposed of. A common example of a situation in which these rules may apply is when land is held on the speculation that it can be sold at a profit without further development.

Farmers are subject to special rules regarding the valuation of inventory (see article 46).

19 Instalment Sales

If selling property to your customers in instalments is part of your business, you should be aware of the tax rules that apply to such sales. To qualify for a tax deferral, the instalment must be for a period of more than two full years. However, if the property sold was land, the instalment need only be for a period that ends after the closing of the fiscal period in which the sale was made.

How much can you defer?

If you qualify, you can spread the profit over a maximum of four years, including the year of sale. The amount you can defer is the pro-rata portion of your profit (i.e., a ratio of the amount not due at each year-end to total sales price). In the third fiscal year following the sale, you must include in your income all the remaining untaxed profit, even if there is still an amount not due until a subsequent year.

EXAMPLE/**Deferring tax**

An airplane manufacturer sells a number of planes to a customer on March 31, 2009, for $1,200,000 and realizes a gross profit of $450,000 on the sale. Terms of the sale require $400,000 to be paid on delivery and another $400,000 to be paid on June 30, 2010, and June 30, 2011. Assuming a December 31 year-end, the amount of profit available for the deferral in each year is calculated as follows:

2009:	($800,000 ÷ $1,200,000) × $450,000	= $300,000
2010:	($400,000 ÷ $1,200,000) × $450,000	= $150,000
2011:	($0 ÷ $1,200,000) × $450,000	= $0

As a result of the deferral, the gross profit of $450,000 will be included in income as follows:

2009:	$150,000
2010:	$150,000
2011:	$150,000

A different set of rules applies to instalment sales of property that are taxed as capital gains (see article 144).

20 Tax Treatment of Lease-Option Arrangements

The CRA used to look at the substance of a lease-option agreement to determine the appropriate tax treatment. Its position was that, for tax purposes, certain types of leases should be treated as a purchase and sale. As a result, instead of deducting the lease payments from income as rent, the payments would have to be capitalized and subject to capital cost allowance (CCA) treatment (see article 7). For example, for tax purposes, a lease arrangement would be treated as a purchase and sale if it was clear at the start of the lease that the lessee could acquire the property at the end of the lease at a price substantially less than its probable fair market value. In such circumstances, the lessee-purchaser rather than the lessor-vendor would be entitled to claim depreciation and any related investment tax credits.

As a result of several court cases dealing with this issue, the CRA changed its position with respect to these types of arrangements. In *Shell Canada Limited v. The Queen*, the Supreme Court held that a situation's economic realities may not be used to recharacterize a taxpayer's bona fide legal relationships. Unless there is a specific provision of the Income Tax Act to the contrary, or a finding that there is a sham, the taxpayer's legal relationships must be respected. As a result, whether a contract is a sale or a lease is based on the legal relationship created by the terms of the agreement, rather than any attempt to determine the underlying economic reality. The CRA now takes the position that a lease is a lease and a sale is a sale, and this position applies to all leases—including financing leases.

TAX TIP

If you have already entered into lease or financing lease agreements and have determined the tax consequences on the basis of the tax agency's old position, you should consult your tax adviser. If you are anticipating entering into a new lease agreement, you should also obtain professional advice to determine the tax consequences. If you want to obtain investment tax credits, you must ensure that the legal relationship creates a purchase.

21 Operating Losses and Prior Years' Taxes

If you carried on a business as a sole proprietor or partner in 2009 and incurred an operating loss, you can apply the loss against your other sources of income, such as investment income, capital gains and employment income. Losses on certain farming businesses may be restricted for the year (see article 46).

How it works

Any business loss realized in a year must be deducted in full against your other sources of income. As a result, you may find you are unable to claim some or all of your non-refundable tax credits, such as personal amounts and medical expenses. To that end, you should check with your tax adviser to assess whether other family members can obtain a benefit from these lost credits.

Should your operating loss exceed your other sources of income, the excess may be carried back three years. To carry back the loss, you must file Form T1A with your return for the year in which the loss arises. Technically, you are supposed to make the request by the filing deadline for the year the loss arises. However, the CRA tends to use its discretion as long as the prior year is still open to reassessment. If you are unable to carry back the loss, or choose not to, it can be carried forward for up to 20 years (10 years for losses that arose in taxation years ending after March 22, 2004, and before 2006, and seven years for losses that arose in taxation years ending before March 23, 2004). You are free to choose the year to which you want to apply the loss. For example, if you expect your marginal rate of tax to increase in the future, you may decide to carry the loss forward rather than back to a prior year.

TAX TIP

When carrying a loss back to a prior year, you have the option of using only a portion of your loss. For example, you might want to claim only part of the loss against income that was taxed at a higher marginal rate and apply the remaining portion of the loss to another year.

22 Apprenticeship Job Creation Tax Credit

If you hire apprentices, you may be able to claim a non-refundable tax credit equal to 10% of the eligible salaries and wages paid to eligible apprentices for employment after May 1, 2006. Eligible wages are those paid during the first 24 months of the apprenticeship. The maximum credit is $2,000 per year for each eligible apprentice. A listing of the trades that qualify can be found at: **www.red-seal.ca/Site/trades/analist_e.htm**

You can claim the credit on your income tax return, using either Form T2038(IND), Investment Tax Credit (Individuals), or Form T2SCH31, Investment Tax Credit—Corporations.

Unused credits may be carried back three years and forward for up to 20 years to reduce federal taxes otherwise payable in those years.

23 Investment Tax Credit for Childcare Spaces

If you create new childcare spaces for children of your employees and the surrounding community, you may be able to claim a non-refundable tax credit. This credit is equal to 25% of eligible expenditures incurred after March 18, 2007, to a maximum of $10,000 per space created. The credit is not available for any of the ongoing or operating expenses of the childcare facility, such as supplies, wages, salaries, utilities, etc.

Unused credits may be carried back three years and forward up to 20 years to reduce federal income taxes otherwise payable in those years. All or part of the credit may be recaptured if, at any time within the five calendar years after the creation of the new childcare space, it ceases to be available or is sold or leased to another person or converted to another use.

24 To Incorporate or Not to Incorporate

If you are currently carrying on a business as a sole proprietor or in an unincorporated partnership, consider whether you should transfer your business to a corporation. It depends on your circumstances and the amount of income you earn. As a first step, you should talk it over with your tax adviser, who can "crunch the numbers" and examine the advantages and disadvantages of being incorporated.

Business income earned as a sole proprietor or partner is subject to income tax at your personal marginal rates. In successful years, you must pay proportionately more income tax, as the extra income places you in a higher tax bracket. However, if you operate your business within a corporation, income that qualifies for the small-business deduction (see article 27) is taxed at a relatively low rate.

If you incorporate your business and can retain earnings in the corporation for growth, you will be able to defer tax to the extent the earnings are not distributed to you as a salary or dividend (see article 32).

As an added benefit, with appropriate planning, shares of a small-business corporation may be able to qualify for the enhanced $750,000 capital gains deduction on their disposition (see article 146).

Transferring your business assets to the corporation on a tax-deferred basis

Most business assets can be transferred to a corporation without incurring immediate income taxes on the transfer. But there are some rules that apply, which means you must follow definite procedures and meet specific criteria. Your tax adviser can advise you on the merits of incorporation and how it might be accomplished on a tax-deferred basis. Provincial transfer taxes, such as property transfer tax and retail sales tax, also have to be addressed. In some cases, these taxes are unavoidable. There may also be GST/HST considerations on the transfer, as well as other non-tax issues.

25 Incorporating Your Professional Practice

Many provinces allow professionals to incorporate their practice. Professional incorporation can confer many of the same tax and non-tax advantages enjoyed by other incorporated self-employed persons. However, professional liability will not be limited through incorporation and, in many provinces, the shareholders of professional corporations are required to be members of the same profession.

One important benefit of incorporation is the fact that corporations enjoy a considerably lower tax rate on income up to a certain amount (see Table 7, page 297). However, this benefit is realized only if the income is kept in the company and used to make capital and operating expenditures and to repay debt. Therefore, incorporating may not be in your best interest unless you are able to retain some of the income within the corporation. It may also be advantageous to incorporate if you are planning to sell all or part of your business. In those provinces that allow non-professionals to own shares in a professional corporation, income splitting is also a benefit.

If you wish to incorporate your practice, you should consult your provincial governing body for the conditions of incorporation specific to your profession. Your tax adviser can assist you in determining whether incorporation would be beneficial, given your specific situation.

26 Integration

The concept of integration is critical to the proper operation of our tax system. According to this concept, income that a corporation distributes to you as either a salary or dividend should attract about the same amount of tax as if you had earned the income directly. Because actual corporate and personal tax rates differ from the rates necessary to achieve perfect integration, integration is not exact. The differences will depend on the type of income, your province of residence and the province in which the company carries on business. In the past, integration was far from perfect when income in excess of the amount that qualified for the small-business deduction (see article 27) was retained in a corporation. Rules introduced in 2006 dealing with the taxation of certain dividends paid after 2005 (referred to as "eligible dividends") were intended to address this issue (see article 153).

Whether it is preferable to earn income directly or through a corporation will depend on your particular circumstances. Active business income that is earned by a corporation, taxed at the small-business rate and distributed as a dividend will usually attract less total tax than if you earned the income directly. On the other hand, income taxed at the top corporate rate and subsequently paid out to you as a dividend could result in more overall tax—particularly if you are in the top tax bracket. However, there can also be a significant tax deferral for as long as the amount remains in the corporation. Also, although it used to be a standard practice to bonus down to the small-business limit (see article 27), the new rules on the taxation of certain dividends (see article 153) mean that this general policy is no longer cut and dried. Although there is generally still a tax advantage to a bonus-down strategy, as opposed to paying current dividends out of high-rate income, the reduced rate of tax for eligible dividends significantly reduces the number of years the funds must be retained in the corporation to make "not bonusing" the better decision. Recent reductions in the general corporate tax rate (see Table 6, page 296) have also resulted in a greater bias to retain profits at the corporate level. The results will vary by province. Consult with your tax adviser in making this determination.

27 The Small-Business Deduction

Canadian-controlled private corporations (CCPCs) are entitled to claim a small-business deduction on active business income earned in Canada. The definition of "active income" is generally intended to exclude corporations created to earn what would otherwise be considered investment income or employment income of the individual shareholder (commonly called "specified investment business" or "personal services business" income).

The small-business deduction currently provides for an 11% federal tax rate on a Canadian-controlled private corporation's active business income. However, only a limited amount of income qualifies for this deduction—that's why it's called the small-business deduction. Prior to 2003, the small-business limit was $200,000. This limit has gradually increased to $300,000, $400,000 and finally to $500,000 (as of January 1, 2009).

The small-business limit is prorated for non-calendar year-ends.

Although all provinces also have a small-business rate, the rate and the amount of income that qualifies for this lower rate varies from province to province (see Table 7, page 297). Both the federal and provincial small-business limit must be shared by an associated group of companies (see article 30).

Restrictions do apply

Larger corporations will find their ability to claim the small-business deduction is restricted. The restriction applies to CCPCs whose taxable capital (generally equal to a company's retained earnings, share capital and long-term debt) exceeds $10 million for the preceding year. If the taxable capital is between $10 million and $15 million, the amount eligible for the low rate is proportionately reduced. Any eligibility ceases if taxable capital surpasses $15 million.

Special rules apply to corporations that are associated with other corporations for income tax purposes (see article 30).

Additional reduction in corporate tax rate

The general corporate tax rate is 28%. However, since 2001, most income that is not subject to the small-business deduction has been eligible for an additional corporate tax rate reduction. As a result of this reduction, at the end of 2007, the federal tax rate on most corporate income that was not subject to the small-business deduction was subject to a federal tax rate of 21%. The general corporate income tax rate was then further reduced as follows:

2008	19.5%
2009	19.0%
2010	18.0%
2011	16.5%
2012	15.0%

At the time these reductions were announced, the government requested the cooperation of the provinces and territories to aim for a 25% combined federal-provincial-territorial statutory corporate income tax rate by 2012. This goal would be reached if all provinces had a general corporate income tax rate of 10% (see Table 7, page 297 for the 2009 corporate rates by province).

The reduced general corporate income tax rate does not apply to investment corporations, mortgage investment corporations, mutual fund corporations or non-resident-owned investment corporations. The general corporate federal rate for such entities remains at 28%.

EXAMPLE/**Lower tax rate**

Suppose a CCPC, earning income from an active business carried on in Canada, has taxable income of $600,000 for its fiscal period ended December 31, 2009. The income eligible for the small-business deduction ($500,000) will be taxed at the lowest federal tax rate of 11%. The $100,000 balance will be taxed at the reduced 19% tax rate.

28 Capital Dividend Account

Because of the integration principle, a private company has an account in which it can accumulate amounts for tax-free distribution to its shareholders. This account is mainly composed of the non-taxable portion of net capital gains, capital dividends received from other companies and the net proceeds of a life insurance policy received on the death of an individual. A positive balance can be distributed to shareholders as a tax-free capital dividend, provided certain prescribed forms are filed with the tax authorities.

Capital dividends are used in a number of planning scenarios, including situations in which a shareholder dies while owning shares in a private corporation.

29 Federal Capital Tax

The federal capital tax—often referred to as the Large Corporations Tax—was eliminated as at January 1, 2006.

Even though the federal capital tax is now eliminated, a company's ability to benefit from the small-business deduction is still reduced when the corporation's taxable capital exceeds $10 million. For this reason, it is still important to calculate a corporation's taxable capital (see article 27). Taxable capital is essentially the liability side of the company's balance sheet (excluding certain short-term liabilities), with a reduction for the cost of certain investments held by the company.

A separate capital tax still applies for financial institutions and insurance corporations. Taxable capital in excess of $1 billion is subject to the tax, at a single tax rate of 1.25%.

30 Associated-Company Rules

To prevent taxpayers from creating more than one corporation to enjoy the benefits of the small-business deduction, there are rules that require the small-business limit to be shared among associated companies. The application of the concept of associated companies is a common one in the Income Tax Act and the definition, like that of many other tax rules, is quite complex. The simplest cases are those in which companies are under common control or one company controls the other.

EXAMPLE/**The ABCs of association**

> Company A controls Company B, so Company A and Company B are associated with one another. If Company A also controls Company C, then companies A, B and C are all associated with each other.
>
> Control of a company is not measured just by ownership of the voting shares. In addition to the traditional voting control test, "control" is recognized if a person or group of persons own more than 50% of the fair market value of all of the issued shares or more than 50% of the corporation's common equity shares. Control can also arise when a person or group of persons have any direct or indirect influence that, if exercised, would result in control "in fact" of the corporation.

Sorting out ownership

Who owns the shares? The tax agency looks through a corporation to deem the ownership in the hands of the shareholders of the corporation. For example, if you own 60% of one company, which in turn owns 30% of another company, you are regarded as owning 18% (60% of 30%) of the company that is owned by your company.

Any shares owned by children under 18 years of age are considered to be owned by the parent. In addition to all the technical rules governing association, there is a general rule stating that companies are considered to be associated if one of the main reasons for their separate existence is to save tax.

The concept of control is quite far-reaching, yet it is possible for related persons to invest in each other's companies and still remain non-associated. To accomplish that, the cross-ownership has to be less than 25%. For example, if you own 100% of Company A and 20% of Company B, and the other 80% is owned by your spouse, Company A and Company B will not automatically be associated. If you own 25% or more of Company B, however, the two companies will be associated. Be aware that the less-than-25% test applies to any class of shares. However, certain types of shares, known as shares of a specified class, are specifically excluded in determining control and cross-ownership.

TAX TIP

Do you have an interest in one or more companies that are related to each other or to other companies? If so, have your tax adviser review the corporate structure to see whether you are deemed to be associated and whether there are ways to prevent association.

31 Salaries and Bonuses to Shareholders

One of the basic principles of taxation is that expenses must be "reasonable" to be deductible. The CRA has had a longstanding administrative position on the reasonableness of salaries and bonuses paid to owner-managers. In general, the CRA will not question the reasonableness of salaries or bonuses paid to principal shareholder-managers of a corporation if the company has a practice of distributing its profits to its shareholder-managers in the form of bonuses. However, this administrative position applies only to shareholders who are Canadian residents actively involved in the day-to-day operations of the company, thus contributing to the income-producing activities from which the remuneration is paid.

Income from the sale of business assets

It was previously the CRA's position that bonuses declared with respect to profits realized on the sale of business assets would also fall under the above policy. However, the CRA has since stated that this is not necessarily the case. A salary or bonus paid out of the proceeds generated from a major sale of business assets would go beyond the scope of the general owner-manager remuneration policy. Where the general policy does not apply, the amount must be "reasonable" to be deductible. Any amount over and above the amount deemed reasonable would not be allowed as a deduction. The CRA has provided little guidance on this revised position. However, in numerous subsequent technical interpretation letters, it has ruled that the full deduction would be allowed when the amount is paid to a shareholder who has been active in the business. The CRA has said that it intends to deem amounts to be unreasonable only in situations where the payment of a bonus creates an "undue tax advantage," but it's not clear what constitutes such an advantage.

TAX TIP

If you're thinking of selling off a significant portion of your business assets, you should contact your tax adviser to determine the most tax-effective way to distribute the after-tax proceeds from the sale.

TAX TIP

If your company earns significant income each year and you're concerned that the CRA might question the reasonableness of amounts paid to shareholders or other related persons, consider the option of paying dividends instead (see articles 26 and 153). The dividends can be paid directly or indirectly through a trust or other corporation.

32 Salary versus Dividends

Once your business is incorporated, you must remember that the corporation's profits are not yours to take. The corporation is a separate legal entity. To extract funds, you must either receive a dividend from the corporation or have it pay you a salary. In addition, if you have loaned money to your company, you can arrange to receive interest on the loan.

The payment of a salary is deductible to your corporation, whereas dividends are paid from after-tax corporate profits. Careful analysis is needed to calculate the best mix of salary, interest and/or dividends for your specific circumstances. The introduction of the eligible dividend regime has further added to the factors that must be considered in making this decision. There are now two tax rates that can apply to dividends, depending on whether it is an eligible or a regular dividend (see article 153). For example, if your company pays a dividend and designates it as an eligible dividend, the shareholder receiving the dividend will pay a reduced rate of tax (see Table 2, page 287). The tax savings can be significant. As noted in article 26, it is no longer a rule of thumb to bonus down to the small-business limit.

TAX TIP

If your salary-to-dividend mix changes from year to year, it can affect your tax instalment requirements. Ensure that you and your corporation are remitting the appropriate amounts.

TAX TIP

Consider paying yourself a salary large enough to make maximum CPP and RRSP contributions.

33 Salary Deferral Arrangements

For the most part, rules relating to unpaid salaries are intended to match the timing of the employer's deduction for paying the salary with the employee's reporting of income. For example, if an employee is entitled at the end of 2009 to receive an amount in a future year, and one of the main purposes for this arrangement is to defer or postpone taxation, the amount will be taxed as a benefit to the employee in 2009. This is referred to as a salary deferral arrangement.

Exclusions

Some plans are excluded from this classification, such as arrangements to fund certain employee leaves of absence. As well, the rules will not apply to bonuses that are paid within three years following the end of the year in which the amount became payable. However, if the bonus is not paid within 179 days from the end of the employer's taxation year, the employer will not be able to deduct the amount until the year it is paid.

TAX TIP

If your corporation's year-end comes after July 6, it can deduct the bonus in the current year and the employee does not have to report the amount as income until the next year. However, the corporation must declare the bonus as of its year-end but not pay it out until after December 31 and within 179 days of the year-end.

34 Directors' Fees

Directors' fees are considered employment income and also constitute earned income for purposes of determining how much you can contribute to an RRSP (see articles 64 and 65).

TAX TIP

If your spouse or common-law partner and/or other family members are directors of your corporation, consider paying them a director's fee for services performed. Such services usually include attending directors' meetings, directing the management and affairs of the business, approving financial statements, declaring dividends, etc.

On the downside, as a director of a corporation, you should be aware of your responsibility should the corporation fail to deduct and remit income taxes on payments to employees or on certain payments to non-residents. Directors can also be held liable for the corporation's failure to collect and remit GST/HST.

Should the corporation fail to deduct and remit, as director, you can be held liable along with the corporation for paying the required amounts, including interest and penalties. However, you will not be held liable if you can demonstrate that you exercised a reasonable degree of care to prevent the failure of withholding and remitting.

Nevertheless, there have been several court cases in which directors have been found liable. Often the moneylender cuts off the line of credit to the business and, as a result, the withholding cannot be paid. Since the withholding is supposed to be in a trust account, this excuse will generally not protect you from liability.

TAX TIP

Do not take your responsibility as a director lightly. If the corporation is in financial difficulty, you should take additional precautions to ensure that withholding taxes are remitted on a timely basis. Consider resigning as a director of a corporation that is having serious difficulties. Ensure that this resignation is in writing and is recorded in the minute book.

35 Loans from Your Corporation

As previously noted, you can withdraw funds from your company by paying yourself either a salary or a dividend. You can also access funds by obtaining a loan from your company. The rules in this area are quite complex. Before borrowing funds from your company, you should thoroughly discuss this strategy with your tax adviser to make sure you are aware of the rules.

Timing of repayment is critical

In general, loans not repaid within one year from the end of the year in which they are made must be reported as income for the year the loan was made. For example, if you borrow $10,000 from your company on June 1, 2009, and your company has a September 30 year-end, if the loan remains unpaid on September 30, 2010, you must report the $10,000 as income on your personal income tax return for the 2009 taxation year.

Some exceptions apply

Shareholders who are also employees can be exempted from the above rules. However, only some types of loans qualify, such as a loan that enables you to acquire treasury stock in your company (or a related company) or finance an automobile to be used in performing your employment duties. There is another exception to these rules if lending money is part of your company's ordinary business. To qualify for any of the exemptions, at the time the loan is taken out, bona fide arrangements must be made to repay it within a reasonable period.

A loan to enable you or your spouse or common-law partner to purchase a home may also qualify—but the rules in this area are complex, and professional advice is recommended. First, to qualify for the exception to the general rule, the loan must be made because of your position as an employee of the company and not because of your shareholder status. To determine whether it is reasonable to conclude that you received the loan because of your employment rather than your share ownership, you must be able to show that a similar loan would be made to employees who were not shareholders of the company. This might be difficult in the case of a low-interest or non-interest-bearing housing loan, particularly if your company employs only family members. Since this rule was introduced, there has been a considerable amount of debate around whether it is still possible for a corporation to make a housing loan to a significant shareholder or to his or her spouse or common-law partner. The CRA's general position in this regard is expressed in CRA Document 2005-0159061E5. This document states that, although it is a question of fact, a housing loan to a 50% shareholder/employee would ordinarily be considered to have been received by virtue of shareholdings, not employment.

One more exception

As a relieving provision, an exception to the general rule covers loans made to an employee who owns less than 10% of any class of shares of the employer corporation and who does not deal at arm's length with the employer corporation. However, be forewarned that if anyone related to you holds shares in the company, the CRA will deem you the owner of these shares for purposes of assessing the 10% rule.

Deemed interest benefit on "excepted" loans

If the loan qualifies for one of the above exceptions, this means only that the amount borrowed does not have to be included in your income. However, you will still have to report a taxable benefit to the extent that the amount of the loan, multiplied by a prescribed interest rate, exceeds any interest actually paid on the loan no later than 30 days after the end of the calendar year. This rate is adjusted quarterly. These rules also apply to most loans to employees (see article 38).

If you use the loan to acquire eligible investments or to earn income, as opposed to using the funds for personal purposes, you can claim the amount of the taxable benefit as a deductible interest expense.

TAX TIP

Did you receive a low-interest or interest-free loan from your company? Did you use the proceeds for a qualified investment purpose? If so, make sure you claim the deemed interest benefit as an offsetting deduction when you file your tax return.

36 Corporate Losses and Change of Control

When you acquire control of a corporation, a number of rules restrict your ability to carry forward losses that were incurred before you took over. At the same time, some of these rules require that certain adjustments be made to various accounts for income tax purposes. The intent is to crystallize any losses inherent in the corporation's assets.

Claiming losses

Claiming non-capital (operating) losses in any period after the change of control requires the business that generated the losses to be carried on throughout the year with a reasonable expectation of profit. In addition, these losses may be claimed only to the extent of the income generated from that business or a similar business. Any unused net capital losses at the time of the change in control may not be used after that point. Similar rules apply with respect to the carry-forward of unused scientific research and experimental development (SR&ED) expenses and business investment tax credits.

TAX TIP

There are some tax-planning techniques available to utilize operating losses that might otherwise be forfeited in the carry-forward period. If you are considering acquiring control of a corporation to utilize its tax losses, before you make your purchase, make sure you are fully aware of the rules as they apply to your situation.

37 Taxable Benefits

If you provide your employees with benefits in addition to a regular salary, an amount must generally be included in their income as a taxable benefit. The most common taxable benefits are company cars (see article 39), employee loans (see article 38) and stock options (see article 42).

In addition, the following less obvious benefits may also have to be included in your employees' income.

Christmas parties and other special events

Did you provide your employees with a Christmas party this year? Following a tax court decision that required an employee to report an income inclusion with respect to the "benefit" he realized from attending his company's Christmas party, the CRA issued guidelines on how it intends to apply the taxable benefit provisions to employer-provided social events.

In general, no taxable benefit will have to be reported for social events that are made available to all employees, provided the cost per employee is $100 or less. Parties costing more than that will generally be considered to be beyond the "privilege" point and may result in taxable benefits.

Gifts and awards

In 2001, the CRA changed its policy with respect to employee gifts and awards to allow up to two non-cash gifts to honour special occasions with a total cost not exceeding $500 per year per employee and up to two non-cash awards to honour achievements (also with a total cost not exceeding $500 per year per employee).

Such gifts or awards are not taxable in the hands of the employee, but are deductible by the employer. The gifts and awards are those given in recognition of milestones and occasions, such as years of service, meeting job safety standards, Christmas, births, marriages, etc.

They are not to be disguised remuneration situations in which every employee gets a $500 non-taxable gift. The policy does not apply to cash or near-cash gifts such as gift certificates. If the value of the gift or award is over $500, it has been the CRA's position that the full fair market value of the gift(s) or award(s) must be included in the employee's income. The CRA has confirmed that the $500 limit is the employer's total cost of a gift or award, including all applicable taxes; that is, PST and GST or HST.

In June 2009, the CRA announced that it plans to change its above administrative policy for non-cash gifts and rewards.

Effective for 2010, the following changes are being made:

1. Non-cash gifts and non-cash awards to an arm's-length employee, regardless of number, will not be taxable to the extent that the total aggregate value of all non-cash gifts and awards to that employee is less than $500 annually. The total value in excess of $500 annually will be taxable.

2. In addition to the above, a separate non-cash long-service/anniversary award may also qualify for non-taxable status to the extent its total value is $500 or less. The value in excess of $500 will be taxable. To qualify, the anniversary award cannot be for less than five years of service or for five years since the employee last received a long-service award.

3. Similar to the current policy, the revised gift and award policy will not apply to non-arm's-length employees.

For clarification, items of an immaterial or nominal value, such as coffee, tea, T-shirts with employer logos, mugs, plaques, trophies, etc., will not be considered a taxable benefit to employees and will not be included in the above $500 threshold. Performance-related rewards (for example, for meeting a sales target) and cash and near-cash awards (such as gift certificates) will continue to fall outside the administrative policy and will be taxable to the employee.

EXAMPLE/**New policy for gifts or awards**

> In 2010, Jennifer received the following gifts and awards from her employer. A T-shirt and mug with her employer's logo ($15 value), a $100 monetary birthday gift, a mantle clock for 10 years service (valued at $225), a wedding gift (art print) valued at $400 and a holiday season gift (theatre tickets valued at $150). The T-shirt and mug have no tax consequences due to their nominal value. The monetary birthday gift is not eligible for the administrative policy since it is cash. The $100 is, therefore, taxable as remuneration. The 10-year anniversary award is eligible under the long-service/anniversary award policy. The total value of the remaining gifts and awards amounts to $550. Jennifer will be considered to have received a taxable benefit in the amount of $50 ($550 – $500).

Employer-paid professional membership fees

Do you pay your employees' professional membership fees? If so, you may have to include in their income the amount paid on their behalf as a taxable benefit.

In general, the payment of a professional membership fee will not be considered a taxable benefit if the employer is the primary beneficiary of the payment. The employer will be considered the primary beneficiary whenever membership in the association is a requirement of employment. In a situation where membership is not a condition of employment, the question of primary beneficiary must still be resolved. The employer is responsible for making this determination.

Non-taxable benefits

Although many benefits received by virtue of employment are taxable, the following benefits are not taxable:

- reimbursement of certain moving expenses, including reasonable expenses related to the reinstallation of services and connection of appliances, as well as the modifications required to install moved property;

- reimbursement of a loss from the disposal of an employee's residence subsequent to a move at the employer's request, up to a maximum of $15,000;
- an expense allowance paid to a member of a municipal organization, to the extent that it does not exceed one-third of the remuneration and allowance received;
- the employer's contributions to a private health services plan;
- the employer's contributions to an RPP, a supplementary employment benefit plan or a DPSP;
- discounts granted to all employees;
- use of the employer's recreational facilities, subject to certain conditions;
- subsidized meals, provided the employee is required to pay a reasonable amount for the cost of food;
- meals or meal allowances of up to $17, where an employee works two or more hours of overtime before or after regular hours, and the overtime is infrequent or occasional (this position is effective for 2009 and subsequent years);
- uniforms and special clothing required for work;
- transportation to the work location where such transportation is provided by the employer;
- meals, lodging and transportation when an employee is performing duties at a remote location or, in some circumstances, at a special work site;
- transportation passes to employees of bus, rail or air companies, except for airline employees travelling on a space-confirmed basis and paying less than 50% of the economy class fare (Administratively, the CRA has allowed for the non-taxable status of surface transit passes provided to transit employees and their families. Effective for 2010, the tax-free status of such passes will apply only for passes provided to the transit

employee for the exclusive use of the employee. Free or discounted passes provided for an employee's family member will represent a taxable benefit to the employee);

- counselling services relating to mental or physical health, re-employment or retirement of an employee;
- allowances paid to a part-time employee for travel expenses, provided that the employee holds another job or carries on a business, the amount is reasonable and this part-time function is performed at a location not less than 80 kilometres from his or her normal place of residence and principal place of employment;
- travel expenses incurred by an employee's spouse, when his or her presence is required by the employer and he or she has a role to play in achieving the business objectives of the trip;
- transportation and parking expenses paid by the employer to a blind or motor-impaired employee;
- membership dues to a sports club paid by the employer, provided it is principally for the employer's own advantage;
- Internet services made available to employees, to the extent that they use it in carrying out their work or when such use mainly benefits the employer;
- loyalty points collected on an employee's personal credit card for business expenses (where the employee is reimbursed for such expenses), as long as the points are not converted into cash and are not indicative of an alternative form of remuneration (this position is effective for 2009 and subsequent years); and
- reimbursement of childcare expenses by an employer to an employee if the employee is required to work out of town at the request of the employer.

TAX TIP

The CRA indicated in a technical interpretation that health care spending account (HCSA) credits provided to employees as part of an incentive pay plan is a tax-free benefit since a HCSA is considered a private health services plan. HCSA credits are utilized to reimburse an employee for his/her medical expenses or his/her dependants' medical expenses not already covered under any other existing medical insurance plan.

TAX TIP

Not all benefits have to be included in your employees' income. An employee may receive certain fringe benefits tax-free. Some examples include employer contributions to registered pension and deferred profit sharing plans (within limits), tuition fees for courses taken for the employer's benefit, employee counselling services paid for by the employer, etc. Your professional adviser can assist you in devising a tax-effective remuneration strategy for your employees.

38 Employee Loans

If an employee is provided with a loan at little or no interest, he or she must include a taxable benefit in income. This benefit is generally calculated as the interest on the loan at a prescribed rate, minus any interest actually paid on the loan within the year or 30 days after year-end.

Special rules apply when you provide your employees with a low-interest or interest-free loan to assist them in buying a home when moving to work at a new location. The taxable benefit arising from such a loan may be partially or entirely offset by a special deduction. To qualify, the new residence must be at least 40 kilometres closer than the old residence to the new work location. In general, this special deduction will entirely offset the taxable benefit arising from low-interest or interest-free loans of $25,000 or less. This deduction applies for a five-year period commencing on the date the loan is made.

Special rules also apply if you provide any of your employees with a "home purchase loan." It is not necessary for the employee to move to a new work location to qualify under this rule. The borrowed money has to be used to either purchase or refinance the debt on the employee's home. The benefit from such loans is calculated by applying either the prescribed rate at the time the loan is granted or the prescribed rate for the particular quarter, whichever is lower. A new base rate on the loan will be established every five years.

39 Personal Use of a Company-Owned Automobile

If your company provides you or any of its employees with a vehicle for personal use, a taxable benefit has to be reported. This benefit comprises two parts: a "standby charge," which reflects the personal access to the car; and an operating benefit, which reflects the personal portion of operating expenses paid by your company.

In general, the standby charge is 2% of the original cost of the car, including PST and GST or HST, for each month in the year the car is made available for use. If the car is leased, the standby charge is generally two-thirds of the lease cost, net of insurance costs.

The standby charge can be reduced if the vehicle is used more than 50% of the time for employment purposes and annual personal driving does not exceed 20,000 kilometres. In this case, the standby charge (as calculated above) is multiplied by the following fraction:

Personal km ÷ 1,667 km per 30-day period (to an annual maximum of 20,004 km)

EXAMPLE/**Pay less tax**

> If you drive your employer-provided vehicle 25,000 kilometres a year for business and 15,000 kilometres for personal use, the standby charge will be approximately 75% (15,000 ÷ 20,004) of the regular standby charge.

The standby charge included in your income as a taxable benefit is reduced by any reimbursement you make to your employer during the year for the use of the vehicle (other than in respect of operating expenses).

Maintaining accurate mileage records to support this claim should be part of your daily routine. In general, travel between your workplace and residence does not constitute employment use. If you stop at a customer's location for employment purposes on your way to or from work, however, this travel may be considered employment related.

Commencing in 2005, Quebec requires employees to keep a mileage logbook to support their personal and business use of a motor vehicle, and to provide a copy of the logbook to their employers within 10 days of the calendar year-end. Employees who do not provide a copy to their employers may be fined $200.

TAX TIP

The standby charge calculation is based on the original cost of the car and does not decrease as the car's value declines with age. After a few years, it may be cheaper to eliminate this benefit by buying the car from the company at its fair market value.

TAX TIP

Previously, it was often recommended that employees buy their own vehicles and receive a travel allowance (see article 41) when business use was less than 90%. With the lower benefit calculation when the vehicle is used more than 50% of the time for employment purposes, it may make sense to revisit this policy and consider whether it is better for the company to provide the automobile.

Employees who sell or lease automobiles may qualify for a reduced standby charge. In these cases, the standby charge is generally calculated at 1.5% instead of 2%. Note that, in such cases, the calculation is based on the average cost of the vehicles acquired by the employer for sale or lease. Your tax adviser can help you with the details of the calculation.

There is an exemption from the automobile benefit provisions for clearly marked police, fire and emergency medical service vehicles. In addition, extended-cab pickup trucks used at remote or semi-remote work sites are also excluded from these provisions. However, there may still be an operating benefit associated with such vehicles.

TAX TIP

If you provide any of your employees with automobiles for personal and business use, the taxable benefit reported on their T4s will have to consider the proportionate amount of personal and business use. You should be advising your employees to closely track their personal versus business use of the vehicles and to advise you accordingly so the benefit can be accurately calculated.

Operating costs

In addition to the standby charge, a separate and additional benefit must be reported when the employer pays any portion of the automobile's operating costs.

The CRA has indicated that virtually all expenses associated with an automobile are operating costs. This includes the cost of gasoline, oil, tires, maintenance and repairs, net of insurance proceeds. Licence and insurance costs are also considered operating costs. However, parking charges are not considered operating costs. To the extent that parking charges paid by the employer are related to use of the car in the course of employment, the charges are non-taxable reimbursements.

Any reimbursement of parking charges incurred for personal use is a taxable benefit.

The operating expense benefit is determined by applying a prescribed amount per kilometre of travel for personal purposes. This amount is currently $0.24 per kilometre of personal use, less amounts reimbursed to the company for the operating costs. This amount includes a GST/HST component. For taxpayers employed principally in selling or leasing automobiles, the prescribed rate is $0.21 per kilometre.

If the automobile is used primarily (more than 50%) for employment purposes, an optional formula—calculated as 50% of the standby charge—can be used to determine the operating cost benefit. To use this method, the employee must inform the employer by the end of the calendar year that she or he would like to use the optional formula to determine the operating cost benefit.

TAX TIP

Employees provided with employer-owned vehicles should keep records detailing the personal and employment use of the car to determine which option is more beneficial. Review the automobile arrangement to ensure that the real benefit, if any, justifies the complex record keeping required. Alternative arrangements of monthly allowances or mileage compensation may provide better real compensation and ease the paper burden.

If your business is registered for GST/HST, the taxable benefit is deemed to be a taxable supply and GST/HST must be remitted on the benefit amount (see article 57).

40 Automobile Expenses

Rather than providing your employees with a vehicle, it may be more tax effective for the vehicle to be acquired by the employee personally. If it is used for business purposes, the employee may be able to claim certain deductions. If this is the case, beware—the rules governing automobile deductions are complex and, as such, cannot be covered here in any great detail. They apply equally to corporations, sole proprietors and partnerships, as well as to employees who qualify to claim automobile expenses against their employment income.

Expenses must first be split into two categories: those that are subject to specific dollar limitations and those that are not. Depreciation, interest and leasing charges are subject to specific dollar restrictions. In general, the amount you can claim with respect to these expenses depends on when the vehicle was acquired. For all vehicles acquired after 2000, the maximum amount that can be depreciated is $30,000 (plus PST and GST or HST on this amount). GST/HST is not included in the depreciation base if it is refunded as an input tax credit. The maximum monthly interest deduction is $300. For all leases entered into after 2000, the maximum monthly lease amount that can be written off for tax purposes is $800 (plus PST and GST or HST on this amount). A separate restriction prorates deductible lease costs when the value of the vehicle exceeds the amount that is deductible for tax purposes.

For unincorporated businesses and employees, the total of the restricted and unrestricted expenses is then prorated between business and personal use, based on the number of kilometres driven for each purpose. Expenses incurred entirely for business purposes, such as parking, can be claimed in full. Corporations do not have to prorate expenses between business and personal use. Expenses can be claimed in full, provided they are reasonable. However, the employee benefit rules may require a benefit to be included in the income of the employee. Also, the employee benefit (standby charge) is calculated based on the original cost of the vehicle rather than the previously noted reduced amounts (see article 39).

If you are a sole proprietor or a partner and you use your vehicle less than 100% for business purposes, the eligible depreciation claim for the year is generally determined by the percentage of business use.

TAX TIP

Detailed records should be kept regarding a vehicle's business and personal use. These records must be accurately maintained to support the percentage claimed for business use. Keep in mind that it is the CRA's position that travel between a taxpayer's regular workplace and home is considered personal.

Recapture and terminal losses

If you dispose of a vehicle without replacing it, and the proceeds from the sale are less than the original cost of the vehicle but more than the undepreciated balance in the CCA class (UCC), you will have to report the excess amount as income. This amount is known as "recapture." Conversely, if there is an amount left in the undepreciated balance but no assets left in the class, you can take the remaining balance as a "terminal loss."

As an exception to this rule, the disposal of a Class 10.1 vehicle cannot create recapture or a terminal loss. A Class 10.1 vehicle is a passenger vehicle costing in excess of the prescribed amount for depreciation purposes (currently $30,000, plus applicable taxes).

EXAMPLE/**Calculating recapture or terminal loss**

> You acquire an automobile for $28,000 in 2004 and sell it in 2009 for $8,000. The vehicle is used entirely for business purposes. If you claimed the maximum CCA each year, the undepreciated amount at the beginning of 2009 would be $5,714. Therefore, you have to include $2,286 as recapture in income in 2009 (i.e., $8,000 – $5,714). In the unlikely event that you sold the vehicle for more than its original cost, you would also have to report a capital gain (to the extent that the proceeds exceeded this cost).
>
> On the other hand, if you were able to sell the automobile for only $4,000, you would have a terminal loss of $1,714 (i.e., $4,000 – $5,714).

41 Tax-Free Travel Allowances

If your employees use their own vehicles for employment purposes, you can eliminate a lot of their paperwork by providing them with a tax-free allowance to cover employment-related travel expenses.

The allowance qualifies for tax-free status if it is reasonable—and only if it is based on the actual number of kilometres that the car is used for employment purposes. Provided the per-kilometre reimbursement is reasonable, 100% of the amounts paid are deductible.

Allowances not based on the number of kilometres driven, such as a flat allowance of $400 per month, must be included in the employee's income. You can reimburse an employee for certain limited expenses (i.e., supplementary business insurance, parking costs incurred for business purposes, and toll and ferry charges) without affecting the tax-free status of the allowance, provided the per-kilometre requirement is met.

If you provide your employees with a combination of flat-rate and per-kilometre allowances (e.g., $200 per month plus $0.25 per kilometre), both components must be included in the employee's income.

TAX TIP

If you currently pay any of your employees a combination of flat-rate and per-kilometre allowance, consider changing the entire allowance to a per-kilometre reimbursement. For 2009, the limit on tax-exempt allowances paid by employers to employees is $0.52 per kilometre for the first 5,000 kilometres driven and $0.46 for each additional kilometre. For Yukon, Northwest Territories and Nunavut, the tax-exempt allowance is $0.04 higher.

TAX TIP

If the employment portion of travel expenses exceeds the amount of the tax-free allowance, the employee may be able to include the allowance in their income and claim related expenses. To do this, the allowance must be considered unreasonable. Since this treatment has been the subject of some recent court cases, professional advice may be required.

As with almost everything else, travel allowances also have GST/HST implications to both the employer and the employee. The treatment varies, depending on whether the payment is taxable to the employee (see article 57).

42 The Score on Stock Options

As an incentive strategy, you may provide your employees with the right to acquire shares in your company at a fixed price for a limited period. Normally, the shares will be worth more than the purchase price at the time the employee exercises the option.

For example, you provide one of your key employees with the option to buy 1,000 shares in the company at $5 each. This is the estimated fair market value per share at the time the option is granted. When the stock price rises to $10, your employee exercises his option to buy the shares for $5,000. Since their current value is $10,000, he has a profit of $5,000.

How is the benefit taxed?

The income tax consequences of exercising the option depends on whether the company granting the option is a Canadian-controlled private corporation (CCPC), the period of time the employee holds the shares before eventually selling them and whether the employee deals at arm's length with the corporation.

If the company is a CCPC, there will not be any income tax consequences until the employee disposes of the shares, provided the employee is not related to the controlling shareholders of the company. In general, the difference between the fair market value of the shares at the time the option was exercised and the option price (i.e., $5 per share in our example) will be taxed as employment income in the year the shares are sold. The employee can claim a deduction from taxable income equal to half this amount, if certain conditions are met. Half of the difference between the ultimate sale price and the fair market value of the shares at the date the option was exercised will be reported as a taxable capital gain or allowable capital loss.

EXAMPLE/**Cashing in on stock options**

In 2008, your company, a CCPC, offered several of its senior employees the option to buy 1,000 shares in the company at $10 each. In 2009, the company performs very well and it is estimated that the value of the stock has doubled. Several of the employees decide to exercise their options. By 2011, the value of the stock has doubled again to $40 per share and some of the employees decide to sell their shares. Since the company was a CCPC at the time the option was granted, there is no taxable benefit until the shares are sold in 2011. It is assumed that the conditions for the half deduction are satisfied. The benefit is calculated as follows:

Employment Income	
Employment income ($20 – $10) × (1,000 shares)	$10,000
Income deduction (50%)	(5,000)
Income inclusion	$5,000
Capital Gain	
Proceeds of disposition ($40 × 1,000 shares)	$40,000
Cost base ($20 × 1,000 shares)	($20,000)
Capital gain	$20,000
	50%
Taxable Capital Gain	$10,000

Public company stock options

If the company granting the option is a public company, or not a CCPC, the rules are somewhat different. The general rule is, in the year the option is exercised, the employee has to report a taxable employment benefit equal to the amount by which the fair market value of the shares (at the time the option is exercised) exceeds the option price paid for the shares. However, since this tax treatment could force the employee to sell some of the shares to pay the resulting tax bill, eligible employees of public companies can elect to be taxed similar to employees of private companies, who generally do not have to pay tax until they sell their shares. This deferral is effective for options exercised after February 27, 2000, and is subject to an annual vesting limit of $100,000 based on the fair market value of the underlying shares at the time the option was granted to the employee.

In general, "eligible employees" must deal at arm's length with their employer and any related corporation. They cannot own 10% or more of the shares of any class of the corporation or any related corporation. In addition, the amount paid by the employee to acquire the security can generally not be less than the fair market value of the security at the time the option was granted. The option must involve a security listed on a prescribed stock exchange. In a situation where the option price goes down because the fair market value of the underlying stock declines in value, the deferral is still available, provided the employee qualifies for it.

Employees who wish to defer taxation of a stock option benefit must file an election with either their employer or the person who is responsible for filing their T4 information slip. This election must be filed by January 15 of the year following the year in which the shares are acquired.

This election is to take the form of a letter containing the following information:

- a request to take advantage of the deferral;
- the amount of the deferral;
- confirmation that the taxpayer was a resident of Canada when the shares were acquired; and
- confirmation that the annual $100,000 limit has not been exceeded.

The onus is on the employee rather than the employer to make the election. The election allows the employer to reduce income tax withholding by the amount of tax related to the benefit being deferred. However, the stock option benefit—deferred or otherwise—is still reported on the employees' T4 slips for the year the option is exercised. Employees then file with their tax return a special form (Form T1212—Statement of Deferred Stock Option Benefits) that keeps track of the stock option benefits deferred. This form must be filed for each year there is a balance of deferred stock option benefits outstanding.

To the extent that the employee does not qualify for the above deferral, the general rule noted above continues to apply: the difference between the option price and the fair market value of the shares at the time the option is exercised will be taxable as employment income in the year the option is exercised. When certain conditions are met, a deduction equal to half the taxable benefit is allowed.

TAX TIP

Consider option arrangements that allow employees to receive, in lieu of shares, a cash payment equal to the value of the options. When the plan gives the employee the choice, the same tax consequences apply to the cash payment as would apply to the issuance of the shares: the employment benefit is included in income and the related 50% deduction is available if certain conditions are met. However, the employer can deduct 100% of the cash payment from the company's taxable income. Professional assistance should be sought to assist in structuring this type of an employee incentive strategy.

Decline in stock value

In the numerical example on page 65, the value of the stock increased between the time the stock was acquired and the time it was sold. But what would happen if the share value declined to $10 at the time of sale in 2011? In this case, the employee would report a net income inclusion of $5,000 and a $10,000 capital loss ($5,000 allowable capital loss). Unfortunately, while the income inclusion is afforded the same tax treatment as a capital gain, it isn't actually a capital gain. It is taxed as employment income. As a result, the capital loss realized in 2011 cannot be used to offset the income inclusion resulting from the taxable benefit.

With the significant decline in the value of some shares, a number of employees have been in the position of paying tax on a benefit no longer reflected in the value of shares acquired. Although this caused concern for a number of taxpayers, the Finance Department has reviewed this situation and concluded that no relief should be granted to such employees. The department's view is that employees who have decided to hold their shares have chosen to accept a market risk as investors. As investors, they are subject to the same general income tax rules as other investors with respect to capital gains and losses on the underlying shares.

Anyone in difficult financial circumstances as a result of these rules should contact their local CRA Tax Services office to determine whether special payment arrangements can be made.

Options held at the date of death

Special rules exist for unexercised options under an employee stock option plan held by an employee on the date of death. In general, the difference between the fair market value of options held immediately before death and whatever price may have been paid to acquire the options is reported as employment income on the taxpayer's final income tax return (subject to a 50% deduction, if certain conditions are met). If the stock option is exercised or otherwise disposed of within the first taxation year of the estate, the legal representative can elect to treat any decline in value—from the date of death to the date of exercise or sale—as a loss from employment income for the year in which the taxpayer died.

43 Qualified Scientific Research Expenditures

Write-offs and tax credits above and beyond your usual business deductions are possible if you conduct scientific research that relates to your business. Scientific research and experimental development (SR&ED) consists of pure research, applied research and experimental development. Of these three activities, experimental development is often the most difficult to evaluate. Part of the problem is the difficulty in defining what constitutes development. It is equally difficult to distinguish exactly when development ceases and production begins—and production does not qualify as research and development. Your accountant can assess if your SR&ED qualifies and tell you what you may have to do to ensure that your SR&ED activities are recognized by the CRA.

What can you deduct?

For purposes of determining the amount that qualifies as an SR&ED expenditure, all qualifying research expenditures of a current nature may be deducted in full the year they are incurred. However, a current-year deduction will not be permitted for accrued amounts that are not paid within 180 days of the end of the taxation year. In addition, subject to the available-for-use rules (see article 7), new equipment purchased solely for qualified research in Canada may be written off in the year it is acquired. As a general rule, expenditures incurred to acquire or rent a building do not qualify as scientific research expenditures.

TAX TIP

You don't have to claim the full amount of eligible SR&ED expenses in the year in which they were incurred. It may make better business sense to carry forward and deduct the amounts in a subsequent year. However, to deduct an amount for SR&ED, you must be carrying on the business to which the research relates in the year you make the claim. For example, in some years you might not want to claim a deduction if it will increase a non-capital loss, especially if you expect to realize losses in future years. By the same token, it might be advantageous to carry the deduction forward to a year in which it can be claimed against a higher marginal tax rate. Unlike non-capital losses, undeducted SR&ED expenses can be carried forward indefinitely.

Claiming SR&ED

To claim special treatment for scientific research expenditures, you must complete Form T661. This requires you to provide a breakdown of the expenditures made, as well as details of the types of projects undertaken, such as the scientific or technological aspects they contained, the advancements they made and the uncertainties they pursued. It is vital that descriptions of projects are complete. Failure to describe the projects properly could result in a rejection of the claim or, at best, a significant delay in processing.

Outlays will not qualify for the beneficial tax treatment afforded research and development expenditures unless Form T661 is filed within 12 months of the filing due date for the taxation year. In other words, if a corporation with a December 31 year-end incurs SR&ED expenditures, Form T661 (for the 2009 taxation year) must be filed by June 30, 2011, because the filing due date of the corporate income tax return is June 30, 2010—six months from the December 31, 2009, year-end.

If your company plans to submit a claim, you should be aware that the CRA is not lenient with taxpayers who file claims late. The claim will be rejected if it is not complete within the 18-month deadline.

For this reason, it is important to file your claim early, ideally with the corporation's income tax return for the year. If any information is missing, the claim will still be accepted, as long as it is complete within the 18-month period. If you file a claim at or near the deadline, it will be essential to ensure that the form is complete at the time it is filed, since it may not be possible for the CRA to advise you in time if anything is missing. The end result is that the tax credits will be lost.

New Form T661

Following consultations with stakeholders on ways to make the SR&ED program more effective, the CRA introduced a new Form T661 and related guide (T4088). The new form is intended to simplify the claim process for SR&ED tax credits. It is effective as of November 10, 2008. However, if you file a SR&ED claim for a tax year ending on or prior to December 31, 2008, the CRA will accept the new or the old version of the form. For tax years after December 31, 2008, the new version of the form must be used.

The new form incorporates the following key changes:

1. a maximum number of words that can be used for scientific descriptions;
2. a new format for presenting financial information; and
3. the requirement to include a technical description for each project claimed.

It's expected that the greatest challenge with the new form will be the new maximum word limit for describing a project. The new form includes three sections for scientific descriptions, each with a word limit, regardless of the project's scope. The first two sections contain a description of advancements and obstacles (uncertainties), each with a 350-word limit. The section on work completed is subject to a 700-word limit. In June 2009, the CRA announced that claimants with more than 20 projects will have to include technical descriptions for only the 20 largest projects in dollar value for tax years ending before

2010. However, for taxation years ending in 2010 and later, claimants must file technical descriptions for all projects claimed.

Investment tax credit

Both current and capital expenditures on scientific research also qualify for a business investment tax credit (ITC). A Canadian-controlled private corporation (CCPC) is entitled to claim a 35% ITC on up to $3 million of qualifying expenditures if it meets certain conditions (prior to February 26, 2008, the limit was $2 million). However, an individual carrying on SR&ED qualifies for only a 20% rate, which is why it's generally recommended that SR&ED be carried on by a private corporation. For example, if you own a small CCPC that incurs $100,000 of qualified scientific expenditures, your company can claim an investment tax credit of $35,000 ($100,000 × 35%). This amount is first deducted from your company's federal taxes payable for the year. If there is any amount remaining, the excess can generate a refund.

This refundable system is available only to individuals and certain CCPCs. SR&ED ITCs earned at the 35% rate are eligible for a 100% refund if the ITC relates to current SR&ED expenditures. For capital expenditures, the refundable portion is equal to 40% of the unused credits. ITCs either reduce the tax cost of the related asset or are included in income in the year following the year the credit is claimed. Other corporations and partnerships earn tax credits at the 20% rate, which must be applied to reduce taxes payable and are not refundable. Alternatively, if it is to your advantage, you can carry unused credits back for up to three years or forward for up to 20 years (10 years for credits earned prior to 2006).

As noted above, a CCPC is eligible for the 35% tax credit rate on up to $3 million of qualifying SR&ED expenditures in the year ($2 million prior to February 26, 2008). However, this maximum limit is available only when the corporation's prior-year taxable income and taxable capital did not exceed certain thresholds. The taxable income limit is the amount that qualifies for the small-business deduction (see article 27) and the taxable capital limit is $10 million. The expenditure limit is gradually phased out when these amounts are exceeded. The upper limit of the phase-out range for the expenditure limit with respect to prior-year taxable income and prior-year taxable capital is $700,000 and $50 million, respectively (prior to February 26, 2008, these limits were $600,000 and $15 million). The increases in the above amounts apply to taxation years that end after February 25, 2008, prorated based on the number of days in the tax year that are after February 25, 2008. The upper limit of the phase-out range for the expenditure limit with respect to prior-year taxable income will increase to $800,000 for 2010 taxation years and will be prorated based on the number of days in the tax year that are after December 31, 2009.

When determining eligibility for this credit, the taxable income and taxable capital include those of the corporation and all associated corporations. Qualifying corporations not eligible for the 35% rate can still earn credits at the rate of 20%.

Filing due date

To claim an investment tax credit, a completed form giving details of the qualifying cost or expense must be filed within 12 months of the due date of the return for the taxation year in which the ITC arises. This filing deadline is the same as the filing deadline for SR&ED expenditures. The details are reported on Schedule 31 (for corporations) and Form T2038 (for individuals). To have proof of timely delivery, given the serious outcome that can result if any part of the claim is misplaced, it's recommended that the claim be sent by registered mail to the appropriate Tax Services centre.

TAX TIP

To qualify for an ITC, you must make sure that all current SR&ED expenditures are paid within 180 days of the year-end.

TAX TIP

In the case of equipment that is used only partially for SR&ED, the cost may not be written off as an eligible SR&ED expenditure. However, if the equipment is used primarily (more than 50%) for SR&ED, the cost may be eligible for a reduced ITC. For equipment to qualify for a tax credit, the equipment must be new.

Overhead expenses

One area that causes confusion is the determination of eligible SR&ED overhead expenses. To simplify matters, you have the option of calculating eligible overhead expenses using a simple formula based on wages and salaries. The amount arrived at in this manner is called the proxy amount. In general, this amount is calculated as 65% of the portion of salaries or wages of employees directly engaged in SR&ED in Canada.

The proxy amount is added to the expenses eligible for an ITC. However, it does not increase the amount of SR&ED expenditures available for deduction. Again, there are special rules that limit the amount of salary to be used in the calculation. These rules apply if the salary has been paid to an employee who does not deal at arm's length with the employer corporation, or to an employee who owns or is related to someone who owns 10% or more of the shares of the employer corporation.

TAX TIP

The use of the "proxy amount" is elective, and if you choose to use this method for a particular year, the election must be made when Form T661 is filed for that year.

A tax court case, *Alcatel Canada Inc. v. The Queen* found that the value of any stock option benefits could also be included as a qualified expenditure for purposes of calculating the company's proxy amount and overall SR&ED claim. However, rules have since been introduced to limit the amount on which an ITC or deduction may be claimed to the amount that has actually been disbursed by the taxpayer. This restriction relates to employee stock options granted and shares issued after November 16, 2005.

Provincial incentives

Some of the provinces also offer investment tax credits and other tax incentives for SR&ED. The qualifying activities must be carried out in the province that grants these tax breaks.

TAX TIP

Not incorporated? Here's another reason to consider it. If you are carrying on a business and conduct scientific research that relates to that business, you should consider incorporating. The provincial incentives, as well as the 35% ITC rate, are available only to corporations.

The rules involved in claiming SR&ED expenditures and related investment tax credits are extremely complex. Consult your tax adviser to ensure that you get the maximum benefit from these tax incentives.

44 Shareholder Agreements

If your corporation has more than one shareholder, a shareholders' agreement should be drawn up to establish the ongoing rights and responsibilities of the shareholders in the ownership and administration of the company.

In the event of death . . .

One of the more important aspects of the shareholders' agreement is that it should specify what should happen in the event of the death or disability of one of the shareholders. This will not only provide for a smooth transition of the business, but also generally establish a purchaser for the shares of the deceased, a formula for determining the purchase price and a method for funding the purchase. By arranging proper tax planning, the buyout can be orchestrated to minimize a drain on cash flow for the company and survivors. A sound arrangement can also minimize or defer the tax liability of the estate.

The most efficient means of funding a buy-sell agreement or share repurchase on the death of a shareholder is generally through life insurance. However, the use of corporate-owned life insurance to fund a share repurchase is subject to special rules that can reduce its tax effectiveness, depending on when the insurance was acquired. It is highly recommended that you speak with your tax adviser to develop a plan appropriate to your situation.

TAX TIP

In situations where it's intended that life insurance proceeds will be used to fund a share repurchase, the rules can get complicated and certain planning may be required. One of the things that should be at the top of your agenda is to undertake a review of your shareholders' agreement. That way, you can ensure that your objectives are met in the most tax-effective manner.

45 Reporting System for Contractors

If you are in the construction business and make payments to subcontractors, you have to report certain payments to the CRA.

Who must report?

Reporting is required by all businesses—whether carried on by an individual, partnership or corporation—whose principal activity is construction. For this purpose, construction is defined as erecting, installing, altering, modifying, repairing, improving, demolishing, dismantling or removing any structure or part thereof.

What payments must be reported?

You must report payments to subcontractors for construction services if the amount paid for services is $500 or more. Payments for goods are not to be included in determining if a payment satisfies this test. The payments can be reported on a calendar-year or a fiscal-year basis.

For example, assume your business's year-end is June 30, 2009. Your reporting return for 2009 can either report all payments from July 1, 2008, to June 30, 2009, or it can report all payments made from January 1, 2009, to December 31, 2009.

What information must be reported?

If you are involved in the construction business and pay a subcontractor for services rendered, you must report the name of the subcontractor, the business address, the amount paid for the reporting period and the subcontractor's business number (BN) or social insurance number (SIN) if no BN is available.

The information can be reported either on a Statement of Contract Payments (Form T5018) or on a line-by-line basis in a column format with the appropriate summary information.

In general, the due date for filing the required information is six months from the end of the reporting period.

Although there is no requirement to provide any information slips to the subcontractors, it is reasonable to assume they will want to know what information is being reported to the CRA.

TAX TIP

If you are in the construction business and pay subcontractors for work performed, you should ensure that you obtain all the information necessary to complete the information return and file it on a timely basis.

46 Farming Businesses

While the term "farming business" is not defined, the tax legislation does state that "farming" includes tilling the soil, raising or exhibiting livestock, maintaining horses for racing, raising poultry, fur farming, dairy farming, fruit growing and the keeping of bees, but it does not include an office or employment under a person engaged in the business of farming.

Case law has established that farming can also include other activities, such as forestry operations or the operation of a game reserve, as well as an artificial incubation business, which includes the purchasing and incubating of eggs, followed by the sale of chicks a few days after they have been hatched.

The CRA has indicated that under certain specific circumstances, farming includes fish breeding, market gardening, the operation of nurseries and greenhouses, and aquaculture and hydroponics.

In addition, to benefit from the specific farming rules, your farming operations have to be of a business nature. The CRA has established the following criteria for determining whether a farming operation is a business:

- The extent of the activity in relation to businesses of a similar nature and size in the same locality. The best criterion is the area used for farming. If your farm property is much too small to generate a reasonable expectation of profit, it can be assumed that it is for the taxpayer's personal use or pleasure.
- The time devoted to farming compared to the time devoted to a job or other means of earning income. If you devote the major portion of your time to the farm during harvesting season, you are likely carrying on a farm business.
- The financial commitments for future expansion in light of your resources. This criterion is based on the capital you have

invested in the operation over a number of years and the acquisition of buildings, machinery, equipment and inventories.

- Your entitlement to some sort of provincial farm assistance.

The fact that your farming operations do not appear to have a reasonable expectation of profit at a particular time does not prove in and of itself that you are not carrying on a farming business. Over the past few years, the courts have taken the position that as long as the activity does not include any personal or recreational component, the activity has to be considered commercial in nature. Proposed changes to the reasonable-expectation-of-profit rules (see article 160) may change this conclusion.

Related businesses

- Raising and maintaining racehorses is considered a farming business to the extent that you can demonstrate it is not a hobby.
- Sharecropping (rent in kind) is defined as an agreement whereby a landowner receives part of the harvest from the tenant as rent. The portion of the harvest that you receive under a sharecropping agreement is considered to be leasing income rather than farming income.
- Even if a woodlot operation is literally a forestry business, if the business is carried on jointly with a farming business the two together are considered a farming business if you elect to report the income on a cash basis.
- If you plant, maintain and harvest Christmas trees, you are deemed to carry on a farming business regardless of whether you pursue other farming activities. If tree sales have not been reported by the sixth year after the trees have been planted (or later, depending on local growing conditions), your operations may be considered forestry, which means that prior years' returns can be amended.
- Payments you receive as consideration for the right to use your marketing quotas (e.g., tobacco, eggs, milk) are considered as income from a farming business.

- If you carry on an active farming business, the proceeds from the sale of sand, gravel and topsoil or similar materials taken from the land are normally income from a farming business.
- If you reforest land with the intention of letting the trees grow until they have matured, i.e., from 40 to 60 years or longer, you are considered to be carrying on a farming business. With the exception of income from occasional cuttings to make clearings, no income can be earned from this operation until the trees have matured. In the meantime, you have to pay the periodic costs, e.g., property taxes, planting, fertilizing and cutting clearings. If the facts indicate that reforestation was carried out on a systematic basis and is managed like a business in accordance with sound forestry practices and provides hope for profits when the trees have matured, the loss created by these costs can be deducted as a business loss, subject to the restricted farm loss rules discussed below.

Methods of reporting income

If you carry on a farming business, you can calculate your farming income using either the cash or the accrual method.

The accrual method is based on generally accepted accounting principles, which means that revenues should be recorded in the year they are earned, regardless of when the cash is received. Similarly, expenses are deducted in the year they are incurred, not when they are actually paid. Inventories at the end of the fiscal year also have to be taken into account.

Under the cash method, you do not account for amounts receivable or payable in computing income. For tax purposes, expenses are recorded when they are paid and revenues when they are received. Inventories are not included in determining income, with the exception of the mandatory and optional inventory adjustment.

You can switch from the accrual method to the cash method simply by filing an income tax return using the cash method. However, if you file a tax return using the cash method, you must continue to do so in subsequent years unless permission is obtained from the minister to do otherwise.

There are specific rules for calculating the inventories of a farm business that effectively prevent you from using inventories to create a loss.

Farming losses

There are two types of farming losses: farm losses and restricted farm losses. A farm loss is your loss for a year from carrying on a farming business that constitutes your principal source of income (i.e., more than 50% of all income). You will have a restricted farm loss if your total income is not principally from farming. In such a case, only a portion of the loss is deductible against your other sources of income. Any excess can be deducted only against farming income.

If farming is just a hobby, you cannot deduct any loss.

Restricted farm losses

In general, the amount of the loss you can claim against your other sources of income for the year is equal to the lesser of:

- The net farm loss for the year; and
- \$2,500 + the lesser of:
    - 50% × (farm loss – \$2,500); or
    - \$6,250

to a maximum of \$8,750.

EXAMPLE/**Restricted farm loss**

> John incurs a \$12,000 loss from his horseracing business in 2009. Raising horses is not his main source of income. The loss he can deduct against his other sources of income is equal to \$7,250; i.e., \$2,500 + (50% × [\$12,000 – \$2,500]). The balance of \$4,750 can be deducted only against farming income earned by John in future years.

Farm losses and restricted farm losses incurred in taxation years ending after 2005 may be carried back for up to three years and forward for up to 20 years (losses incurred prior to 2006 were limited to a 10-year carry-forward period). Farm losses are deductible against all sources of income, whereas restricted farm losses can be applied only against farming income.

Capital gains deduction for qualified farm property

Subject to certain conditions, if you sell or transfer a qualified farm property, you can take advantage of a capital gains deduction with respect to the capital gain on the sale or transfer. For qualifying dispositions after March 18, 2007, the maximum deduction that can be claimed is $750,000. Prior to this time, the maximum deduction was $500,000. This limit is a cumulative lifetime limit and is reduced by prior capital gains deduction claims, regardless of whether the claim related to farm property. A qualified farm property includes:

- a building used in carrying on a farm business;
- a share of the capital stock of a family farm corporation;
- an interest in a family farm partnership; or
- a qualified capital property used in carrying on a farm business, e.g., a quota.

In general, to take advantage of this deduction, you or your spouse, common-law partner, child, grandchild, father or mother has to have actively participated in carrying on the farming business. While the tax laws do not define the term "actively participated," it is understood to mean a certain amount of activity, but not necessarily full time.

The rules related to the capital gains deduction are quite complicated and can be affected by numerous factors, such as your cumulative net investment loss (CNIL) balance and allowable business investment loss (ABIL) claim. You should consult your tax adviser if you plan to claim the deduction to offset a capital gain on farm property (see also article 147).

Intergenerational transfers

There are rules to permit a deferral of all or part of the income tax arising on the transfer of a farm property to a child, grandchild or great-grandchild. If you transfer or sell farm property to such a person, you can elect proceeds of disposition for the property at any amount between the tax cost and the fair market value. However, if you simply give the farm property to a child, grandchild or great-grandchild, or if you sell it for less than its tax cost, the proceeds of disposition will equal the property's tax cost.

Similar rules govern the transfer of farm property on death.

There is also an intergenerational tax-deferred rollover for woodlot operations provided you or a family member is actively involved in the management of the woodlot to the extent required by a prescribed forest-management plan.

47 Fishing Businesses

Measures were introduced in 2006 to provide fishing businesses with tax incentives similar to those available to farming businesses.

Capital gains deduction for qualified fishing property

For dispositions after May 1, 2006, the enhanced $500,000/$750,000 capital gains deduction is extended to include dispositions of qualified fishing property (see article 148). This includes:

- real property and fishing vessels used in a fishing business;
- eligible capital property, such as an interest in a fishing license;
- a share of the capital stock of a family fishing corporation; or
- an interest in a family fishing partnership.

In general, to take advantage of this deduction, you or your spouse, common-law partner, child, grandchild, father or mother has to have actively participated in carrying on the fishing business. For purposes of applying these rules, the definitions will parallel those used for farmers (see article 46).

Intergenerational transfers

Similar to farmers, if you transfer qualified fishing property to your child or grandchild after May 1, 2006, the transfer can take place on a tax-deferred basis. This means that you can give the fishing property to a child or grandchild without having to report any income or gain on the transfer—the child will inherit the property's tax cost.

Again, definitions and related measures will parallel the existing rules for intergenerational transfers of farm property (see article 46).

48 Transfer Pricing

A transfer price is the amount charged between related parties involved in international transactions—for example, where a Canadian resident buys goods and services from or sells products to a related non-resident corporation. The government's concern centres on ensuring that the price charged is equal to the amount that would be agreed upon by parties dealing at arm's length. If it is not, taxable profits may be shifted from one jurisdiction to another.

The Canadian rules on transfer pricing are similar to those that have been put in place in other industrialized countries, such as the United States, the United Kingdom and Australia. The rules require Canadian taxpayers to adopt the arm's-length principle in setting transfer prices for transactions with related non-resident persons and to document the basis for their transfer prices.

The arm's-length principle has always been required in transactions with related persons, but there are now specific documentation requirements. These standards stipulate that the documentation for a particular tax year must be completed by the due date for filing that year's tax return. Failure to complete the required documentation can result in a penalty of 10% of the transfer pricing adjustment, even where no additional tax arises as a result of that adjustment.

This area can be quite complex, as transfer prices must be developed that are acceptable to the tax authorities of both countries: the home country of the non-resident entity and Canada.

TAX TIP

If you have transactions with related non-resident persons, have your tax adviser review your transfer pricing polices, as well as your related documentation, to determine whether they comply with the transfer pricing legislation.

49 Thin Capitalization Rules

The thin capitalization rules are directed at preventing non-residents of Canada who own shares in Canadian resident corporations from withdrawing profits in the form of interest payments that will be subject to a low rate of withholding tax and reduce Canadian taxable income. The impact of these rules is to limit the amount of interest that can be deducted by a Canadian corporation where the amount of outstanding debts payable to specified non-resident shareholders exceeds a certain amount.

In general, a "specified shareholder" is a shareholder who, either alone or together with persons with whom she or he is not dealing at arm's length, owns shares of any class of the corporation that give the holder 25% or more of the votes or fair market value of the corporation.

Effective for tax years commencing after 2000, if the amount of debt to such persons exceeds two times the "equity" of the Canadian resident corporation, a prorated portion of the interest paid or payable in the year to such non-residents is not allowed as a deduction in calculating the income of the Canadian resident corporation. A corporation cannot correct an equity deficiency by having specified non-residents subscribe for additional share capital immediately prior to year-end.

TAX TIP

If your corporation pays interest to specified non-residents, contact your tax adviser to determine whether it is subject to these rules. If so, planning strategies may be available to reduce or eliminate their impact.

50 Interest Deduction for Investments in Foreign Affiliates

The 2007 federal budget included tax measures that would severely restrict the deductibility of interest on money borrowed by a corporate taxpayer to invest in shares or debt of a foreign affiliate. In general, a foreign affiliate is a non-resident corporation in which the Canadian taxpayer's equity ownership is at least 10%.

Based on recommendations in a report from the Advisory Panel on Canada's System of International Taxation, the government repealed this proposed legislation. Therefore, the rules to restrict the interest deduction for investments in foreign affiliates will not become effective.

51 Withholding Tax on Interest Payments

In December 2008, an updated Canada–U.S. tax treaty entered into force. One of the key changes was the elimination of the 10% withholding tax on cross-border interest payments. Withholding tax on interest payments between non-related (arm's-length) parties is eliminated retroactive to January 1, 2008. Withholding tax on interest payments between related (non-arm's-length) parties will be reduced to:

- 7% in 2008;
- 4% in 2009; and
- 0% in 2010 and subsequent years.

Where excess amounts were withheld during the 2008 year, the refund request should be made on Form NR7-R.

The updated treaty deals with only payments between Canada and the United States. The tax rules also provide that the Canadian withholding tax on interest paid to all arm's-length non-residents (regardless of their country of residence) is eliminated effective January 1, 2008.

52 Withholding Tax for Non-Resident Actors

If you pay amounts to a non-resident who acts in films or videos made in Canada, you are required to withhold 23% of the gross amount paid to the non-resident (either to the individual or a corporation related to the individual). These rules apply to only acting income—they do not apply to other services performed in the movie and television industry, such as directing, producing and other work behind the scenes. Also, these rules do not apply to persons in other sectors of the entertainment industry, such as musical performers, ice or air show performers, or international speakers.

Non-resident actors have the option of filing a tax return to recover some of the amount withheld. Regardless of whether the recipient chooses this option, you are still required to withhold and remit to the Receiver General 23% of any amounts paid.

53 Payments to Non-Residents for Services Rendered in Canada

All Canadian residents making payments to non-residents for services rendered in Canada (other than in the course of employment) must withhold and remit tax at a rate of 15%. However, the service provider can reduce or eliminate the withholding tax if they have obtained a treaty-based or income-and-expense waiver from the CRA. Failure to deduct and remit this tax to the CRA can make you liable for the outstanding amount, plus interest and penalty.

The 15% withholding tax applies to a fee, commission or other amount paid to a non-resident individual, partnership or corporation with respect to services rendered in Canada other than in the course of regular and continuous employment.

Non-residents who are employed in Canada are subject to withholding tax deductions in the same manner as Canadian residents (i.e., using graduated tax rates) unless the employee has obtained a treaty-based exemption. To obtain this exemption, the employee must make a request in writing and send it to the tax services office for the area where the services will be provided.

TAX TIP

If you make payments to non-residents for services rendered in Canada and fail to comply with the withholding requirements, you may be liable for significant penalties and interest in addition to the 15% withholding tax. Amounts should be withheld and remitted on any payments to a non-resident unless a waiver has been obtained.

54 The Goods on the GST/HST

In 1991, the GST replaced the old federal sales tax as a consumption tax on most goods and services provided in Canada. Unlike provincial retail sales taxes that are imposed only at the time of a sale to a consumer, the GST is a multi-level tax collected every time a taxable good or service is provided. Registered businesses must charge GST on their revenues that are taxable for GST purposes. As the GST is a value-added tax, most businesses can recover the GST paid on expenses they incur to earn taxable revenue. This is claimed in their GST return as an "input tax credit," Although GST was originally set at the rate of 7%, the rate was reduced to 6% effective July 1, 2006, and again to 5% on January 1, 2008.

In 1997, Newfoundland and Labrador, New Brunswick and Nova Scotia replaced their respective provincial sales taxes and harmonized them with the federal GST to create the Harmonized Sales Tax (HST). The HST operates in the same manner and is generally applicable to the same base of goods and services as the GST, but it is applied at a rate of 13% (15% before July 1, 2006, and 14% from July 1, 2007 to December 31, 2007). A business registered for the GST is automatically registered for the HST and both are filed in the same return. It is proposed that Ontario will also harmonize its sales tax system, effective July 1, 2010.

Quebec has largely harmonized its provincial sales tax, the QST, with the federal GST/HST. It is applied on a similar basis as the GST and taxed on the consideration plus the GST. Similar to the GST, the QST paid on expenditures incurred to earn taxable income is also refundable as an input tax credit. However, some restrictions may apply in Quebec. Similar restrictions on claiming ITCs are also proposed for the 8% provincial component of the harmonized Ontario tax.

The other provincial retail sales taxes are not value-added taxes like the GST/HST or QST. Instead, they apply to most goods and certain services, unless an exemption is available. Unlike the GST/HST or QST, most businesses cannot recover the provincial retail sales taxes.

Supplies of goods or services are taxed in three ways. Most goods and services are rated as taxable supplies and are taxed at 5% outside the HST-participating provinces and 13% in the HST provinces. In general, all tax collected is to be remitted. Any GST/HST–registered business that makes only taxable supplies can recover as an input tax credit all the GST/HST it pays on supplies it purchases for use in its commercial activities. Tax is not collected on zero-rated supplies, but full input tax credits are claimed for the GST/HST paid on related inputs. Zero-rated supplies include most basic foods, agricultural products, prescription drugs, medical devices and most goods and services that are exported.

Exempt supplies are not subject to GST/HST, but a business making them is not entitled to claim an input tax credit for the GST/HST on related costs. In effect, a business making exempt supplies bears the cost of the GST/HST and must factor it into the price of the goods and services sold. Long-term residential rents, health care services and financial services are some of the most common types of exempt supplies.

55 GST/HST Registration, Collection and Remittance

Businesses that have $30,000 or less in annual worldwide taxable sales are not required to register and collect tax. However, to determine if your business meets this threshold, the worldwide revenues of associated entities are included in measuring annual taxable sales. Associated businesses can include related parties, such as shareholders, corporations, partnerships, trusts or individuals. If their combined taxable revenues exceed the $30,000 threshold, all of the businesses must be registered.

A business that is not required to register because it has less than $30,000 in annual taxable sales is called a small supplier. Such businesses can volunteer to register and collect tax, as this enables them to claim input tax credits for any GST/HST they pay on supplies purchased for use in their commercial activities (see article 56). This is generally advisable if the recipient of the supply is also registered for the tax.

Separate thresholds are used to determine whether charities and public sector bodies are required to register.

New businesses

Starting a new business? In most cases, it's generally a good idea to register for GST/HST as soon as you're allowed. Provided your business makes taxable or zero-rated supplies, early registration ensures that GST/HST paid on costs incurred is recoverable, since any tax paid prior to registration can generally be recovered in limited circumstances and only on the purchase of inventory, capital property and prepaid services still on hand at the time of registration. Be sure to register early because, in many situations, registering late can result in not recovering any GST paid before registration.

When to report

Every business has a reporting period based on the revenue of the associated group. Most businesses are required to report quarterly. However, large businesses (over $6 million in annual taxable supplies for the associated group) must report monthly, while smaller businesses (under $1,500,000 in annual taxable supplies for the group) are generally put on an annual filing frequency. However, they can elect to file either on a quarterly or monthly basis. New GST/HST registrants with annual taxable supplies of under $1,500,000 for the group are automatically assigned an annual reporting period unless they choose to file more frequently. Prior to 2008, the small-business filing threshold was $500,000.

TAX TIP

> You can elect to report more frequently than required. This is advisable if you are generally in a net refund position, as businesses that sell a large percentage of zero-rated goods (e.g., businesses that export goods to customers outside Canada) often are.

Certain businesses that have either a nil balance or a refund of $10,000 or less can use GST/HST TELEFILE to file their GST/HST returns. Another option is to use GST/HST NETFILE, which allows you to file your GST/HST return directly to the CRA over the Internet.

56 Input Tax Credits

If you have paid GST/HST on goods and services used in making taxable and zero-rated supplies, you can recover the GST paid by claiming input tax credits on your GST return. To ensure that your claim will be allowed, you must have supporting documentation in your records in case your claim is ever challenged. You should go over the detailed rules that govern the content of this supporting documentation thoroughly to ensure that you have complied with each stipulation. Audit problems often arise through deficient documentation, even if the deficiency is minor.

If input tax credits claimed in a reporting period exceed the tax owing, the excess is refunded to the business.

In general terms, the following chart outlines the prescribed information that needs to be included as supporting documentation for the purposes of claiming input tax credits.

Information Required	Total Sale under $30	Total Sale of $30 to $149.99	Total Sale of $150 or More
Vendor's business or trading name	✔	✔	✔
Invoice date	✔	✔	✔
Total amount paid or payable	✔	✔	✔
An indication of the total GST/HST		✔	✔
An indication of which items are taxed at what rate			
Vendor's Business Number (GST/HST number)		✔	✔
Buyer's name or trading name		✔	✔
Brief description of goods or services			✔
Terms of payment			✔

Shorter time frame for recovery of input tax credits

Listed financial institutions and certain registrants, whose annual taxable supplies (including the supplies of associated businesses) exceed $6 million for each of the preceding two years, have only two years to claim input tax credits. The CRA, on the other hand, still has four years to audit a GST/HST return. Therefore, it is essential that large businesses of these types ensure that their systems accurately and completely capture and claim all GST/HST paid. Businesses with taxable supplies of 90% or more in either of the two immediately preceding fiscal years are excluded from the two-year restriction, as are charities. These, and all other registrants, maintain the ability to claim input tax credits for a period of four years.

Allocation of tax between taxable and exempt supplies

Businesses that make both taxable and exempt supplies must allocate between the two types of supplies the recovery of the GST paid on purchases. Any reasonable method of allocation is acceptable. It is not necessary to use the same method from year to year, though the same method must be used consistently during the course of the year. The allocation of input tax credits allows you some scope for planning. However, for financial institutions, specific rules will apply for allocation methods.

EXAMPLE/**Allocation methods**

> A GST registrant involved in both taxable and exempt activities incurs GST of $3,200 on its occupancy costs. If 70% of the total floor space is used in commercial activities, based on the square footage, the registrant may choose to use this allocation method and claim $2,240 (70% × $3,200) as an input tax credit. Alternatively, the registrant may choose to base the allocation on the number of employees working in each particular activity. A 2004 tax case, *Bay Ferries Ltd. v. The Queen*, concluded that there is no "right" method of allocation and that it is not necessary to use the most reasonable method.

TAX TIP

> A business that must allocate the tax paid on purchases of both taxable and exempt supplies for the purpose of claiming input tax credits should review its method of allocation each year. Inherent changes in business activity may make it advantageous to change the allocation, since it may result in a higher recoverable percentage.

It is important that you thoroughly document whatever method of allocation you choose. In the event of an audit, providing this documentation to the CRA will allow them to clearly understand how the allocation was determined.

57 GST/HST and Automobiles

The complexity of the automobile rules is taken a step further by the GST/HST factor.

Passenger vehicles that cost more than a prescribed amount (currently $30,000, net of PST and GST or HST) are included in a separate depreciable class identified as Class 10.1. For such vehicles, the input tax credit is limited to the tax on $30,000, excluding PST and GST or HST. This means the maximum input tax credit that can be claimed for passenger vehicles subject to the 5% GST is $1,500. The maximum credit available in those provinces subject to the HST is $3,900. Upon the subsequent sale of a Class 10.1 vehicle, it may be possible to recover a portion of the unclaimed GST/HST.

Special rules apply to GST/HST–registered sole proprietors and partnerships where the vehicle is used less than 90% in a commercial activity. In such cases, GST/HST is recovered based on annual deductible capital cost allowance (CCA) claims. Upon the subsequent sale of the passenger vehicle, it may be possible to recapture a portion of the unclaimed GST.

EXAMPLE/**GST and your auto**

> You are a sole proprietor and registered for the GST. On August 1, 2009, you purchase an automobile for $28,000, including GST. The vehicle is used 60% in commercial activities and 40% for personal use. The maximum capital cost allowance you may claim on the automobile in the year of purchase is $2,520 (1/2 × 30% × $28,000 × 60%).
>
> Because you use the automobile less than 90% in commer-

cial activities, you are entitled to claim an input tax credit of $120 (5/105 × $2,520). If you live in a province that is subject to the HST, the recoverable factor is 13/113.

If all that isn't enough, the GST/HST must also be considered if a vehicle is sold or traded in. The rules differ depending on the status of the vendor. Is the vendor registered for the GST/HST? Is the vendor a corporation, a sole proprietor or a partnership? Was the vehicle used exclusively in a commercial activity? Your tax adviser can help you avoid any pitfalls in this regard.

GST/HST also has to be considered if you provide your employees with vehicles for their personal use or pay for any of their vehicles' operating expenses. If your company is a GST/HST registrant, the resulting taxable benefit is deemed to be a taxable supply and GST/HST must be remitted on the benefit amount. Your company must remit the tax on its GST/HST return that covers the last day of February each year—in other words, for the period that includes the due date for filing T4 slips for the relevant year. The GST/HST with respect to vehicles provided to shareholders who are not employees must be reported on the GST/HST return that includes the last day of the taxation year.

How much do you owe?

The GST/HST to be remitted is calculated by a formula that varies with the nature of the benefit and whether the employee or shareholder who is being taxed on the benefit works or lives in a participating province. The remittance for 2009 is calculated as follows:

	Standby Charge	Operating Cost Benefit
Outside participating provinces	4/104	3%
Participating provinces	12/112	9%

TAX TIP

If personal use of the automobile is high, and the employee or shareholder incurs most but not all of the operating costs, the taxable operating cost benefit and related GST remittance may be higher than the portion of actual operating costs paid by the employer. It's not a bad idea to review employment arrangements from time to time to determine if any changes should be made.

EXAMPLE/**Remittance for operating cost benefit**

During 2009, an automobile is made available to an employee in a non-participating province, and that person drives 15,000 personal kilometres and only 5,000 business kilometres in the year. The employer pays $500 of the operating costs and the employee pays the remainder. An operating cost benefit of $3,600 ($0.24 per personal kilometre) must be reported and the employer must remit $108 of GST on the benefit ($3,600 × 3%). If the employee reimburses the employer $500 by no later than 45 days after the year-end, no amount has to be reported as an operating cost benefit and no amount has to be remitted for GST.

Employee or partner expenses rebate

Finally, certain employees and partners may be able to claim a GST/HST rebate for particular expenses that are deductible in calculating income for tax purposes. The rules in this area are complex as well. For example, if you receive a tax-free travel allowance that you include in income and you claim offsetting expenses, you cannot claim the rebate. A GST/HST–registered employer, however, may be entitled to claim a notional input tax credit for the amount paid. The rules are just the reverse if you receive a travel allowance that has to be included in income—for example, a flat allowance of $400 a month. You may be able to claim the rebate, but the employer cannot claim an input tax credit.

For 2009 and subsequent taxation years, this rebate is calculated as 5/105 of eligible expenses in those provinces subject to the GST and as 13/113 of eligible expenses in those provinces subject to the HST. Although the rebate claim can be filed with your personal tax return, you have up to four years to make a claim. To claim the rebate, the employer must be registered for GST/HST and cannot be a listed financial institution such as a bank, credit union, insurance company or an investment or insurance business.

As noted above, there may be situations in which an employer is entitled to claim a notional input tax credit for travel allowances paid to employees. For qualified allowances paid after 2007, the amount that can be claimed is 5/105 (13/113) of the amount paid. If the employer is entitled to claim the notional input tax credit, the employee cannot claim the rebate.

TAX TIP

Confused about the application of GST/HST to automobiles and allowances? Don't be surprised—the rules in this area are extremely complex. It may be well worth a trip to your tax adviser to make sense of the GST/HST rules as they apply to your business.

58 GST/HST and Real Property Sales

As a general rule, real property transactions are taxable, even when the vendor is a small supplier. In such cases, the vendor must collect and remit the tax (unless the purchaser is a GST/HST registrant—see discussion that follows). However, the sale of used residential property and certain sales of real property by an individual who is not engaged in a business are generally exempt from GST/HST. In the case of bare land, if the property has been subdivided into more than two parts, even an individual must charge GST/HST when the property is sold, unless it is sold to a related individual.

Sales of real property to a registrant

A vendor is generally not required to collect the tax where real property is sold to a GST/HST registrant. A business selling real property should ensure that the purchaser is a GST/HST registrant before concluding that no tax will be collected on the sale. Where the purchaser is registered, the sale remains taxable; however, the purchaser is obligated to report the tax on a self-assessment basis. If the property is used primarily in making taxable supplies, an offsetting input tax credit can usually be claimed on the same GST/HST return that reports the liability. If 90% or more of the supplies are taxable, a full input tax credit is available (except for financial institutions) and no tax has to be remitted. However, if the property will not be used primarily in making taxable supplies, the purchaser must remit the applicable GST/HST using a special GST/HST form. Under these circumstances, a partial input tax credit may still be available.

TAX TIP

When a non-registrant sells real property and the deal is subject to tax, the vendor can claim back any GST/HST previously paid on the acquisition or improvement of the property that has not already been recovered. The eligible amount is claimed by filing a rebate form. If the vendor collects tax on the sale, the result is that the vendor sends the CRA the net amount of the tax collected minus the rebate amount. If the vendor does not collect tax on the sale (because the purchaser is registered), the rebate will be paid to the vendor directly by the CRA. The rebate application must be filed within two years of the date of sale.

59 GST/HST and Buying and Selling a Business

Where a business or a part of a business has been sold, a purchaser and vendor may be able to file a special election to avoid paying GST/HST on the purchase of the assets. This election is usually available if the purchaser is acquiring the ownership, possession or use of all the property needed to carry on the business or part of the business. However, this is often not an easy determination to make. The big difficulty is in determining whether the business assets being sold qualify for this election. Before signing the papers, you should consult your tax adviser to determine if you qualify to make this election.

SECTION 2

Individuals

IN THIS SECTION

60 Filing a Tax Return
61 Your Return Is Due . . .
62 GST/HST Credit
63 Why Buy an RRSP?
64 How Much Can You Contribute?
65 RRSP Contribution Limits
66 RRSP Overcontributions
67 RRSP Carry-Forward Rules
68 Self-Directed RRSPs
69 Retiring Allowances and RRSPs
70 RRSPs and Loans
71 Transfer of Pension Income
72 Using an RRSP to Buy a Home
73 Using an RRSP to Finance Higher Education
74 Death and the RRSP
75 Retirement and the RRSP
76 Company Pension Plans
77 Individual Pension Plans
78 New Tax-Free Savings Account
79 Pension Income Splitting
80 Old Age Security Clawback
81 Childcare Expenses
82 Alimony and Maintenance
83 Deductibility of Legal Fees During Separation or Divorce
84 Deductibility of Other Legal Expenses
85 Moving Expenses
86 Scholarship Income
87 What Is a Tax Credit?
88 Federal Personal Tax Credits
89 Child Tax Credit
90 Disability Tax Credit
91 Tax Credits for Charitable Donations
92 Political Donations
93 Medical Expenses
94 Attendant Care/Disability Supports Deduction
95 Attendant Care in a Retirement Home
96 Adoption Expense Credit
97 Tuition Fees, Education and Textbook Credits
98 Interest on Student Loan Credit
99 Claiming Your Spouse or Common-Law Partner's Unused Credits
100 Pension Credit
101 Age Credit
102 First-Time Home Buyers' Tax Credit
103 New Home Renovation Tax Credit
104 Canada Employment Credit
105 Working Income Tax Benefit
106 Public Transit Credit
107 Children's Fitness Credit
108 Canada Child Tax Benefit
109 Universal Child Care Benefit
110 Taxation of Common-Law Couples
111 Special Rules for Artists and Entertainers
112 Apprentice Mechanic Deduction for Tools
113 Tradespeople's Tool Expenses
114 Northern Residents Deduction
115 Special Rules for the Clergy
116 Taxation of Emergency Volunteers
117 Principal-Residence Rules
118 Selling Personal-Use Capital Property

IN THIS SECTION

119 Transfers and Loans to Family Members
120 Registered Education Savings Plans (RESPs)
121 Registered Disability Savings Plan (RDSP)
122 Splitting CPP Benefits with Your Spouse or Common-Law Partner
123 Income Splitting with Family Members
124 Income Splitting Using Family Trusts
125 Retroactive Lump-Sum Payments
126 Some Income Is Tax-Free
127 Taxation of Non-Competition Payments
128 Taking Up Canadian Residence
129 Giving Up Canadian Residence
130 Temporary Assignments Outside Canada
131 Canadian Residents Working in the U.S.
132 Canadian Tax Obligations for Non-Residents
133 Disposition of Taxable Canadian Property by Non-Residents
134 U.S. Citizens Resident in Canada
135 U.S. Social Security Payments
136 U.S. Real Estate Owned by Canadian Residents
137 Withholding Tax on Income from U.S. Sources
138 U.S. Estate Tax
139 U.S. Residency Regulations
140 Succession and Estate Planning
141 Deceased Taxpayers
142 Taxation of First Nations

Individuals face a tough challenge in trying to understand all the tax rules that could affect them. However, with proper tax planning, many pitfalls can be avoided. By reviewing the tax articles in this section, you should find a number of ways to reduce your tax liability.

In this section, we address the most common areas that can affect your tax situation. We provide details on the various tax credits you can claim, many of which are often not used because many Canadians are unaware that these tax-relief measures are available. We also comment on some new credits, such as the Home Renovation Tax Credit, as well as other new credits that have been introduced in the past few years.

Other areas covered include the rules for Registered Retirement Savings Plans (RRSPs); some comments on the new Tax-Free Savings Account (TFSA); the tax implications of owning more than one piece of real estate; how you can reduce your tax load by splitting income with family members (including pension income splitting); what's involved in becoming a Canadian resident; and what happens when you give up your Canadian residency. And last, but certainly not least, are details on one of the most overlooked but vitally important areas for you to consider—estate planning.

As with the other sections of this book, there are many tips to help you make smart choices as you develop a tax strategy for your particular circumstances.

60 Filing a Tax Return

You are required to file an income tax return for a taxation year if you

- have tax payable for that year (in excess of amounts withheld on your behalf);
- sold or disposed of capital property in the year, regardless of whether you had a gain or loss on the property;
- claimed a capital gains reserve on your 2008 return, even if the application of losses, exemptions or a new capital gain reserve results in no tax owing;
- have to repay Old Age Security or Employment Insurance benefits;

- you and your spouse or common-law partner elected to split pension income for 2009;
- you received Working Income Tax Benefit advance payments in 2009 and you want to apply to WITB advance payments for 2010;
- want to apply for the Goods and Services Tax (GST) or Harmonized Sales Tax (HST) credit or provincial tax credits;
- want to apply for the child tax benefit (both you and your spouse or common-law partner must file a return);
- want to reapply for the Guaranteed Income Supplement;
- have self-employed earnings of $3,500 or more in the year and must make CPP contributions, even if your income is otherwise below taxable levels;
- have not fully repaid amounts you withdrew from your RRSP under the Home Buyers' Plan or Lifelong Learning Plan (see articles 72 and 73);
- ceased to be a resident of Canada in the year and owned capital property at the time of emigration; or
- receive a request to file from the CRA.

Non-residents of Canada who receive certain types of income from Canada may also be required to file returns.

Even though you may not be required to file a return, you may still want to do so for the following reasons:

- if no tax is payable, but tax has been withheld, you must file a return to obtain a refund;
- you may be entitled to claim federal or provincial tax credits; for example, the Goods and Services Tax Credit;
- you were a student in the tax year and you have excess tuition/education/textbook amounts to be carried forward (see article 97); or

- you had "earned income" in the year for RRSP purposes (see article 64).

TAX TIP

Anyone, including minors, with earned income for RRSP purposes should consider filing an income tax return. Your RRSP contribution room, which may be used in subsequent years, will accumulate only if a tax return is filed.

61 Your Return Is Due . . .

Most individuals are required to mail their income tax returns on or before April 30 of the following calendar year. In other words, your 2009 return will be due by April 30, 2010. This date is particularly important if you owe the government a tax payment. Interest on outstanding amounts begins to accumulate after that deadline. If you are owed a refund, it doesn't make any sense to wait until that date—much less past that date. File as soon as you have all your documentation. After all, the refund is your money and it's not doing you a lot of good sitting in the government's treasury.

There is one major exception to the April 30 rule. If you or your spouse or common-law partner carry on a business as a sole proprietor or in a partnership (other than as a member of a limited partnership) during the year, you both have until June 15 of the following year to file your returns.

EXAMPLE/**Due dates**

> If you and your spouse or common-law partner were both employed full-time, and you also had a part-time consulting business in 2009, each of you will have until June 15, 2010, to file your returns. However, any taxes owed by you and your spouse or common-law partner must be paid by April 30, 2010, to avoid interest charges.

TAX TIP

Anticipating a refund? Then you should still file your return as early as possible. Interest on refunds will be paid only starting from whichever of the following three dates is latest: May 31, 2010; the 31st day after you file your return; or the day after you overpaid your taxes.

62 GST/HST Credit

The GST/HST credit is intended to offset GST/HST paid by lower-income individuals and families during the year. It is paid in quarterly instalments—in January, April, July and October. An individual's GST credit entitlement for the calendar quarter will be based on the individual's family circumstances at the end of the previous calendar quarter.

Subject to income restrictions, you are eligible to claim the credit. But you must, at the end of the year, be a resident of Canada and either 19 years of age or over, married or a parent. No credit can be claimed for a person who died during the year.

What's it worth?

For 2009, the basic GST/HST credit for an individual is $248. For families, the credit is $248 for you and $248 for your spouse or common-law partner (or other parent of your child). An eligible child will be credited with $130. There is also a GST/HST supplement credit of up to $130 for certain low-income single persons and single parents. If you live with your spouse or common-law partner (or other parent of your child), only one of you may claim the credit for the family unit, and it doesn't matter which of you claims the credit.

However, the total credit you may claim is reduced by 5% of your combined adjusted net incomes in excess of a specified threshold, which is currently $32,312. (This amount is adjusted annually for inflation.) Therefore, a married couple with two eligible children qualify for the full credit of $756 if their combined family income is $32,312 or less. Their entitlement decreases to zero once family income exceeds $47,432.

Eligibility for the credit

GST/HST payments can be impacted due to changes in family circumstances during the year, such as the birth of a child. As a result:

- Following the birth of a child, a family will receive an additional amount for that child with the next quarterly payment.
- The credit will be available to an individual in the quarter immediately following the individual's 19th birthday.
- Individuals who get married, or become separated or widowed,

will have their credits adjusted in the quarter following their change in marital status.

- New or returning residents to Canada will be eligible for the credit in the quarter following their entry or return into Canada.

To claim any added benefits, you should inform the CRA of relevant changes in your status. Call 1-800-959-1953.

TAX TIP

To apply for the GST credit, you should file an income tax return—even if you have no income to report. After you file your tax return, the CRA generally lets you know whether you qualify for the credit and, if so, how much you will receive. For example, payments based on your 2009 income tax return will be issued in July and October 2010 and January and April 2011 (generally issued on the 5th day of each quarter).

TAX TIP

Any children who will turn 19 before April 1, 2011, should apply for the GST credit on their 2009 tax return. They will start getting the credit on the first payment date after they turn 19.

63 Why Buy an RRSP?

There are three compelling reasons for contributing to a Registered Retirement Savings Plan. First, your contribution is tax deductible—and the higher your marginal tax rate, the greater your tax savings. Second, the income generated by the plan is taxed only on withdrawal from the plan (usually when you are retired and possibly in a lower tax bracket). That means you can build up quite significant earnings inside your plan on a pre-tax basis. Finally, all or a portion of your annual eligible contribution may be contributed to a plan set up for your spouse or common-law partner.

Spousal plans

Setting up a spousal RRSP is a good idea if you expect your spouse or common-law partner to be in a lower tax bracket than you on retirement. When funds are withdrawn from the spousal RRSP, they are taxed in your spouse's or common-law partner's hands at his or her lower tax rate (this arrangement is subject to special rules to prevent abuse). This reduces your family's total tax bill. This strategy also means that benefits such as the pension credit can be made available to both of you, and you may reduce your exposure to the Old Age Security clawback (see article 80).

Regardless of the pension income-splitting rules (for 2007 and subsequent tax years—see article 79), it's expected that spousal RRSP contributions will still have a role to play. Since the pension income-splitting rules limit the ability to income split to 50% of the amount received, a spousal RRSP may still allow for greater income splitting since 100% of the payments from the spousal RRSP can be taxed in the hands of the spouse with the lower income. Spousal RRSPs can also be useful in situations where the funds put aside are not always intended for retirement—for example, where both parties want to access RRSP contributions to purchase a home (see article 72) and one spouse has not had sufficient income to benefit from making his or her own RRSP contributions.

The majority of Canadians do not focus on retirement planning early in their careers. Yet contributing to an RRSP as early as possible, even if it is not the maximum allowable amount, is a very powerful retirement-planning strategy. Once you invest in an RRSP, you can earn income that compounds on a pre-tax basis. Depending on the type of investment products in your RRSP, this additional growth can often be far more substantial than the initial savings realized through the tax deduction.

TAX TIP

If you don't have an RRSP, don't worry—you're not alone. Despite the benefits of an RRSP, many Canadians don't have one. But better late than never. RRSPs are not at all hard to establish. Talk to a financial planner or your bank's financial services staff, who can set up an RRSP with a minimum of fuss or confusion. As for the type of RRSP to select, you should consider a self-directed plan (see article 68)—you don't really have to manage it, but it gives you much more flexibility in your financial and tax-planning strategies.

64 How Much Can You Contribute?

Your maximum annual RRSP contribution is based on earned income in the previous year. Earned income includes salaries, employee profit sharing income, business income, disability pensions (issued under the Canada and Quebec pension plans), taxable alimony or maintenance and rental income. Remember, too, your earned income is reduced by business losses, rental losses, union dues, employment expenses and deductible alimony or maintenance paid. Retiring allowances, investment income, capital gains, pension income and business income earned as a limited partner are not classified as earned income.

Estimating your contribution limit

If you are not a member of a registered pension plan (RPP) or a deferred profit sharing plan (DPSP), you will be able to contribute 18% of your 2008 earned income to an RRSP in 2009 to a maximum of $21,000. That contribution must be made within 60 days of the end of the calendar year, which is March 1, 2010 for the 2009 taxation year. If you were not able to make the maximum contribution to your plan in any or all the years from 1991 to 2008, you can also make up the difference in 2009 (see article 67). Your 2009 earned income will determine your 2010 contribution limit.

TAX TIP

Making the maximum RRSP contribution in 2009 will require earned income of at least $116,667 for 2008. Check the Notice of Assessment that the CRA sent you after the assessment of your 2008 return. It will tell you how much you can contribute. This amount should take into account any undercontributions since 1991. It will also tell you if you have made any contributions that you have not yet deducted for income tax purposes.

RPP and DPSP members

If you are a member of an RPP or DPSP, your RRSP contribution limit will be reduced by an amount called the pension adjustment (PA). This adjustment represents the present value of the pension benefits you earned for the previous year in your RPP or DPSP. PA reporting is required as part of the T4 reporting process in February of each year.

Another thing to consider is an adjustment made where benefits are enhanced for post-1989 service. This particular adjustment—the past service pension adjustment (PSPA)—reduces your RRSP contribution limit for any given year. In general, your maximum deduction for any one year will be calculated as follows: RRSP contribution room carried forward (see article 67), plus 18% of your prior year's earned income (to a stated maximum), plus any pension adjustment reversal (PAR—see below), less your PA for the prior year, less any PSPA for the current year.

EXAMPLE/**Adjustments and your RRSP**

> If your earned income for 2008 was $90,000, and a PA of $4,000 was reported on your 2008 T4, you will be able to contribute $12,200 to an RRSP in 2009—$16,200 less the $4,000 PA. However, if a $3,000 PSPA was also reported on slip T215, you would be able to contribute only $9,200 to your RRSP in 2009—$16,200, less the $4,000 PA and $3,000 PSPA.

Pension adjustment reversals

For members of an RPP or DPSP who leave before retirement, the pension entitlement received is often less than the RRSP contribution room that was given up in favour of the pension plan. Recognizing this inequity, the government introduced a pension adjustment reversal (PAR) that is intended to restore lost RRSP contribution room to individuals who leave an RPP or DPSP before retirement.

Generally, the PAR increases the RRSP contribution limit by the amount by which the PAs exceed the termination benefit—thereby restoring the RRSP room that would otherwise be lost. RPP and DPSP administrators are required to report the PAR to the CRA. The PAR is added to the RRSP deduction room for the year of termination.

EXAMPLE/**Applying the PAR**

> Suppose you were laid off by your employer in 2009 and, based on your earned income for 2008, your 2009 RRSP contribution room was $14,500. If your former employer reports a PAR of $5,000 with respect to your participation in its pension plan, your revised 2009 RRSP deduction room will be increased to $19,500.

Age limits

Subject to age restrictions, you may contribute any amount up to your maximum to your RRSP, an RRSP set up for your spouse or common-law partner, or a combination of both. Prior to 2007, a contribution could not be made to an RRSP if the beneficiary of the plan was 70 or older at the end of the year. For years after 2006, RRSP annuitants may retain their RRSP and continue to make contributions to the plan until the end of the year they turn 71 (as opposed to 69). However, if you have earned income and your spouse or common-law partner will be under 72 at the end of the year, you can still make a contribution to his or her plan even if you are 72 or older.

Converting your RRSP

Normally, you have until March 1, 2010, to make your 2009 contribution. However, if the beneficiary of the plan turned 71 in 2009, the contribution must be made by December 31, 2009. That's because RRSPs must be converted into a Registered Retirement Income Fund (RRIF) or life or term annuity by December 31 of the year in which the beneficiary turns 71.

A huge word of warning: If you turned 71 in 2009 and your RRSP is not converted into one of these plans by December 31, 2009, the full amount of the RRSP will be brought into your income and will, therefore, be taxable.

For a taxpayer who dies in 2009, the executor or legal representative can make a spousal RRSP contribution on behalf of the deceased until March 1, 2010, provided the spouse otherwise satisfies the age requirements.

TAX TIP

If you turned 71 in 2009, you may be able to make an extra contribution to your RRSP for 2010 before collapsing the plan at the end of 2009. Just before you wind it up in 2009, make a contribution equal to your 2010 contribution room. The amount of your 2010 contribution room is based on your 2009 earned income. Payments can then be claimed as a deduction in 2010. This tax-planning tip requires that you have earned income in 2009. It is important to note that the contribution may trigger a penalty of 1% per month from the date of the contribution to December 31, 2009 (see article 66). Therefore, it would be wise to make this extra contribution as late in the year as possible.

Before proceeding with this option, you and your tax adviser should review your financial situation carefully in light of your contribution room, the amount of the contribution, the penalty tax, etc. Also, you still have the opportunity to contribute to a spousal RRSP in the future if you have earned income and your spouse or common-law partner is under 72 years of age.

65 RRSP Contribution Limits

The maximum you could contribute to an RRSP remained at $13,500 for several years. Starting in 2003, the maximum contribution limit increased $1,000 per year, to a maximum of $16,500 in 2005. The contribution limit for 2006, 2007, 2008 and 2009 then increased to $18,000, $19,000, $20,000 and $21,000 respectively. The limit for 2010 is $22,000 (indexed for inflation for 2011 and subsequent years).

There will be corresponding increases to the maximum limits for money purchase and defined benefit pension plans.

TAX TIP

To make the most effective use of your RRSP, there are several things you can do:

1. Depending on the type of investment, you can either contribute to your RRSP early in the year (for fixed income investments) or at regular intervals throughout the year (for most mutual funds) rather than at the end of the contribution year. That way, you can benefit from income sheltering and dollar cost averaging (for investments that fluctuate in value).
2. If you make regular contributions to an RRSP, consider applying to have your income tax withholdings reduced on your paycheque, which will improve your monthly cash flow. To do this, simply submit Form T1213 to the CRA for authorization. Once authorized, your employer will be able to reduce the amount of taxes withheld from your pay.
3. Even though your RRSP administration fee is not tax deductible, you should consider paying it directly, instead of from inside your RRSP—this helps maintain capital in your plan, allowing it to grow on a tax-deferred basis.
4. You don't need to deduct your contribution in the year it is made. If you are expecting to be in a higher tax bracket in the future, consider delaying your deduction until that time—you will receive a larger tax savings if the deduction is taken when you're in a higher tax bracket.
5. Consider filing tax returns for children or other low-income earners to create contribution room that can be used in the future.

66 RRSP Overcontributions

You are permitted to overcontribute a cumulative lifetime total of $2,000 to your RRSP without incurring a penalty tax (this limit is increased to $8,000 for anyone who had an overcontribution prior to February 27, 1995). An overcontribution is not deductible from income in the current year, but the advantage lies in the fact that you are able to inject extra cash into your RRSP, where it can compound on a tax-deferred basis for as long as it remains in the plan. Overcontributions may be deducted in a subsequent year when your actual RRSP contribution is less than the maximum allowed. A penalty tax of 1% per month applies to the amount of any overcontribution in excess of $2,000 (or $8,000 where that limit applies). The CRA has recently become more stringent in going after taxpayers who have overcontributed to their RRSPs in excess of the allowable amount. If you think you are in an overcontribution position, you should contact your tax adviser to determine the steps you need to take. The calculation of the penalty tax and the filing of the forms to withdraw the excess amount is not part of the normal engagement to prepare your personal tax return.

TAX TIP

Before overcontributing to an RRSP, you are usually better off to pay down debt on which interest is not deductible, such as a large outstanding personal credit card balance or a personal home mortgage. Check with your tax or financial adviser to determine your best course of action. If you decide to overcontribute, work with your adviser to ensure that you stay within the allowable limit. One of the reasons the government permits an overcontribution is to provide you with a cushion against possible errors and unforeseen events, such as a pension adjustment or past service pension adjustment.

TAX TIP

Consider using your $2,000 overcontribution when you quit working. The earned income you have in your final year of employment will entitle you to an RRSP deduction in the following year.

67 RRSP Carry-Forward Rules

For many individuals, it is not always possible to make a full RRSP contribution in any given year. To remedy this situation, you are allowed to carry forward the unused portion of your contribution room to subsequent years. That means that if you were eligible to contribute $10,000 to an RRSP each year from 1991 to 2008 but only contributed $7,000 each year, you will be able to contribute an additional $54,000 over and above your annual maximum limit.

If you expect a change in your income in the near future—a change that might see you bumped up into a higher tax bracket—it might make sense to consider delaying your RRSP contributions until then. However, you must also consider the loss of tax-sheltered investment growth by building up your RRSP later rather than earlier.

TAX TIP

To accumulate RRSP contribution room, you must file an income tax return. If you have "earned income" for RRSP purposes, but you are not required to file an income tax return, you should consider filing a return anyway. While an RRSP may not be a significant consideration at this point, there will probably be a time when you have enough cash to make a contribution and can benefit from the deduction.

TAX TIP

Will you have low taxable income in 2009, unused contribution room and enough excess cash to make an RRSP contribution? Then consider making the contribution for 2009 but not claiming the deduction on your 2009 return. As long as the amount is not claimed as a deduction, your unused contribution room will remain intact. You can still claim the deduction in a future year, preferably when your taxable income is higher. In the meantime, the investments in the RRSP will compound on a tax-deferred basis.

68 Self-Directed RRSPs

Self-directed RRSPs are subject to special rules. Despite the annual administration fee—which unfortunately is not tax deductible—a self-directed RRSP will give you more flexibility and may provide you with the opportunity to realize better returns. However, you should have a little time to give it the attention it needs.

In a self-directed plan, you make your own investment choices. These decisions can be based on information given to you by your financial or tax adviser. In fact, many Canadians allow their financial planners to look after their self-directed plans. However, as the owner of the plan, you always have the final say in how it's managed and the types of investments purchased.

Should your plan acquire a non-qualified investment, the value of that investment is included as income on your return. There are no longer any restrictions on the amount of foreign investments you can hold in your RRSP.

Transferring investments

You can transfer other investments you own into your self-directed RRSP as part of your deductible contribution. Should their fair market value at the time of the transfer exceed your cost, the difference must be reported as a capital gain. However, if you transfer the investment, or sell the investment and have the RRSP purchase the same investment within 30 days before or after you sold it, you are out of luck if your cost exceeds the fair market value—you cannot deduct the capital loss. Therefore, it's not the best idea to sell or transfer losing investments to your RRSP.

It is also possible to hold the mortgage on your home in your RRSP—it takes a bit of effort to set up and there are costs involved, but this arrangement can offer some advantages.

EXAMPLE/**Investment transfers**

> You acquired 100 shares of ABC Co. in 2004 for $10 per share. Now, in December 2009, you are considering a contribution to your RRSP and are reviewing your available options. If the shares of ABC are trading at $15 per share, and you transfer all of the shares to your RRSP, your RRSP contribution will be $1,500 and you will report a capital gain of $500—in other words, $1,500 less the original $1,000 cost of the investment.
>
> Now, if those shares are trading at $8 per share, your RRSP contribution will be $800 but you will not be able to claim a capital loss of $200 ($800 – $1,000) on the transfer. As an alternative, you could sell your shares for $8 per share and contribute the cash proceeds to your RRSP. In that case, your RRSP contribution will still be $800, but you will be able to claim the $200 capital loss, provided the RRSP does not acquire the shares of ABC Co. within 30 days before or after you sold the shares.

TAX TIP

If you have a self-directed RRSP, transferring some of your non-registered investments to it may be a way to get your annual RRSP deduction without actually laying out any cash. However, there are some drawbacks to holding shares in an RRSP. Since shares generate capital gains and dividend income (which is tax-preferred) it might make more sense to keep these investments outside your RRSP and fill up your contribution room with investments that generate interest (e.g., savings bonds, GICs, etc.) which are usually taxed at a less advantageous rate.

In certain situations, your RRSP can invest in shares of a Canadian private company if it carries on its business primarily in Canada. Certain types of business activities do not qualify. The rules are extremely complicated, however, and you should be aware of how they may affect your potential investment before your RRSP acquires such shares. Talk to a knowledgeable adviser first.

When considering long-term investments, such as five-year guaranteed investment certificates (GICs), within your RRSP, keep in mind that you may have a problem if you need to withdraw the funds before the investment matures.

69 Retiring Allowances and RRSPs

Individuals who will receive or have received an amount from their former employers upon dismissal or retirement in 2009 may be eligible to contribute an extra amount to their RRSP or RPP. These retiring allowances are a key item in personal tax planning, and they're doubly attractive because they are also deductible for the payer. In addition, amounts transferred to your RRSP or RPP are not taxable until they are withdrawn from the plan.

What amounts are involved?

The maximum amount that can be transferred to your RRSP or RPP is $2,000 multiplied by the number of years you worked for your employer before 1996. You can also add in $1,500 multiplied by the number of years you were employed prior to 1989 in which your employer did not make vested contributions to a registered plan on your behalf. The contribution, which is in addition to your regular contribution limit, must be made to your own retirement plan, not your spouse's.

TAX TIP

If the portion of your retiring allowance that is eligible to be transferred to your RRSP is paid directly to your RRSP, your employer will not be obligated to withhold income tax.

70 RRSPs and Loans

Interest on loans taken out to invest in an RRSP is not deductible. Therefore, your investments should be structured to take maximum advantage of the interest deductibility rules.

TAX TIP

Consider cashing in an existing investment to contribute to your RRSP and then, if you wish, borrowing funds to acquire another investment that is held outside your registered plan. This way, you receive a deduction for your RRSP contribution, and the interest on the loan borrowed for investment purposes should also be tax deductible provided certain conditions are met (see article 160).

71 Transfer of Pension Income

Are you entitled to a lump-sum payment out of a registered pension plan (RPP) or a deferred profit sharing plan (DPSP)? If you wish, that amount may be contributed to another RPP, DPSP or RRSP. However, the lump-sum payment must be made directly from one plan to another, and then only if certain conditions are met.

If you want to transfer to your RRSP a lump-sum payment or withdrawal from a foreign plan, you should get professional tax advice. For example, the tax implications of transferring amounts from a U.S. individual retirement account (IRA) to a Canadian RRSP are complex. Your adviser can explore all the options and potential tax obligations of such transfers.

72 Using an RRSP to Buy a Home

Previously, the Home Buyers' Plan allowed you to withdraw as a loan up to $20,000 from your RRSP without paying tax. For withdrawals after January 27, 2009, you are now permitted to withdraw up to $25,000 from your RRSP for qualifying home purchases. Form T1036 needs to be filed to report the withdrawal. Under this plan, only first-time homebuyers are eligible to participate, unless the special rules for persons with disabilities (discussed below) apply. You are considered to be a first-time buyer if, during the four calendar years prior to the year of withdrawal and up to 30 days before the withdrawal, neither you nor your spouse or common-law partner owned a home in which either of you resided. Loan repayments must take place over a period of 15 years, or less if desired, beginning in the second year following the year of withdrawal. If the required repayment is not made, an amount will have to be included as income in the year of the shortfall.

TAX TIP

If you contribute an amount to your RRSP, you cannot make a withdrawal under the Home Buyers' Plan within 90 days of that contribution, or your ability to claim a deduction for the contribution may be restricted. As a general rule, you should make your RRSP contribution more than 90 days before the withdrawal. After a waiting period of 90 days or more, your deduction may generate a refund, which can then also be applied toward your down payment.

In a related move, if you have money on hand for a down payment and you have accumulated some RRSP contribution room, open an RRSP. Then you can deposit the money into the plan, wait 90 days, be eligible to partake in the Home Buyers' Plan and at the same time use whatever refund is issued to bolster your original down payment amount. Be sure to run this by your tax adviser to ensure it is a sound strategy for your particular financial circumstances.

If you have previously participated in the Home Buyers' Plan, there are certain situations in which you may be able to participate a second time. First of all, the full amount previously withdrawn must be paid back into your RRSP before the beginning of the given year in which you wish to participate a second time. Also, you must still qualify as a first-time homebuyer.

TAX TIP

Each spouse or common-law partner can withdraw eligible amounts under the Home Buyers' Plan from any RRSP under which he or she is the annuitant, including spousal RRSPs. Also, each person may withdraw up to the $25,000 limit, or $50,000 in aggregate (if purchasing the property jointly).

Persons with disabilities

If you are already a homeowner and you have a disability, or if you are a relative of a person who has a disability, you may withdraw funds from your RRSP under the Home Buyers' Plan if the withdrawal is to assist you or your disabled relative to purchase a home.

Some conditions must be met first:

- You or your disabled relative must qualify for the disability tax credit (see article 90).
- The home must be more accessible or better suited for the care of the person with a disability.
- If you are not disabled, your disabled relative must live in the home or plan to occupy it within one year after the acquisition.

73 Using an RRSP to Finance Higher Education

Tax-free RRSP withdrawals can also be made to assist you in financing full-time training or education for you or your spouse or common-law partner. Withdrawals are limited to $10,000 per year over a period of up to four calendar years and subject to a cumulative total of $20,000.

To qualify, you or your spouse or common-law partner must be enrolled or committed to enrol as a full-time student in a qualifying education program of at least three months' duration at a designated educational institution. The full-time criterion is dropped for disabled students.

Withdrawals must be repaid to the RRSP over a maximum 10-year period starting in the year after the last year in which the qualifying individual was enrolled as a full-time student. However, the repayments must commence no later than the sixth year after the initial withdrawal, even if full-time enrolment continues. If the required repayment is not made, an amount will have to be included in income. As with many tax situations, special rules apply.

74 Death and the RRSP

Should you die while you still own your RRSP, its entire value must be included in your income in the year of your death unless your spouse or common-law partner or your financially dependent child or grandchild is entitled to the funds. If you designate your spouse or common-law partner or financially dependent child or grandchild as beneficiary of your RRSP, the proceeds from the plan will be taxable in your beneficiary's hands in the year they're received, unless they are transferred into his or her own tax-deferred plan.

If none of the above is designated as the beneficiary of your RRSP, its value may still be taxable in his or her hands on your death, provided he or she is a beneficiary of your estate. This approach may provide more flexibility, but more paperwork will be involved.

For the purpose of these rules, a "financially dependent" child or grandchild is one whose income for the year preceding your death is less than the basic personal amount for the year or if the child is infirm, equal to or less than the basic personal amount plus the disability amount for the year (see Table 1, page 282). Where the child's income exceeds this amount, he or she will be financially dependent if this dependency can be established. In such cases, your estate's representative should write to the tax services office outlining the reasons the CRA should consider him or her to be financially dependent.

Other rules apply if you die after your plan has matured and you were receiving annuity payments from your RRSP or RRIF.

As noted above, the general rule is that the fair market value of investments held in a RRSP or RRIF must be included in the income of the deceased for the year of death. However, what happens if the value of those investments declines from the date of death to the time of distribution to the beneficiaries? In today's economy, this is likely a fairly common scenario. Until recently, there was no provision to recognize this decrease in value. New rules were introduced in the 2009 federal budget to address this situation. Where the final distribution from the RRSP or RRIF occurs after 2008, the post-death decrease can be carried back and deducted against any RRSP/RRIF income inclusion on the deceased's final tax return. For further information, please contact your tax adviser.

Two conditions must generally be met for this deduction to be available:

1. the RRSP/RRIF must be wound up by the end of the year following the year of death, and
2. the RRSP/RRIF must have held no investments other than qualifying investments during the post-death period.

EXAMPLE/**Claiming the deduction**

Your widowed mother dies in June 2008 (at which time the fair market value of the assets in her RRIF is $120,000). In March 2009, her estate distributes $80,000 to you (her sole beneficiary) and the RRIF is wound up. Income of $120,000 would have been reported on your mother's final T1 income tax return. Under these new rules, a deduction of $40,000 can be claimed to offset this income inclusion.

75 Retirement and the RRSP

Are you considering withdrawing funds from your RRSP? Then you should be aware of the options available to you.

For 2007 and subsequent years, you are required to take the funds out of your RRSP by the end of the calendar year in which you reach the age of 71. Prior to 2007, the age limit was 69. When you collapse your RRSP, you may transfer the funds on a tax-deferred basis into a Registered Retirement Income Fund (RRIF) or a life or term annuity. The third option is to withdraw the funds and pay tax on the full amount. The choice will be based on your retirement objectives, tax implications and cash flow requirements. If you want, you can do all three—you can put some of the funds into a RRIF, some into an annuity and (if necessary) withdraw a portion in cash.

How RRIFs work

A RRIF provides you with varying amounts of income during retirement. If the payments are structured properly, a RRIF can continue indefinitely, essentially providing income for life. Payments from a RRIF are quite flexible. You can withdraw as much as you want, although you must take a minimum amount each year. As an exception to this rule, if you have a RRIF and you turn 71 in 2009, the minimum withdrawal for 2009 is nil. The minimum amount increases slightly each year, based on a specific formula. RRIF payments are subject to tax in the year of receipt.

How annuities work

If your RRSP funds are transferred to an annuity, periodic payments from the annuity will also be taxed in the year of receipt. Annuities can be arranged to provide payments for either a fixed term (e.g., to age 90) or life. The main advantage of an annuity is that you can have some form of guarantee of the amounts you will receive.

For instance, if you opt for a life annuity, you or you and your spouse or common-law partner can be guaranteed a specific income stream regardless of how long either of you survive. Nevertheless, an annuity is not as flexible as a RRIF. Once you purchase a life annuity, and the funds are deposited and registered, they are locked in. You generally cannot deregister or cash in the plan or amend the terms of the contract.

Tax implications

If you withdraw funds from your RRSP, you will pay a withholding tax on the amount withdrawn. The plan holder is required by law to withhold a certain percentage of the amount and remit it to the CRA. Any additional tax on the withdrawal is paid when you file your tax return for the year. The end result is that you will pay tax on the withdrawal at your marginal tax rate. The higher your other sources of income for the year of withdrawal, the more tax you will pay. There are many options available to you when you decide to cash in your RRSP. Become familiar with the various alternatives and their tax consequences so you can make an informed choice.

76 Company Pension Plans

In general, if you are a member of a company pension plan, your RRSP contribution room is reduced by your pension adjustment (PA). As noted in article 64, this adjustment is intended to represent the present value of the pension benefits you earned for the previous year in your registered pension plan (RPP) or deferred profit sharing plan (DPSP).

There are two main types of RPPs: defined benefit plans, in which pension benefits are specified in the plan, and money purchase plans, in which pension benefits are based on combined employer and employee contributions, plus earnings in the plan.

Defined benefit plans

As a member of a defined benefit plan, you are entitled to deduct 100% of all required contributions for current or post-1989 past service. You are also entitled to deduct a maximum of $3,500 per year for past service contributions for service prior to 1990 while you were not a contributor to a pension plan. This deduction is subject to an overall limit of $3,500 multiplied by the number of years of pre-1990 service bought back. This is in addition to any deduction for post-1989 or current service.

For years of pre-1990 service during which you were a contributor to the plan, the annual deduction is limited to $3,500 less the amount of other contributions deducted in the current year. This includes amounts for the current year, post-1989 past service, and pre-1990 past service while you were not a contributor. The $3,500 annual limit for deductibility of pre-1990 service contributions is disregarded in the year of death. You should consult your tax adviser if you are subject to these complicated rules.

EXAMPLE/**Defined benefit past service contribution**

> Assume you make a $4,000 contribution to your defined benefit plan in 2009 with respect to two years of service prior to 1990 while you were not a contributor to a pension plan. Your maximum deduction is $3,500 in 2009. The remaining $500 can be deducted in 2010.

Money purchase plans

You are entitled to deduct the amount you contributed to a money purchase plan during the year, subject to certain maximum amounts that parallel the RRSP rules. Money purchase plans do not allow for past service contributions.

The benefits you earn in your defined benefit pension plan, or total contributions to a money purchase plan, determine how much you can also contribute to your RRSP (see article 64).

TAX TIP

> If you leave a registered pension plan before retirement, you may be able to have your lost RRSP contribution room restored. The pension adjustment reversal is the mechanism designed to achieve this. Pension adjustment reversals will be added to your RRSP contribution room for the year of termination (see article 64).

Money purchase plans can pay pension benefits in a Life Income Fund (LIF) which provides a similar income stream currently permitted under a RRIF. However, while a RRIF has only minimum withdrawal limits, LIFs also limit the maximum amount that may be withdrawn on a yearly basis. Therefore, with a LIF you have to withdraw between a minimum and maximum amount from your money purchase account each year, beginning no later than the year in which you reach age 72.

Additional provisions were implemented in 2008 to increase the flexibility of accessing funds in a LIF under certain circumstances. Subject to transitional rules, LIF contracts entered into after May 8, 2008, must include the option of permitting funds in the LIF to be transferred into a new type of locked-in retirement account called a Restricted Life Income Fund (RLIF). In the year you turn 55, or in any subsequent year, you will be allowed to transfer up to 50% of the RLIF's value into a tax-deferred savings vehicle (i.e., RRSP or RRIF) with no maximum withdrawal limit, as long as this transfer happens within 60 days of the creation of the RLIF. This is a one-time 50% unlocking provision.

The new provisions also allowed for an increase in the maximum amounts that certain individuals can withdraw from their LIF on a yearly basis. Individuals facing financial hardship (e.g., low income, high disability or medical-related costs) are entitled to withdraw up to $23,150 a year from their LIF. This maximum is adjusted annually, based on the Year's Maximum Pensionable Earnings.

Deferred profit sharing plans (DPSPs)

An alternative to the RPP is a deferred profit sharing plan (DPSP). Under this type of arrangement, your employer makes payments to a trustee, who holds and invests the contributions for your benefit. Unlike RPPs, however, employee contributions are not allowed.

The maximum contribution your employer can make on your behalf in 2009 is, in general, equal to 18% of your earned income or $11,000, whichever is less. Similar to an RPP, employer contributions to a DPSP on your behalf reduce your RRSP contribution room. The contribution your employer makes to your DPSP in 2009 will have an impact on your 2010 RRSP contribution room.

77 Individual Pension Plans

Prior to 1991, employees who held at least 10% of their company's shares were not permitted to participate in a company registered pension plan unless the value of benefits provided to non-shareholder employees was at least equal to the value of the benefits provided to themselves. However, since 1991, employees have been able to become members of a single-member pension plan, regardless of their share ownership.

What is an IPP?

The individual pension plan (IPP) is simply a defined benefit pension plan for one member. IPPs specifically benefit owners of companies or executives of incorporated companies who do not participate in an employer pension plan and who have annual earnings in excess of $120,000. Ideally, individuals should be 50 years of age to derive the maximum benefits from the plan. However, such plans have been set up by persons as young as 40. The contribution advantage of using an IPP versus an RRSP increases with age.

Subject to certain limitations, a defined benefit plan will provide for an annual pension equal to a percentage of your highest earnings over a given period. One of the benefits of these plans is that the annual contribution limits are generally a great deal higher than those allowed for RRSP accounts. Therefore, such plans may be a very good option if you have not regularly contributed to an RRSP in the past and are nearing retirement. Another added benefit is that such plans are protected from creditors.

These plans can be either 100% funded by the employer or employer/employee-funded. In general, you will not be able to fund more than 50% of the cost of the pension.

IPPs are not for everyone. It is an individual decision based on several factors—your age, current and projected income level, the rate of return earned on the plan's assets, whether you are an owner-manager or an arm's-length executive and several other considerations. Due to their complex nature, it is recommended that you consult your tax or financial adviser before investing in one of these plans.

78 New Tax-Free Savings Account

One of the more popular announcements in the 2008 federal budget was the introduction of a new Tax-Free Savings Account (TFSA), which the Finance Minister described as the "single most important personal savings vehicle since the introduction of the RRSP."

Basically, starting in 2009, every Canadian resident individual (other than a trust) who is 18 years of age or older will be able to contribute up to $5,000 a year (indexed for inflation to the nearest $500) to a TFSA. A TFSA will generally be permitted to hold the same investments as a Registered Retirement Savings Plan (RRSP). This includes mutual funds, securities listed on a designated stock exchange, Guaranteed Investment Certificates (GICs), bonds, and certain shares of small-business corporations. However, you are prohibited from holding investments in any entities that you do not deal with at arm's length, such as shares in a corporation you control. You are also entitled to make "in kind" contributions of qualifying investments to your TSFA. The amount of your "in kind" contribution will be equal to the fair market value of the property at the time of your contribution.

Unlike RRSPs, you will not obtain a deduction for contributions to a TFSA in calculating income for tax purposes. However, you will not include in income for tax purposes any income, losses or gains from investments held within a TFSA, or amounts withdrawn from it. The amounts withdrawn from a TFSA will also not be included in determining your eligibility for income-tested benefits or credits, such as the medical or age credit (see articles 93 and 101) or OAS clawback (see article 80). If you do not contribute to a TFSA in one year, the amount can be carried forward indefinitely to future years. Any amounts withdrawn from a TFSA can also be recontributed without impacting your contribution room. For example, if you contribute $5,000 in each of 2009 and 2010 and then withdraw $6,000 in 2011, you will be able to contribute $16,000 to your TFSA in 2012 ($5,000 contribution room in 2011 and 2012 plus the $6,000 withdrawn in 2011). Interest on money borrowed to invest in a TFSA will not be deductible.

If you can afford it, this new plan can prove to be a worthwhile savings vehicle. A TFSA can also provide you with some interesting opportunities to manage your retirement income. The one problem with this plan is that not everyone can afford to make regular, annual contributions. Even though unused TFSA contribution room can be carried forward until you have the available funds, the ability to earn tax-free income is lost in the intervening period.

TAX TIP

You should generally pay off your personal interest-bearing debt before contributing amounts to this plan. Also, in most cases, it's expected that the present value (PV) of the tax savings from making an RRSP contribution will exceed the PV of the tax paid on its withdrawal. Therefore, you should also try to maximize your RRSP contributions before contributing to a TFSA.

TAX TIP

If your spouse cannot afford to contribute to a TFSA, you can contribute to your spouse's TFSA as well as your own without any negative tax consequences. This will allow you to reduce your family's total tax bill.

TAX TIP

U.S. citizens who are also Canadian residents should obtain tax advice before investing in a TFSA. If you are a U.S. citizen resident in Canada you are subject to the tax rules of both countries. Although income earned within the TFSA will be tax-free in Canada, the income will be taxable under U.S. tax rules.

Your tax adviser can assist you in determining what savings vehicle is the best option for you, given your particular circumstances.

79 Pension Income Splitting

One of the most significant changes to the personal income tax system for 2007 and subsequent years is the introduction of pension income splitting. If you are receiving income that qualifies for the pension income tax credit (see article 100), you will be able to allocate up to half of that income to your spouse or common-law partner (and vice versa) Although pension income can also be split in the year of death, there are special rules that apply depending on whether it is the pension income recipient or transferee that has passed away.

The extent to which pension income splitting will be beneficial will depend on the marginal tax bracket of you and your spouse or common-law partner, as well as the amount of qualifying income that can be split. In many cases, the optimal allocation will be less than the allowable 50% maximum.

EXAMPLE/**Splitting your income**

Your total income for 2009 is $90,000, of which $60,000 is qualifying pension income. Your spouse has no pension income and only $5,000 in other sources of income. You can allocate up to $30,000 of your pension income to your spouse. In this case, you will report taxable income of $60,000 and your spouse will report taxable income of $35,000. Both of you can claim the pension income credit (see article 100) and you will no longer be subject to the Old Age Security (OAS) clawback (see article 80). The overall savings can be considerable.

To qualify for income splitting, the pension income must satisfy certain criteria. If you are 65 years of age or older, eligible pension income includes lifetime annuity payments under a registered pension plan (RPP), a Registered Retirement Savings Plan (RRSP) or a deferred profit sharing plan (DPSP), and payments out of or under a registered retirement income fund (RRIF). If you are under 65 years of age, eligible pension income includes lifetime annuity payments under a registered pension plan and certain other payments received as a result of the death of your spouse or common-law partner. Eligible pension income does not include payments under the Canada Pension Plan (CPP) or OAS payments.

If you opt to pension split, a special election form (Form T1032) must be signed by you and your spouse or common-law partner and filed with the CRA. If you file your return electronically (see article 172), you should keep the election form on file in case the CRA asks for it. Another result of pension splitting is that the income tax withheld from your pension income will be reported on your spouse or common-law partner's return, proportional to the amount of income being split.

EXAMPLE/**Splitting the tax withheld**

Using the figures from the example above, you elect to split 50% of your pension income with your spouse. On your T4A, $10,000 was deducted for income tax. You will report 50% of this amount as tax withheld (or $5,000) and your spouse will report the other $5,000. If you had elected to split only 30% of your pension income, $3,000 of income tax withheld would be reported on your spouse's return.

80 Old Age Security Clawback

The government imposes a special tax—the "clawback"—on your Old Age Security (OAS) payments if your net income for the year exceeds a certain annual threshold. For 2009, the threshold is $66,335. The amount of the clawback is equal to your OAS payments or 15% of the amount by which your net income exceeds the threshold, whichever is less. Based on January to June 2009 OAS payment rates, the full amount of the OAS benefit will be eliminated when your net income reaches $107,692. The clawback amounts are repaid through withholdings from your monthly OAS payments.

Benefits paid to you are calculated on the basis of your income for the previous year. It is therefore not necessary to repay benefits when filing a return for the year. Moreover, non-residents wishing to continue receiving OAS benefits must file a return reporting their worldwide income.

How it works

Each OAS payment you receive is reduced by an estimate of the clawback tax. The reduction for the period from January through June 2009 is based on your 2007 net income. The reduction in the payments for July to December 2009 is based on your net income for 2008.

When you file your 2009 income tax return, the CRA will calculate the actual OAS clawback based on your net income for the year. This amount will be compared to the amounts withheld from your monthly payments during the year. Any excess withheld will be refunded or applied against any other tax liability. Conversely, where the amount withheld falls short, you will be required to remit the difference.

TAX TIP

If your income is over the $66,335 clawback threshold, and your spouse or common-law partner's net income is below it, consider splitting your pension income (see article 79) or splitting your Canada Pension Plan (CPP) benefits with him or her if that will bring your net income below the threshold (see article 122).

TAX TIP

If you are considering making the election to include all of your spouse or common-law partner's taxable Canadian dividends in your income (see article 154), make sure you are not subjecting yourself to the OAS clawback by using this strategy.

81 Childcare Expenses

Work commitments may qualify you or your spouse or common-law partner (or other supporting individual) to deduct eligible expenses for daycare and/or other forms of childcare. Eligible costs include daycare or babysitting, boarding school and certain camp expenses. Medical expenses, education costs, clothing and transportation expenses are not eligible. You are also not allowed to deduct payments made to persons under 18 years of age who are related to you. As with most qualifying expenses, there is a specified limit.

TAX TIP

After-school recreational programs can qualify as an eligible childcare expense if the fees are incurred to allow the parent to work. For example, a 2006 court case found that a mother who paid $984 to a gymnastics club for after-school classes was allowed to claim the amount as a childcare expense. She needed to make arrangements for the care of her daughter after school until she finished work.

Who can claim?

When the child lives with both parents, the parent with the lower net income must claim the expense deduction. A parent with no income is considered to have the lower income and, therefore, must claim the expenses. The supporting parent with the higher income may claim a deduction only during the period in which the lower-income spouse or common-law partner is mentally or physically infirm, confined to a bed or a wheelchair, attending full-time at a secondary school or a designated educational institution, or incarcerated in a correctional facility.

The amount that can be claimed for childcare is subject to special rules when the lower-income spouse or common-law partner is in part-time attendance at a designated educational institution. Special rules also apply for single parents and those who have separated during the year or are divorced.

How much can you deduct?

In general, you can deduct up to $7,000 annually for each child who is aged six or under at the end of the year, and up to $4,000 for each child aged seven to 15 at any time in the year. This limit is increased to $10,000 annually for each child who is eligible for the disability tax credit (see article 90). In general, the total deduction cannot exceed two-thirds of the salary or business income of the parent who is required to claim the deduction. However, it is limited by the actual amounts paid in the year for childcare.

EXAMPLE/**Deducting childcare expenses**

> You and your spouse are both employed and earn $36,000 and $65,000 per year, respectively. You incurred $12,000 in eligible childcare expenses in 2009 for your five-year-old child. Since your income is less than your spouse's, you are required to deduct the childcare expenses. The maximum you can deduct is $7,000 or two-thirds of your net income (2/3 × $36,000 = $24,000), whichever is less. Therefore, you can deduct $7,000 for childcare expenses in 2009.

82 Alimony and Maintenance

Rules regarding alimony and maintenance payments changed significantly as of May 1, 1997. The main change was to treat child support payments differently from spousal support payments.

What hasn't changed?

Periodic payments for spousal support continue to be taxable to the recipient and deductible by the payer, provided certain conditions are met (see discussion below on agreements or court orders prior to May 1, 1997).

What's changed?

For new or varied child support agreements made after April 30, 1997, the recipient will not pay tax on the payments and the payer will not receive a tax deduction for them. If the agreement or court order does not identify an amount as being solely for the support of a spouse or common-law partner, it will be treated as child support. Similarly, any third-party payments that are not clearly identified as being solely for the benefit of the spouse or common-law partner will be treated as child support.

The changed rules can also apply to older agreements and court orders—for example, where a previous court order or agreement is varied or amended after April 30, 1997, and results in a change in the amount of child support. In addition, parties to an agreement or court order entered into before May 1, 1997, may jointly elect to have the changed rules apply.

TAX TIP

If you are party to an agreement or court order entered into before May 1, 1997, and you want the changed rules to apply, you must jointly elect by filing Form T1157. In some cases, you may also be required to file a copy of the agreement itself.

Registration of agreements

In some cases, you may be required to file Form T1158 with the CRA, along with a copy of the agreement or court order,. Generally, these requirements extend to situations in which payments will continue to be deductible—for example, if an agreement is entered into after May 1, 1997, and it contains a requirement either for spousal payments only or for separate amounts for spousal and child support. Agreements entered into before May 1, 1997, may also have to be filed if they provide for spousal or spousal and child support payments and the agreement becomes subject to the new rules.Your tax adviser will be able to provide you with details on these filing requirements.

Child support payments from a U.S. resident are not taxable under the Canada–U.S. tax treaty.

Agreements or court orders prior to May 1997

Generally, the rules remain unchanged for alimony and maintenance payments made pursuant to a written separation agreement or court order in place before May 1997.These amounts are deductible for tax purposes if they meet certain criteria. Also, if the person making the payments is allowed to deduct them, the person receiving the payments must include the amounts in income.

In general, to be deductible, the payments must be periodic, for the maintenance of your spouse and/or children and made pursuant to a written separation agreement or court order. Payments made in the same year (as well as those in the preceding year), before the agreement was signed, may also be deductible, provided the agreement or court order recognizes these payments.

Payments to a third party

There are also rules regarding the tax treatment of alimony and maintenance payments that have been paid to a third party rather than directly to your spouse, former spouse or common-law partner. Such payments, which can include medical bills, tuition fees and mortgage payments, may qualify for a deduction to the payer and a corresponding income inclusion to the recipient. To qualify, the expense must have been incurred at a time when you and your spouse, former spouse or common-law partner were separated and living apart, and such payments must have been specifically provided for in the court order or written agreement.

Where the child support is not taxable, deductibility to the payer and taxability to the recipient apply to only third-party payments that are not considered to be child support payments.

83 Deductibility of Legal Fees During Separation or Divorce

The tax treatment of legal fees paid during a separation and divorce is a complex subject. Although most of the legal fees incurred are not deductible since they are considered a personal or living expense, legal fees incurred with respect to support payments may be deductible. Their deductibility will depend on whether you are the payer or the recipient of the support payments.

From the payer's standpoint, legal costs incurred in negotiating or contesting an application for support payments are not deductible, nor are any of the costs incurred to terminate or reduce the amount of such payments. Legal expenses relating to custody or visitation rights are also non-deductible.

From the recipient's view, some or all of the legal fees may be deductible—depending on the circumstances outlined below.

Legal expenses incurred to obtain a lump-sum payment

Legal expenses incurred to obtain a lump-sum settlement are generally not deductible unless the lump-sum payment specifically relates to a number of periodic child support payments that were in arrears.

Legal expenses incurred to obtain periodic support payments

The CRA's position is that the following legal costs are deductible:

- costs incurred to obtain periodic child support payments or to enforce pre-existing rights (regardless of the fact that the amount received for child support may not have to be reported as income);

- costs incurred to enforce pre-existing spousal support;
- costs incurred to obtain spousal support; and
- costs incurred to obtain an increase in support or to make child support non-taxable.

TAX TIP

If you have incurred legal fees as part of a separation or divorce, you should contact your tax adviser to determine whether any of the amounts may be deductible. You may also be able to apply for a refund with respect to amounts paid in prior years.

84 Deductibility of Other Legal Expenses

Most legal expenses are personal in nature and are not deductible. However, legal costs paid to collect or establish a right to salary or wages from your employer or former employer are deductible. In addition, legal expenses paid to collect or establish a right to a retiring allowance or pension benefit are also deductible within a seven-year carry-forward period. The deduction is limited to the amount of retiring allowance or pension benefits received, less any portion that has been transferred to an RPP or RRSP.

85 Moving Expenses

If you moved from one location to another within Canada in 2009, you may be able to deduct your eligible moving expenses on your 2009 return. You must have started work or carried on a business at your new location. In addition, your new residence must be at least 40 kilometres closer to your new work location. A court case has concluded that this distance should be measured using the shortest route normally open to the travelling public.

Costs you can claim

Eligible moving expenses include travelling expenses incurred in connection with the move and the cost of transporting your household goods. The cost of meals and temporary accommodation for a period not exceeding 15 days is eligible, as are the costs of selling your old residence or, if you were renting, of breaking your lease. Any loss incurred on the sale of your former residence cannot be deducted.

To a maximum of $5,000, you can also claim mortgage interest, property taxes, insurance premiums, and costs associated with maintaining heat and power payable with respect to a vacant former residence. However, you must be able to show that you were making a reasonable effort to sell the former residence. The costs of revising legal documents to reflect the taxpayer's new address, replacing driver's licences and automobile permits, and having utilities connected and/or disconnected are also eligible for deduction.

If your employer paid for your moving expenses, however, you may not claim them as a deduction. If your employer pays or reimburses you for part of your moving expenses, you may deduct all of your eligible moving expenses but must report the amounts paid by your employer as income. Eligible expenses are deductible from only employment or business income earned at the new location. Amounts not deducted in the year of the move may be carried forward to another year to the extent of the employment or business income earned in that year.

TAX TIP

If you are moving to a new work location, any relocation payments should generally be structured as a reimbursement of actual expenses incurred. Payments received as a blanket lump-sum allowance, rather than a reimbursement of costs already incurred, may leave you open to tax implications. Talk to your tax adviser about how the payments can be structured to avoid or minimize tax.

Amounts received from your employer

Numerous court cases have addressed the tax status of amounts received from an employer following relocation for employment. Is the amount a taxable reimbursement? Due to the inconsistent court decisions and resulting uncertainty in this area, rules were introduced in 1998 to provide that all subsidies paid directly or indirectly by an employer with respect to the financing of an employee's new or former residence will be taxable. Half of any amounts in excess of $15,000 paid directly or indirectly to an employee by an employer to compensate for a loss on the disposition of the former residence will also be taxable.

TAX TIP

If you have to start a job at a new location, but a permanent move to that area is not possible until the following year, you won't lose any of your eligible deductions because the two events do not coincide. The courts have ruled that where a taxpayer commences employment at a new location but does not move until a subsequent year, the taxpayer can claim moving expenses incurred in that subsequent year.

Student eligibility

Students may claim moving expenses if they move to begin a job (including summer employment) or to start a business. If the move is to attend a full-time post-secondary institution, the expenses can be deducted, but only to the extent of the student's scholarship or research grant income included in the student's taxable income for the year (but see article 86, which comments on the taxation of scholarship and bursary income).

Optional method for claiming certain moving expenses

If you moved to a new work location in 2009 and would otherwise be entitled to claim moving expenses, you have the option of using a simplified method for claiming your meal and vehicle expenses.

Under the current detailed method, you have to keep all related receipts for meals and vehicle expenses and submit them on request. Vehicle expenses include operating expenses such as fuel, oil, tires, licence fees, insurance, maintenance and repairs, and ownership expenses such as depreciation (CCA), provincial tax and finance charges.

Under this method, you also have to keep track of the number of kilometres you drove in that time period, as well as the number of kilometres you drove specifically for the purpose of moving. Your claim for vehicle expenses is the percentage of your total vehicle expenses that relate to the kilometres driven for moving.

For example, if you drove 20,000 kilometres during the year, and 1,000 kilometres of that was related to your move, you can claim 1/20 of the total vehicle expenses on your tax return.

The optional rules are as follows:

- Meal expenses: In 2008 you were permitted to claim a flat rate of $17 a meal, to a maximum of $51 per day per person without receipts. At the time of writing, it's not yet known if this rate will remain the same for 2009.

- Vehicle expenses: This method involves the use of various pre-established flat rates. If you choose this option, you do not need to keep receipts. Instead, you simply keep track of the number of kilometres you drove during the tax year for your trips relating to the move. To determine the amount you can claim, multiply the number of kilometres by the cents-per-kilometre rate that applies for the province or territory from which the travel begins. These rates can be found on the CRA's website.

86 Scholarship Income

Prior to 2006, the first $3,000 of scholarship, fellowship or bursary income that you received with respect to post-secondary education or occupational training did not have to be included in your income.

For 2006 and subsequent years, such amounts are fully exempt from taxation, regardless of the amount received. To qualify for the full exemption, you must be entitled to claim the education credit amount for your enrolment in the educational program (see article 97). These amounts must be reported on an information slip.

For 2007 and subsequent years, elementary and secondary school scholarships are also subject to a full tax exemption.

87 What Is a Tax Credit?

Several of the articles that follow refer to a tax credit. Although there is a substantial difference between a tax credit and a tax deduction, it is easy to get the two confused. A tax deduction reduces your taxable income, with the actual amount of tax saved depending on your personal tax rate. If you are in the highest tax bracket, the deduction is generally worth anywhere from $0.39 to just over $0.48 on the dollar (depending on your province of residence—see Table 2, page 287). If you are in the lowest bracket, it is generally worth around $0.20 on the dollar (again, this will differ depending on your province of residence). If you have no taxable income, a deduction will not save you any tax at all.

A tax credit, on the other hand, is a deduction from tax owing. Provided the credit can be used, each taxpayer receives the same tax relief with a tax credit regardless of their particular tax bracket.

Prior to 2000, in all provinces except Quebec, personal income tax was calculated as a percentage of basic federal tax. All provinces now use taxable income—commonly called the TONI (Tax ON Income) system—rather than basic federal tax as their assessment base. Under this system, each province is free to either follow the federal tax credit system or introduce tax credits that are unique to the particular province. In many cases, the amount of the provincial credit will differ from its federal counterpart. Table 1, page 282, summarizes the federal and provincial amounts for some of the main tax credits.

Because of the changes to the provincial tax systems, the sections that follow that refer to tax credits will generally just comment on the federal tax credit. Keep in mind that the provincial tax credits may or may not parallel the treatment provided at the federal level.

EXAMPLE/**What they are worth**

Assume you live in Ontario and are in the highest federal tax bracket (29%). Your combined federal and provincial marginal tax rate in 2009 is 46.41% (see Table 2, page 287). A $100 tax deduction will save you $46.41 in tax. Your tax savings will be reduced where you are in a lower tax bracket.

Most federal tax credits are calculated using the lowest federal rate of tax (15% for 2009). Therefore, if you have $100 that is eligible for a tax credit, you will save $15 in federal income tax. The same amount will result in an Ontario tax credit of $6.05. So the combined tax saving is $21.05, regardless of your tax bracket.

88 Federal Personal Tax Credits

For 2009, federal personal tax credits are calculated as 15% of specified "personal amounts" (see Table 1, page 282) and are allowed as a deduction in calculating your federal tax liability.

You may claim personal exemption credits for yourself, your spouse or common-law partner and certain other persons who are related to you by blood, marriage or adoption. These credits are discussed more fully below. Federal personal tax credits are also indexed for inflation.

Basic personal credit

For 2009, everyone is entitled to claim a basic personal amount of $10,320.

The spouse or common-law partner credit

You may claim the spouse or common-law partner amount if, at any time in the year, you were married or had a common-law partner (see article 110) and you were not living separately because of a breakdown of the relationship. For 2009, the spouse or common-law partner amount is also equal to $10,320. This amount is reduced on a dollar-for-dollar basis by the dependant's net income. For example, if your spouse's net income is $3,000 for 2009, the spouse amount will be $7,320.

The provinces all have their own personal credit amounts, which can differ greatly from the federal amount (see Table 1, page 282).

The eligible dependant credit

If you were unmarried or separated from your spouse or common-law partner at any time in the year, you may be entitled to claim a personal tax credit known as the eligible dependant credit. To qualify, you must have maintained a home in which you and your qualifying dependant lived. As well, your dependant must be related to you and dependent on you for support. The dependant must be your parent, grandparent or child and must be either under 18 years of age at any time during 2009 or mentally or physically infirm. Two or more supporting relatives cannot split this tax credit. This credit is calculated the same way as the spouse or common-law partner credit. Therefore, the maximum claim for 2009 is $10,320.

The infirm dependant credit

You may claim the infirm dependant tax credit for a relative who is 18 years of age or older before the end of the year, provided the individual is dependent on you because of mental or physical infirmity. In addition, the individual must be dependent on you for support at any time in the year. Unlike the credits above, it is not necessary that the dependant live in the same residence as you, nor does the disability have to be severe enough that the dependant qualifies for the disability tax credit (see article 90). The CRA's position is that the dependency must be brought about solely by reason of the infirmity, and the infirmity must be such that it requires the person to be dependent on the individual for a considerable time.

For 2009, the infirm dependant amount is $4,198. This amount is reduced on a dollar-for-dollar basis by the dependant's income in excess of $5,956.

The caregiver credit

Because of the above income threshold, most taxpayers who provide care to an elderly relative living with them cannot claim the eligible dependant credit because payments under the Old Age Security and Guaranteed Income Supplement programs are well in excess of the threshold. As a result, there is another tax credit available if you reside with and provide in-home care for a parent or grandparent who is 65 years of age or older. The age restriction is removed if the relative is dependent on you by reason of mental or physical infirmity.

As with the infirm dependant amount, the maximum caregiver amount is $4,198. The major difference is the dependant's net income threshold at which the credit begins to be reduced. For 2009, the net income threshold is $14,336. No credit will be available if the dependant's income exceeds $18,534. Also, the caregiver credit will not be available if any person claims an eligible dependant or infirm dependant tax credit with respect to the dependant.

89 Child Tax Credit

This non-refundable tax credit was introduced in 2007. When it was first introduced, it was equal to $2,000 for each child under the age of 18 at the end of the taxation year. For 2009, this amount is increased to $2,089 per child.

Where the child resides together with the child's parents throughout the year, either of those parents may claim the credit. In other cases, the credit can generally be claimed by the parent who is eligible to claim the eligible dependant credit for the year for that child. The full amount of the credit can also be claimed in the year of birth, adoption or death. Any unused portion of the credit can be transferred to the parent's spouse or common-law partner.

90 Disability Tax Credit

Individuals suffering from a severe and prolonged mental or physical impairment can claim a federal disability amount of $7,196. If the person with a disability is a child under 18, there is an additional supplement of $4,198, for a total disability amount of $11,394. To qualify, a doctor must certify on Form T2201 that there exists a severe and prolonged impairment that "markedly restricts" the individual's daily living activities. The impairment must have lasted, or can reasonably be expected to last, for a continuous period of 12 months. Once obtained, the form continues to be valid until the cessation date noted on the form or until there is a change in condition. There is no requirement to file a new certificate each year.

Recent changes have extended eligibility for the disability tax credit to individuals who would be markedly restricted if therapy to sustain one of their vital functions was not administered to them at least three times a week, for a total duration averaging not less than 14 hours a week (e.g., individuals on kidney dialysis and cystic fibrosis sufferers). The types of activities that constitute life-sustaining therapy have also been better defined. For example, where the therapy has been determined to require a regular dosage of medication that needs to be adjusted on a daily basis, such as for children with severe cases of Type 1 diabetes, the activities directly involved in determining the appropriate dosage will be considered part of the therapy. As a result, many children with severe Type 1 diabetes should now qualify for the disability tax credit.

For 2005 and subsequent years, the ability to claim the disability tax credit has also been extended to individuals with multiple restrictions where the cumulative effect results in a marked restriction in a basic activity of daily living.

Those making a new application for this credit will find that the CRA will review the claim to determine eligibility before assessing the tax return. For this reason, if you are claiming the disability tax credit for the first time, you must paper-file your tax return. Once approved, this credit can continue to be claimed as long as circumstances do not change.

Transferring the credit

If you can't take advantage of this credit, it may be able to be transferred to your spouse, common-law partner or other supporting person. The list of supporting relatives who can claim a person's unused disability tax credit includes a parent, child, brother, sister, aunt, uncle, nephew or niece. Key to making the claim is that the person on whose behalf it is made must be "dependent on the taxpayer for support." This is not defined in the Act. The CRA has provided numerous technical interpretations in this area, basically concluding that whether a person is dependent on another "is a question of fact to be determined in each case." Consideration must be given to the availability and quantity of support provided. In general terms, support involves the provision of the basic necessities of life, such as food, shelter and clothing.

A court case, *Fleury v. The Queen*, addressed the meaning of "support" for purposes of this provision. In this case, the taxpayer's son suffered from severe epilepsy and lived in a care facility that was paid for by the Quebec government. Although the taxpayer dedicated significant amounts of time to the physical, moral and psychological development and care of his son, he did not expend any of his own funds for the care of his son. The Tax Court agreed with the Minister that the taxpayer could not claim the transfer of the disability tax credit. The existing jurisprudence concerning the definition of "support" indicated that "support" for credit purposes was restricted to financial support.

However, no claim can be made for a person with a disability under this provision if anyone has claimed a medical expense credit relating to a full-time attendant or nursing home care for that person. On the other hand, the attendant care deduction (see article 94) and the disability tax credit can both be claimed at the same time, as long as no additional attendant or nursing home claim has been made on behalf of the same taxpayer. To confuse this issue even further, the disability tax credit can also be claimed where an amount is claimed as a medical expense for attendant care (see article 93), to a maximum amount of $10,000 per year.

TAX TIP

If you or anyone else paid for an attendant or for care in a nursing home or other establishment because of your impairment, consider whether the amounts should be claimed as a medical expense instead of claiming the disability tax credit. In some circumstances, both may be claimed (subject to certain restrictions).

The rules relating to this area of credits are exceedingly complex and often confusing. Before filing a return, it is recommended that you have a tax adviser analyze your particular circumstances to determine the appropriate claim or combination of claims.

Disability tax credit—certificate issued after death

As previously noted, to qualify for the disability tax credit, a medical doctor must certify that the individual has a severe and prolonged mental or physical impairment that is expected to last more than 12 months. This certification can be made after the taxpayer dies where it is based on a prognosis made by an appropriately qualified person before the individual died, and where the individual's severe impairment was reasonably expected to last for a continuous period of at least 12 months.

91 Tax Credits for Charitable Donations

Donations made to registered charities, registered Canadian amateur athletic associations, Canadian municipalities, the federal government or a provincial government are eligible for a tax credit. As a general rule, donations to U.S. charitable organizations qualify for the credit, provided you also have U.S.–source net income that is taxable in Canada.

Donations can be claimed only after they are paid—pledges don't count. Unused claims may be carried forward for up to five years and donations made in the year of death may be carried back one year.

The general annual limit on charitable donations as a percentage of net income is 75%. However, the limit on gifts by individuals in the year of death (and the prior year) is 100%.

Save those receipts

To qualify for the donation credit, you must attach to your tax return the original official receipts issued by the registered charity or association. These receipts will include the registration number of the given institution. Photocopies of receipts are not acceptable, and filing cancelled cheques is not good enough either. If you are filing your return electronically or by using NETFILE or TELEFILE (see article 172), you are not required to file these receipts with your return, but you must keep them on hand in case the CRA asks to see them.

For 2009, the federal credit is 15% on the first $200 of donations claimed in the year and 29% on the amount in excess of $200. After factoring in provincial tax savings, donations in excess of $200 will save you anywhere from 39% to just over 48% depending on your province of residence.

TAX TIP

If you and your spouse or common-law partner donate more than $200 in any one year, the tax credit will be larger if one of you claims the entire amount. That way, only one $200 amount is credited at 15%.

EXAMPLE/**Joining forces**

Suppose you donated $700 in 2009 and your spouse donated $800. Rather than claiming the amounts individually, where each of you receives a 15% federal credit on the first $200, you should pool the amounts and have one of you claim it. That way, one of you receives a 15% credit on $200 and a 29% credit on $1,300.

Donating property

Subject to special rules outlined in what follows (see "Art and other charitable donation arrangements"), if you donate capital property to a registered charity you can elect to value the gift at any amount not less than its adjusted cost base and not more than its fair market value. The amount claimed as a donation must also be reported as your proceeds of disposition of the property.

To account for the fact that the disposition may result in taxable income to the donor, the general annual limit of 75% of net income is increased to effectively allow 100% of the donor's taxable income created by the disposition to be offset by tax credits. In addition, donors of depreciable assets, such as buildings and equipment, will be entitled to increase the net income limit for such a donation to ensure that the donor has enough tax credits to more than offset the tax arising from the recaptured depreciation and/or the taxable capital gain that may be incurred.

If you donate "eligible property" to a charity, you are entitled to additional tax relief. Eligible property includes securities, such as shares and bonds listed on a prescribed stock exchange, as well as mutual fund units. For such donations made before May 2, 2006, the taxable capital gain resulting from the disposition of the property was reduced by 50%. For donations made after May 1, 2006, the taxable portion of the gain is reduced to nil. Prior to March 19, 2007, this tax relief did not extend to gifts of eligible property to a private charitable foundation. However, for gifts made after March 18, 2007, this tax relief also extends to qualifying donations made to private foundations.

EXAMPLE/**Sharing the wealth**

Your net income for 2009 is expected to be $150,000. In 1990, you purchased 2,000 bank shares for $10,000. In March 2009, you donate 1,000 of the shares, now with a fair market value of $50,000, to your favourite registered charity. The following outlines the impact on your 2009 net income:

Net income	$150,000
Taxable capital gain [(0% × 50% × $40,000)]	$0
Total net income	$150,000

The donation amount eligible for tax credit is calculated as follows:

75% of net income	$112,500
25% of taxable capital gain	$0
Limit	$112,500
Available for credit (donation amount)	$50,000

Assuming your marginal tax rate is 45%, the tax saving arising from the donation is $22,500 (45% × $50,000). There is no tax on the gain resulting from the disposition.

TAX TIP

If you are planning to make significant donations to a charitable organization, consider giving shares of public corporations so that you may benefit from the special rules on these donations. Keep in mind that you can now get the same tax relief if you donate the shares to a private charitable foundation.

Other gifts

Donations do not always have to be in the form of money or tangible property. Donating a life insurance policy to a registered charitable organization qualifies for the credit (see article 140), provided certain conditions are met. It is the CRA's current administrative position that the amount eligible for the credit is the fair market value of the life insurance policy at the time it is gifted to the charity. Under certain conditions, the gift of a residual interest in a trust or estate may also qualify for the credit. Your tax adviser can provide additional information in these areas.

Charitable gifts made on the death of an individual may qualify for the charitable donation tax credit in the year of death and the prior year. The charitable donation tax credit can also be claimed for donations of RRSP, RRIF and insurance proceeds that are made pursuant to a direct beneficiary designation.

Art and other charitable donation arrangements

For several years prior to 2000, there was a tax arrangement whereby taxpayers would buy a series of works of art for, say, $200 each, and would then dispose of them to a registered charity or university at a much higher appraised value (say $1,000 each). No capital gain was reported on the disposition due to the "personal-use property rules" (see article 118), which deemed the cost to the taxpayer for purposes of calculating capital gains to be $1,000 per piece of art. The donor received a charitable donation receipt for the artwork's appraised value. Since that time, numerous charitable donation arrangements have arisen that involve the purchase of property at a discounted price and the subsequent donation of the property to a charity at a much higher value.

Over the past few years, the government has looked for ways to put a stop to these planning strategies. In 2000, rules were introduced to provide that the personal-use property rules would not apply to property acquired after February 27, 2000, where it was reasonable to assume that it was acquired as part of an arrangement whereby it would be gifted to a charity. But this didn't go far enough. In December 2003, the government announced that for gifts made after 6:00 pm EST on December 5, 2003, the fair market value of the property is deemed to be whichever is less—the actual fair market value or the donor's cost of the property where the property is (1) donated under a gifting arrangement that is a tax shelter; (2) donated within three years of its acquisition; or (3) acquired by the donor within the past 10 years in contemplation of making the donation.

You should note that all donations in kind will be caught by this rule—not just those that are made as part of a gifting arrangement. Therefore, if you acquire a gift of art in January 2009 for $1,500 and donate it to a charity in December 2011, at which time its estimated fair market value is $2,500, you can receive a donation receipt for only $1,500. You must wait three years from the time of acquisition to receive a receipt for the higher amount. However, if you acquire any property as part of a gifting arrangement that is a tax shelter, the donation receipt will always be restricted to the cost of the property—regardless of how long you hold it. There are certain exceptions to this rule where property is donated as a result of a taxpayer's death and for donations of certain types of property, such as inventory, real property located in Canada, Canadian cultural property, ecological property and qualifying public securities. Provided certain conditions are met, the exception will also apply where a shareholder of a closely held company donates company shares to a charity or where the company donates property that it acquired from a shareholder on a tax-deferred basis.

Special rules apply if the donated property was previously acquired by a person related to the donor. If a non-arm's-length person owned the property within the three- or 10-year period noted above, prior to the time the donation is made, the cost of the property for purposes of these rules is deemed to be the lowest cost amount to the donor or non-arm's-length person. This rule applies to gifts made after July 17, 2005.

EXAMPLE/**Limiting the cost amount of the donation**

> Mary acquires a piece of art for $2,000 at an auction on December 1, 2005. In May 2009, it is valued at $5,000. She sells it to her daughter, who donates it to a charity in August 2009. For charitable donation receipt purposes, the cost of the property is limited to $2,000.

What about bulk donations made before 6:00 pm EST on December 5, 2003?

Several Federal Court of Appeal decisions (*Klotz*, *Nash*, *Tolley* and *Quinn*) have addressed the tax treatment of bulk donations made before the introduction of the above rules.

All of these cases dealt with the valuation of works of art for charitable donation receipt purposes. In each case, the taxpayers acquired groups of limited edition prints, which they subsequently donated to charities and universities. The taxpayers each received a donation receipt for an amount that was significantly greater than the purchase price of the prints. The Minister of Revenue argued that the donation amount should be limited to the amount actually paid for the prints and the Federal Court of Appeal agreed. The Supreme Court has refused to hear the taxpayers' appeal.

Such cases no longer have to be handled by the courts. Rules introduced in December 2003 have now officially legislated the amount that can be reported on a charitable donation receipt in similar "buy low, donate high" gifting arrangements.

Other receipting guidelines for charities

In general, a charitable organization can issue a tax receipt for the amount of a gift made to the charity. In some cases—for example, when the donor receives some benefit as a result of making the donation—the actual amount of the gift may not be clear. To help resolve some of the uncertainty in this area, the CRA has issued guidelines to describe how the amount of the gift should be determined in various fundraising methods commonly used by the charitable sector, such as fundraising dinners, charity auctions, concerts, shows and sporting events, golf tournaments, etc.

In all of these situations, the donor generally receives some type of benefit or advantage as part of making the gift. The guidelines assist in clarifying how the amount of the gift should be valued. The eligible amount of the gift will be the amount by which the value of the property transferred to the charity exceeds the amount of the advantage.

In many cases, the charity should consider obtaining an independent valuation to substantiate the amount of the advantage.

EXAMPLE/**Fundraising event**

> Your favourite charity holds a fundraising dinner for which 500 tickets are sold for $250 each. A comparable meal could be purchased for $100. Each donor is entitled to receive a charitable donation receipt in the amount of $150. There may be further adjustments where the event has door prizes or provides attendees with other complimentary gifts.

For gifts made after February 18, 2003, the amount of the advantage received by the donor will include any limited recourse debt associated with the gift. Although many donation plans have been structured on the basis that the associated debt is not limited recourse debt, the rules introduced in 2003 have considerably broadened the definition of such a debt to include arrangements involving loans that the donor has little or no risk of repaying.

TAX TIP

Some donation arrangements are being promoted on the basis that they are not caught by the above rules. You should be particularly wary of plans that sound too good to be true. In such cases, you should consult with your tax adviser to determine the impact these rules could have on your ability to receive a charitable donation tax credit.

92 Political Donations

Contributions made to registered political parties generate tax credits (within limits), not tax deductions. Political contributions to federal parties can be applied only against federal income taxes.

For 2009, the credit is calculated as follows: 75% of the first $400, 50% on the next $350 and 33 1/3% of any contribution over $750, up to $1,275. The maximum credit allowed is $650. Some provinces provide similar credits against provincial income taxes for contributions made to provincial political parties. To claim the credit, you must attach to your return a copy of the receipt.

For both federal and provincial purposes, the credit can reduce only taxes paid or payable. If you are not liable for any taxes in 2009, the credit is lost. It cannot be carried forward to 2010. Note that contributions to local mayoral campaigns do not qualify for the political donation tax credit.

TAX TIP

Consider spreading your political contributions over two years. For example, if you contribute $750 in 2009, your federal tax credit will be $475. If, instead, you contribute $375 in 2009 and $375 in 2010, your political contribution tax credit will be $281.25 in each of 2009 and 2010, for a total of $562.50.

93 Medical Expenses

Medical expenses paid within any 12-month period ending in the year are eligible for a tax credit claim. Expenses reimbursed by either your employer or a private or government-sponsored health care plan are not allowed.

The list of eligible medical expenses is extensive and includes:

- payments to medical practitioners, dentists or nurses, or to public or licensed private hospitals with respect to medical or dental services provided to the patient;

- payments for eyeglasses or devices for treatment or correction of vision, lab tests and dentures where these have been prescribed by a medical practitioner or dentist, as the case may be; payments for drugs and medication where these are prescribed by a medical practitioner or dentist and recorded by a pharmacist (except for drugs and medications that can be purchased without a prescription—see below);
- premiums paid by the taxpayer to private health services plans;
- payments for real-time captioning services or sign-language interpretation services, to the extent that the payment is made to a person in the business of providing such services;
- the cost of voice-recognition software, provided the need has been certified in writing by a medical practitioner;
- additional costs related to the purchase of gluten-free food products compared to the cost of comparable non-gluten-free food products for a patient who has celiac disease, provided it has been certified in writing by a medical practitioner;
- expenses paid for training courses for the taxpayer or a related person with respect to the care of a related person with a mental or physical impairment who lives with or is a dependant of the taxpayer, provided it has been certified in writing by a medical practitioner;
- the cost of purchased or leased products, equipment or devices that provide relief, assistance or treatment for any illness or condition, such as an artificial limb, an oxygen tent, a guide dog or a van for a wheelchair;
- premiums (including deductible and co-insurance portions) under a provincial drug insurance plan;
- amounts paid as remuneration for tutoring persons with learning disabilities or other mental impairments if the need for such services is certified in writing by a medical practitioner and provided by a person whose normal business is to provide such services;
- talking textbooks prescribed by a medical practitioner for an individual with a perceptual disability, in connection with the individual's enrolment at an educational institution in Canada;

- payments to a person engaged in the business of providing transportation services for transportation from where a patient lives to a location at least 40 kilometres away where a medical service will be provided, as long as it has been certified in writing by a medical practitioner;
- reasonable travel expenses incurred to obtain medical services at a location that is at least 80 kilometres away from where a patient lives, provided it has been certified in writing by a medical practitioner;
- reasonable moving expenses incurred for the purpose of moving to a more accessible dwelling, up to a maximum claim of $2,000 by all persons with respect to the move;
- reasonable supplemental expenses for the construction of a principal residence considered necessary to enable a person with a serious, prolonged mobility impairment to gain access to this residence or to be mobile or functional within it;
- reasonable expenses for renovations or alterations to a dwelling to enable a person who has a severe and prolonged mobility impairment to gain access to, or to be mobile or functional within, the dwelling. Rules have recently been introduced to clarify the types of expenses that qualify as home renovation expenses. Following some court cases that tended to interpret this measure quite broadly—most notably to include the cost of installing hardwood floors or a hot tub as an eligible expense—a two-criteria test has been established for determining whether a home renovation expense qualifies as a medical expense. First, the expense must not typically be expected to increase the value of the home. Second, it must be of a type that would not typically be incurred by persons without such impairment. These changes are effective for expenses incurred after February 22, 2005;
- amounts paid for a full-time attendant or for full-time care in a nursing home for a person with a disability who is entitled to the disability tax credit;
- amounts paid for full-time nursing home care for a person certified in writing by a qualified medical practitioner to lack

"normal mental capacity" and who is dependent now and in the foreseeable future on others for personal needs and care;

- amounts paid for a full-time attendant for a patient in a self-contained domestic establishment in which the patient lives. This rule does not require that the patient qualify for the disability tax credit, but it does require a qualified medical practitioner to certify in writing that due to physical or mental infirmity the patient is in need of the full-time attendant. The attendant cannot be a dependant of the person claiming the medical expense credit or be under 18 years of age;
- an amount paid as remuneration for attendant care (which need not be full-time attendant care) for a person who qualifies for the disability tax credit (to a maximum of $10,000 per year or $20,000 in the year of death). This amount can be claimed in addition to the disability tax credit (see article 90). This amount can be claimed for certain retirement home expenses (see article 95);
- amounts paid as remuneration for the care and supervision of a person eligible for the disability tax credit who resides in a home exclusively for such persons;
- the cost of phototherapy equipment for the treatment of skin disorders;
- amounts paid for drugs purchased under Health Canada's Special Access Program and the cost of medical marijuana. To qualify as an expense, the marijuana must be purchased from either Health Canada or a designated grower, and the taxpayer must be authorized to use the drug for medical purposes under Health Canada's Medical Marijuana Access Regulations or an exemption under Section 56 of the Controlled Drug and Substances Act;
- the cost to purchase, operate, and maintain the following devices, provided they are required by a medical practitioner:
    - altered auditory feedback devices for the treatment of a speech disorder;
    - electrotherapy devices for the treatment of a medical

condition or a severe mobility impairment;

- standing devices for standing therapy in the treatment of a severe mobility impairment; and
- pressure pulse therapy devices for the treatment of a balance disorder;

- certain expenses for service animals that are specially trained to assist someone who is severely affected by autism or epilepsy. The types of expenses that can be claimed include the cost and the care and maintenance of the service animal, as well as reasonable travel expenses incurred by the individual to receive training in the handling of such an animal.

In recent years, court cases have been decided in the taxpayer's favour, allowing vitamins and herbal supplements to be claimed as a medical expense, provided they have been prescribed by a qualified medical practitioner. This was not the intent of Parliament. As a result, the 2008 federal budget introduced measures to clarify that drugs and medications that can be purchased without a prescription will not qualify for the medical expense tax credit. This new rule is effective for expenses incurred after February 26, 2008.

The above list is not all inclusive. The government is continually amending the list of expenses that qualify for this credit.

You may claim medical expenses for yourself, your spouse or common-law partner, and certain related persons (discussed below).

TAX TIP

On the year of death tax return, the legal representative of a deceased taxpayer may claim any medical expenses paid by the taxpayer or his legal representative within any 24-month period that includes the date of death. The same expense may not be claimed more than once.

For 2009, total eligible medical expenses paid for you, your spouse or common-law partner or minor child must first be reduced by 3% of your net income or $2,011, whichever is less. The tax credit is 15% of the amount remaining.

TAX TIP

Select your 12-month period to maximize the tax credit. The 12-month period ending in the year may vary from year to year, but you cannot claim the same expense twice. Keep your receipts for next year if some of your 2009 expenses are not claimed as a credit in 2009.

A refundable medical expense supplement is also available to eligible individuals who have business and/or employment income of at least $3,116. The refundable credit is 25% of medical expenses that qualify for the regular medical expense tax credit, up to a stated maximum. It is reduced by 5% of the taxpayer's (and spouse or common-law partner's) income in excess of a specified amount ($23,633 per family in 2009). This credit is in addition to the tax credit for medical expenses. The maximum refundable medical expense supplement is $1,067 for the 2009 taxation year.

EXAMPLE

> Sally incurs medical expenses of $3,500 for prescription drugs. She recently began working at a job and reported net income of $20,000 for 2009. Sally can claim both a federal medical expense tax credit of $435 [15% × ($3,500 – $600)] and a refundable medical expense supplement of $725 [25% × ($3,500 – $600)].

What you cannot claim as medical expenses

Many items do not qualify as medical expenses—for example, non-prescription birth control devices, drugs and medications that you can purchase without a prescription (see above), funeral and burial costs, and gym memberships, to name a few. In addition, you cannot claim medical expenses for which you are reimbursed or are entitled to be reimbursed.

Medical expenses of dependants other than a spouse or common-law partner

Subject to special rules, you may also claim medical expenses you have paid for a dependant. In general, a "dependant" is a person who is dependent on you for support at any time in the year, and who is the child, grandchild, parent, grandparent, brother, sister, uncle, aunt, niece or nephew of you or your spouse or common-law partner.

Claims for the medical expense credit for minor children are grouped with claims for you and your spouse or common-law partner. Medical expenses paid for other dependant relatives must first be reduced by 3% of that dependant's net income, to a maximum of $2,011 in 2009. The maximum amount that can be claimed for each "other dependant" is $10,000.

EXAMPLE

Kelly supports her adult daughter, Michelle, who has a disability. Michelle has a part-time job and earned $10,000 in 2009. Kelly pays all of Michelle's medical expenses, which total $4,000 for the year. Kelly can claim $3,700 of Michelle's medical expenses, for a federal tax reduction of $555, calculated as follows:

Medical expenses incurred on behalf of Michelle	$4,000
Less: 3% of Michelle's net income	($300)
Net medical expense claim	$3,700
Federal income tax reduction ($3,700 × 15%)	$555

TAX TIP

If you pay medical expenses for a dependant other than your spouse or common-law partner or minor child, the ability to claim a medical expense credit is based on the dependant's net income, not your own. As a result, even limited payments can qualify where the dependant's income is quite low. Don't forget to claim these amounts when you file your tax return. If you forgot to make a claim in the years 2005 to 2008 and you think you might qualify, you can request an adjustment to your prior year's return.

94 Attendant Care/Disability Supports Deduction

If you are entitled to claim the disability amount (see article 90), you may deduct expenses paid for attendant care from your income. This attendant care must allow you to earn income from employment or self-employment or to take an occupational training course for which you receive a training allowance. The deduction is limited to two-thirds of your earned income, which is basically salary and business income.

Although subject to certain limitations, this deduction may also be claimed by people who require an attendant to go to school.

As an alternative, for purposes of the medical expense tax credit (see article 93) you can claim the cost of attendant care incurred as a medical expense, even if you are not earning income. The maximum annual amount that can be claimed is $10,000 ($20,000 in the year of death).

The list of expenses that qualify for this deduction have recently been expanded to include sign-language interpreters and talking textbooks, job-coaching services, reading services and deaf-blind intervening services. In addition, Bliss symbol boards, Braille note takers, page turners, and devices and software designed to enable a person with a disability to read print are also eligible for this deduction where the need for the device or software is certified by a medical practitioner. Any expenses claimed under this deduction will not be eligible for the medical expense tax credit (see article 93).

TAX TIP

If you are disabled, and your taxable income is over $40,726, the deduction for attendant care is worth more to you than claiming the medical expense tax credit. You will likely be further ahead economically if you take the deduction.

95 Attendant Care in a Retirement Home

In general, payments made to a nursing home or long-term care facility qualify for the medical expense tax credit, provided the individual meets all the criteria to claim the disability tax credit. The issue has been less clear with respect to amounts paid to a retirement home. However, it is now the CRA's position that seniors who live in a retirement home and are eligible for the disability tax credit can claim attendant care expenses as medical expenses. The maximum amount that can be claimed under this provision is $10,000 per year ($20,000 in the year of death).

To make the claim, you must have a receipt from the retirement home showing the portion paid for attendant care and be eligible for the disability tax credit.

TAX TIP

If you think you (or someone you know) might have qualified for this credit but it was not claimed in a prior year, contact your tax adviser about filing a T1 adjustment request.

96 Adoption Expense Credit

If you adopt a child, you are able to claim a non-refundable tax credit for certain expenses you incur as part of the adoption process.

Eligible expenses include court, legal and administrative expenses, reasonable travel and living expenses, fees paid to an adoption agency licensed by a provincial or territorial government, any other reasonable expenses required by such an agency, mandatory fees paid to a foreign institution, mandatory expenses paid with respect to the immigration of the adopted child and document translation fees.

The maximum amount that can be claimed for 2009 is $10,909.

97 Tuition Fees, Education and Textbook Credits

For the 2009 tax year, students are entitled to a tax credit equal to 15% of tuition fees paid to qualifying educational and training institutions. They are also entitled to an education credit of 15% of $400 per month (or $60) for the number of months in the year they were full-time students. This includes full-time post-secondary students enrolled in correspondence courses.

The education credit is also available to part-time students registered at an educational institution in Canada where the eligible post-secondary program covers at least three consecutive weeks and 12 hours of courses per month. In such cases, the credit is 15% of $120 per month (or $18). Part-time students eligible for the disability tax credit or who cannot be enrolled on a full-time basis because of the student's mental or physical impairment are entitled to the full-time education credit.

In the past, employed individuals were not entitled to claim the education tax credit for the cost of programs related to their current employment. However, the education tax credit can now be claimed for education related to such employment when the costs are not reimbursed by the employer.

Effective for 2006 and subsequent taxation years, students can also claim a textbook tax credit. This credit is calculated as follows:

- $65 for each month for which the student qualifies for the full-time education tax credit amount; and
- $20 for each month the student qualifies for the part-time education tax credit amount.

Part-time students eligible for the disability tax credit or who cannot be enrolled on a full-time basis because of the student's mental or physical impairment are entitled to the full-time textbook tax credit.

What's covered?

Qualifying fees include those for attending a Canadian university, college or other educational institution providing courses at a post-secondary level. If you attend a primary or secondary school that provides courses at the post-secondary level, you may also qualify for the tuition credit, provided the course paid for is at the post-secondary level. If the institution has certification from the Ministry of Human Resources and Skills Development, courses that allow you to obtain or improve an occupational skill may also qualify. To qualify for the tuition credit, the total fees for the year paid to each institution must be at least $100. Subject to certain restrictions, tuition fees paid to universities outside Canada may also qualify for the credit.

All of the above credits are claimed on a calendar-year basis. Where the student attends a post-secondary institution in Canada, the claims for these credits are normally supported by Form T2202 or T2202A, which is completed by the educational institution. Currently, this supporting document does not have to be filed with the return, but it must be available if requested by the CRA. Where tuition fees are paid to a qualifying institution outside Canada, Form TL11A (for a foreign university), TL11C (for commuters attending post-secondary institutions in the U.S.), or TL11D (for deemed residents of Canada) must be completed and filed with the return.

It used to be the CRA's position that tuition fees for foreign courses required physical attendance at the foreign institution. However, in *Valente* and *Kuwalek*, the tax court ruled that tuition fees for courses in England provided essentially by the Internet qualified for the tuition credit. In light of these decisions, the CRA published an opinion saying that it now accepts that a student enrolled at a university outside Canada and taking courses over the Internet may be able to claim a tuition tax credit for the related tuition fees, provided the student is able to demonstrate their attendance constituted "full-time attendance." This new position applies to tuition fees paid for the 2007 taxation year, unless a notice of objection was filed and is still outstanding, or can still be filed for a prior period.

Students are entitled to carry forward unused tuition, education and textbook credits indefinitely. As a result, any amount not used by the student in the current year and not transferred to an eligible person (see below) can be carried forward by the student and claimed in a subsequent year.

TAX TIP

Students must provide all necessary information to the CRA to establish the carry-forward. This will require filing an income tax return, even if one is not otherwise required.

Transfer of tuition, education and textbook credits

If a student is unable to use all or a portion of these credits, he or she can transfer up to $5,000 to an eligible person. That translates into a $750 federal tax credit. Transfer to an eligible person is available only for credits earned in the current year. To make this designation, the student must complete and sign Form T2202. To support the amount claimed, a copy of this form should be kept by the designated person and, if applicable, by the student. Currently, the form does not need to be filed with the return, but it must be available if requested by the CRA.

TAX TIP

If you cannot fully utilize your tuition, education and textbook tax credits to reduce taxes payable to zero, all or a portion of the unused credits may be transferred to a spouse or common-law partner or supporting parent or grandparent.

There are special rules for calculating the transfer of provincial tuition and education amounts between students and parents residing in different provinces.

98 Interest on Student Loan Credit

Many students obtain loans to finance their post-secondary education. You can claim a tax credit of 15% of the interest paid in the year or in any of the five preceding years (if not previously claimed) on a federal or provincial student loan provided for post-secondary education. Interest on other loans such as bank loans obtained for post-secondary education does not qualify for this tax credit.

99 Claiming Your Spouse or Common-Law Partner's Unused Credits

TAX TIP

If your spouse or common-law partner has little or no taxable income and cannot use all the federal tax credits to which he or she is entitled, you are in a position to claim the portion of the qualifying credits that your spouse is unable to use. However, you cannot claim these credits if you were separated at the end of the year and for a 90-day period that commenced at any time in the year. The unused credits that can be transferred include the tuition fee and education and textbook tax credits (see article 97), the pension credit (see article 100), the disability tax credit (see article 90) and the age credit (see article 101).

To determine how much your spouse or common-law partner can transfer to you, you must calculate his or her federal tax liability before applying any of these credits. Then you subtract from this amount his or her basic personal tax credit (see article 88 and Table 1, page 282) and the amount of any tax credits arising from EI and/or CPP contributions, plus any tuition, education and textbook carry-forward credits that arose in prior years. If there are no federal taxes payable after applying these credits, then the full amount of his or her unused credits can be transferred to you. If, after deducting these credits, your spouse or common-law partner still owes federal tax, the qualifying credits must be applied first to eliminate her or his remaining federal tax liability. The remaining portion can be transferred to you.

EXAMPLE/**To your credit**

Suppose you earn $100,000 of employment income and your spouse reports $12,000 of RRSP income in 2009. Your spouse also attended university full-time for four months and paid $4,500 in tuition fees. Your spouse would have taxable income of $12,000 and an eligible tuition, education and textbook amount of $6,360 [$4,500 + (4 × $400) + (4 × $65)]. The amount of credits transferable to you is calculated as follows:

Spouse's Tax Liability	
Taxable income	$12,000
	15%
Federal tax (before tax credits)	$1,800
Personal tax credit (15% × $10,320)	$1,548
Federal tax (before tuition credit)	$252
Tuition credit needed to reduce taxes payable to zero	($252)
Federal tax	$0

As shown above, your spouse must use a portion of the credit ([$ 252 ÷ 15%] or $1,680) to eliminate his or her federal tax liability. Although the unused amount is $4,680 ($6,360 – $1,680), only $3,320 is eligible for transfer to your 2009 tax return, since the maximum amount that can be transferred is limited to $5,000 minus the amount required to reduce your spouse's tax liability to zero. The remaining amount of $1,360 can be carried forward by your spouse and can be deducted from his or her income in a subsequent year.

100 Pension Credit

The first $2,000 of eligible pension income qualifies for a non-refundable tax credit (prior to 2006, the amount was $1,000). The type of pension income that qualifies for this credit differs depending on whether you were 65 or older in the year. If you were under 65 as of December 31, 2009, "qualifying pension income" includes life annuity payments out of a superannuation or pension plan and certain payments received as a result of the death of a spouse or common-law partner.

If you were 65 or older in 2009, other defined payments such as lifetime annuity payments out of your RRSP, deferred profit sharing plan (DPSP) or RRIF also qualify for the pension credit. Qualifying pension income does not include Canada Pension Plan (CPP), Old Age Security (OAS) or Guaranteed Income Supplement (GIS) payments.

TAX TIP

If you don't already benefit from the pension income tax credit and you are 65 years of age or older, consider creating pension income by purchasing an annuity that yields $2,000 of interest income annually. Alternatively, you can use some of the funds in your RRSP to purchase an annuity or a RRIF to provide you with $2,000 of annual pension income.

101 Age Credit

Canadian taxpayers 65 or older are entitled to claim an age amount of $6,408. The resulting credit is one that can be transferred between spouses or common-law partners (see article 99). It is reduced at a rate of 15% where a taxpayer's income exceeds a prescribed threshold, currently $32,312, and it is fully eliminated once income exceeds $75,032.

TAX TIP

Are you able to manage your income level but require more than $32,312 a year on average? Then you may find it beneficial to receive larger amounts of income in one year and a reduced amount the next. This will ensure that the age credit amount is reduced in only one year. This strategy can also be used to reduce the total Old Age Security clawback (see article 80).

102 First-Time Home Buyers' Tax Credit

The 2009 federal budget introduced a new non-refundable tax credit for first-time home buyers. Subject to certain limitations, the $5,000 credit applies to first-time home buyers who acquire homes after January 27, 2009. Since the credit is based on the lowest marginal tax rate of 15%, this new credit will reduce federal income taxes by $750. The rules to qualify as a first-time home buyer are generally the same as those that apply under the Home Buyers' Plan (see article 72).

103 New Home Renovation Tax Credit

The 2009 Federal budget introduced a temporary 15% non-refundable home renovation tax credit (HRTC) for certain eligible expenditures made after January 27, 2009 and before February 1, 2010 with respect to a taxpayer's principal residence. Eligible expenditures include amounts incurred for labour, material, equipment rentals and permits in relation to a renovation or alteration of an eligible dwelling provided the expenditures are on personal-use areas of the residence.

The credit will apply to expenditures in excess of $1,000 but not more than $10,000, resulting in a maximum credit of $1,350. The credit will apply only to the 2009 taxation year and will be claimed on your 2009 income tax return (including expenditures made in January 2010). The claim must be supported by receipts. The HRTC will not be reduced by any other tax credits or grants to which you may be entitled under other government programs.

The following expenditures will not qualify for the credit:

- the cost of routine repairs and maintenance normally performed on an annual or more frequent basis;
- expenditures for appliances and audio-visual electronics;
- financing costs associated with a renovation;
- other indirect expenditures that retain a value independent of the renovation (e.g., furniture and draperies); and
- expenditures for goods and services provided by a non-arm's-length person, unless that person is registered for the GST/HST.

104 Canada Employment Credit

Compared to a self-employed individual, an employee is extremely limited with respect to the deductions he or she can claim against employment income.

To help offset some of an employee's work-related expenses, the Canada Employment Credit was introduced in 2006. This credit is indexed for inflation. The maximum amount of this credit is $1,044 for 2009.

105 Working Income Tax Benefit

To provide incentives for low- and mid-income Canadians to enter or remain in the workforce, the 2007 federal budget introduced a new working income tax benefit (WITB). For the 2008 taxation year, this benefit comprised a refundable tax credit of up to 20% for each dollar earned in excess of $3,000 to a maximum credit of $510 for single individuals and $1,019 for couples and single parents. The credit is reduced by 15% of net family income in excess of a specified amount. In the 2009 federal budget, the government announced that it plans to double the tax relief provided by this benefit. The final parameters of the enhanced WITB for the 2009 taxation year will be announced once the government has consulted with the provinces and territories. Advance payments for 2009 will be based on the 2008 rates. Adjustments will be made and full entitlement will be paid out based on the announced increases when the 2009 tax return is filed, providing Schedule 6 of the return (which calculates the WITB) is completed.

The WITB also includes an additional disability supplement for each individual, other than a dependant, who is eligible for the disability tax credit (see article 90). British Columbia, Nunavut and Quebec adjust the WITB calculation based on specific social and economic conditions.

For the purposes of calculating this benefit, earned income means the total amount of an individual's or family's income for the year from employment and business, and is determined without reference to any losses arising or claimed in that year.

To qualify for the WITB, you must be a resident of Canada and at least 19 years of age at the end of the year or the primary caregiver to a dependent child in Canada. Full-time students with no dependent children will not qualify for this benefit.

The maximum benefit levels and thresholds are indexed for inflation.

Prepayment

If you are eligible for the Goods and Services Tax (GST) credit, you may also be able to apply for a prepayment of half your estimated WITB. You must apply to the CRA to receive the prepayment. To qualify, you must provide adequate evidence of anticipated earned income and proof of residency in Canada. This application is made annually. If approved, the prepayments will be made as part of your GST credit payments.

106 Public Transit Credit

If you and or your family members rely heavily on public transit throughout the year, this tax credit can provide substantial tax savings.

Starting July 1, 2006, the cost of eligible travel on a local bus, streetcar, subway, commuter train, commuter bus or ferry qualifies for this non-refundable tax credit. It can be claimed by you, your spouse or common-law partner for eligible transit costs incurred by you, your spouse or common-law partner and any dependent children under 19 years of age. When these rules were first introduced, an eligible public transit pass was defined as being a pass that was valid for a period of at least 28 days of public transit. For 2007 and subsequent years, this credit was extended to more innovative fare products, such as electronic payment cards and weekly passes. Electronic payment cards will qualify for the credit provided the cost relates to the use of public transit for at least 32 one-way trips during an uninterrupted period not exceeding 31 days. Weekly passes will qualify, where an individual purchases at least four consecutive weekly passes that provide a passholder with the right to unlimited public transit use within a period of between five to seven days.

If your employer reimburses you for your travel costs the total eligible costs must be reduced by the amount you receive, unless the amount of the financial assistance is included in your income for tax purposes (as a taxable benefit).

While no support is required to be filed with your tax return, you should, at a minimum, keep your expired transit passes. Provided the transit pass includes the date or period for which it is valid, the name of the transit authority or organization, the amount paid for the pass and the identity of the rider (either by name or a unique identifier), the expired passes will serve as sufficient support for the tax credit claimed. However, if the pass does not have all of this information, you may also have to have receipts, cancelled cheques or credit card statements to support the claim. The CRA has also indicated that it will accept receipts or letters generated by taxpayers' employers or Employer Pass Program Coordinators, provided the receipts/letters note the amount and purpose of the payments, the date of the payments and the name of the payee. Finally, although the CRA doesn't generally consider a bank statement to be a valid receipt, it will accept bank statements as support for the credit claim if the statement clearly indicates the debit to the bank statement pertains to public transit pass purchases.

TAX TIP

If you want to make a claim for this credit, you must keep your receipts to support the claim. Remember to keep the receipts for all eligible family members. There is no maximum limit to the amount that can be claimed.

107 Children's Fitness Credit

This credit will be of interest to you if you have children under the age of 16 at the beginning of the year.

For 2007 and subsequent taxation years, you may claim a tax credit of up to $500 for eligible fitness expenses paid for each of your eligible children. The expenses can be paid by you, your spouse or common-law partner with respect to the children of either of you.

On December 19, 2006, the Department of Finance released information explaining what programs of physical activity would qualify. To qualify for the tax credit a program must be:

- ongoing (either a minimum of eight weeks duration with a minimum of one session per week or, in the case of children's camps, five consecutive days);
- supervised;
- suitable for children; and
- substantially all of the activities must include a significant amount of physical activity that contributes to cardio-respiratory endurance plus one or more of muscular strength, muscular endurance, flexibility or balance.

EXAMPLE: **Amounts that qualify**

In July 2009, you sent your 10-year-old son to an away-from-home hockey camp for children. The all-inclusive registration fee is $1,100 for the two-week camp. This fee includes $400 for accommodation and $250 for meals. The portion of the fee that qualifies for the children's fitness tax credit is $450 ($1,100 – $400 – $250).

Memberships and mixed-use facilities can also qualify for the credit provided either more than 50% of the programs are eligible or more than 50% of available time is devoted to eligible programs for qualifying children. If neither of these tests are met, a receipt can be issued for a prorated amount. The portion of a family membership can also qualify if it is attributable to a qualifying child's participation in an eligible program or activity.

It is up to the organization to determine to what extent the fees paid qualify for the credit and to prepare suitable receipts for income tax purposes. It is important to note that the year in which the tax credit can be claimed is determined by the date when the fees are paid, not when the activity takes place.

EXAMPLE: **Timing of payment**

Jill registered her daughter Jane in an eligible physical activity program and paid the $800 fee on August 30, 2009. This program started on September 15, 2009, and will end on April 30, 2010. She also registered her son John in an eligible physical activity program and paid the $750 fee on December 28, 2009. This program will start on January 6, 2010, and will end on June 30, 2010. She registered her other son Jim in the same program, but did not pay his $750 fee until January 2, 2010. On her 2009 income tax return, Jill will be allowed to claim the maximum amount of $500 for Jane and John.

TAX TIP

You should either receive, or ask for, a receipt from organizations providing eligible programs of physical activity in which your child is enrolled. The organizations are supposed to determine the part of the fee that qualifies for the tax credit.

For the purposes of this credit, the age limit is increased by 2 years to under 18 years of age at the beginning of the year for children eligible for the disability tax credit. There is also a separate $500 non-refundable amount for such children (subject to spending a minimum of $100 on registration fees for an eligible program).

108 Canada Child Tax Benefit

The Canada Child Tax Benefit (CCTB) is a federal tax measure to assist lower-income families with children. The CCTB has three components: the CCTB base benefit for low- or mid-income families; the National Child Benefit (NCB) supplement for low-income families; and the Child Disability Benefit (see discussion below).

How it works

A monthly non-taxable payment is issued to those who qualify, and each payment is based on the number of children and the prior year's combined income of you and your spouse or common-law partner. Payments for the first six months of the year are based on net income from two years ago, and payments for the next six months are based on net income from last year. In 2009, the family income threshold at which the NCB supplement is fully phased out and the CCTB benefits begin to be phased out is $40,726. This income threshold will have an impact on the July 2009 to June 2010 payments.

TAX TIP

To qualify for this program and receive child benefit payments, you and your spouse or common-law partner must each file an income tax return.

There is additional assistance for families entitled to the NCB supplement. For each child born after 2003, the Canada Learning Bond (CLB) program provides a $500 bond at birth, with subsequent annual instalments of $100 until age 15 in each year that the family is entitled to the NCB supplement. The maximum CLB payment per child is $2,000. Children born after 2003 who do not initially qualify for the $500 CLB but become entitled in a subsequent year will get the $500 CLB at that time. The bond will be paid into a Registered Education Savings Plan (see article 120).

Low- and mid-income families with disabled children are entitled to receive a Child Disability Benefit supplement. Eligibility for this income-tested benefit is based on the same eligibility criteria used for the disability tax credit. The full supplement is provided to all families with disabled children who currently receive the NCB supplement. Beyond that income level, the benefit is reduced.

109 Universal Child Care Benefit

The Universal Child Care Benefit (UCCB) was introduced on July 1, 2006. This benefit is paid to all families with eligible children, regardless of the family's income level.

Families are entitled to a childcare allowance of $100 per month ($1,200 annually) for each child under six years of age. Although this allowance will be taxable in the hands of the spouse or common-law partner with the lower income, amounts received will not be taken into account for the purpose of calculating income-tested tax benefits.

The UCCB is administered under the Canada Child Tax Benefit (CCTB) program.

TAX TIP

If you have a child under the age of six and you have never applied for the Canada Child Tax Benefit, you will need to complete an application form to receive this benefit. The application form and additional information can be found on the CRA's website at **www.cra-arc.gc.ca/bnfts/uccb-puge/menu-eng.html.**

110 Taxation of Common-Law Couples

Common-law couples are treated the same way as legally married couples for all provisions of the Income Tax Act. A common-law partner is defined as a person who has lived with you in a conjugal relationship throughout the 12-month period that ends at that time, or who is the natural or adoptive parent of your child. Since 2001, a common-law partner also includes a same-sex partner. As a result, common-law couples are:

- able to claim the married credit;
- permitted to contribute to spousal RRSPs;
- able to benefit from the new pension income-splitting rules (see article 79);
- required to combine their incomes to determine entitlement to the GST credit and the child tax benefit;
- subject to the income attribution rules;
- allowed to transfer assets to a surviving partner on a tax-deferred basis upon the death of the other partner; and
- subject to all other income tax provisions that formerly applied only to married persons.

111 Special Rules for Artists and Entertainers

Artists and entertainers are entitled to special treatment under the Income Tax Act.

If you are employed as a musician and are required to provide a musical instrument as a condition of your employment, you may deduct the cost of maintenance, rent or capital cost allowance (see article 7) and insurance for the instrument. The amount deducted for musical instrument costs cannot exceed the income from employment as a musician after you deduct all other employment expenses.

Artists and entertainers receiving employment income are entitled to deduct related expenses actually incurred, up to a maximum of 20% of such income but not more than $1,000. This deduction is in addition to the deductions that all employees may be entitled to for most other expenses, such as automobile and related travel expenses. However, it is reduced by the sum of the amounts claimed for interest and capital cost allowance on an automobile and for musical instrument costs (see above).

TAX TIP

Expenses incurred in the year but restricted by the 20% or $1,000 limit may be carried forward indefinitely. Don't overlook these carry-forward balances when calculating your income from artistic employment.

112 Apprentice Mechanic Deduction for Tools

Before they can gain employment, apprentice mechanics are often required to purchase a tool set that can cost thousands of dollars. To provide relief, the cost of new tools acquired by an eligible apprentice mechanic is deductible in calculating income, subject to certain limits.

The deductible amount cannot exceed the amount determined by a specified formula (which, in general, allows a deduction for the total cost of the tools less the greater of $1,500 or 5% of the individual's apprenticeship income for the year).

The deduction is optional, and if the employee chooses not to deduct all or a portion of the deductible amount, it can be carried forward and deducted in a subsequent taxation year.

EXAMPLE / **Calculating the deduction**

John earns $35,000 as an apprentice mechanic in 2009 and acquires new tools with a cost of $5,000. John can deduct $3,250 as an apprentice mechanic deduction for tools [$5,000 – (5% × $35,000)].

Since the apprentice is basically denied a deduction when the cost of the tools in any given year is less whichever is the greater of $1,500 or 5% of his or her apprenticeship income for the year, the timing of the acquisition could be important.

The cost of a tool is reduced pro rata by the deductible portion of the cost. If it is sold, the proceeds are included in income to the extent that the proceeds exceed the cost.

To be eligible for this deduction, the tools must be acquired while the apprentice is registered with a provincial or territorial body in a program leading to a designation as a mechanic licensed to repair automobiles, aircraft or any other self-propelled motorized vehicles.

In addition, the mechanic's employer must certify in prescribed form (Form T2200) that the tools were required as a condition of and for use in the apprentice's employment.

113 Tradespeople's Tool Expenses

If you are an employed tradesperson, you may be entitled to a tax deduction for the cost of new tools used in carrying out your employment duties.

For 2009, the amount you can claim is equal to the cost of new tools in excess of $1,044 that you are required to purchase as a condition of your employment, subject to a maximum claim of $500. This measure applies to new tools, other than electronic communication devices and electronic data-processing equipment (such as computers, pagers and cell phones), and is in addition to the Canada Employment Credit (see article 104). If you qualify for the tax deduction, you will also be able to claim a rebate for the GST/HST paid on the portion of the equipment that qualifies for the deduction.

The CRA has noted that since there is no definition of "tradesperson" in the Act, it should take on its everyday meaning such as "a person, other than an apprentice, who works for remuneration at any designated trade." It is the CRA's view that any person engaged in an occupation that demands a certain level of skill may be considered a "tradesperson" for purposes of this deduction.

If you are an apprentice vehicle mechanic, you will also be eligible to claim this tax deduction in addition to the existing apprentice vehicle mechanics' tools deduction (see article 112).

114 Northern Residents Deduction

You may qualify for the northern residents deduction if you lived in a prescribed area in northern Canada on a permanent basis for a continuous period of at least six consecutive months commencing or ending in the taxation year for which a return is being filed. The deduction is claimed by filing form T2222 with your return.

The prescribed northern zone includes all of Labrador, Yukon and the Northwest Territories, and certain areas of each province except Nova Scotia, Newfoundland (except for Labrador), New Brunswick and Prince Edward Island. The prescribed intermediate zones are in each province except the four Atlantic provinces (except for Sable Island in Nova Scotia, which is an intermediate zone). You can review the CRA publication T4039, *Northern Residents Deduction—Places in Prescribed Zones*, to determine if you live in a prescribed northern or intermediate zone.

There are two northern residents deductions:

- a **residency deduction** for living in a prescribed zone; and
- a **travel deduction** for taxable travel benefits you receive from employment in a prescribed zone.

Residency deduction

If you live in a prescribed northern zone, you can claim $8.25 for each day in the taxation year that you lived there and an additional residency amount of $8.25 per day if you're the only person in your household claiming the residency deduction (prior to 2008 the daily amount was $7.50). For example, if you and your spouse or common-law partner live in a prescribed northern zone, you can each claim $8.25 per day or either you or your spouse or common-law partner can claim $16.50 per day. If you live in an intermediate northern zone, the residency deduction is half the above amounts.

The residency deduction is reduced by the non-taxable benefit for board and lodging at a special work site (box 31 of your T4 slip, or from the footnotes area of your T4A slip).

The maximum residency deduction you may claim is limited to 20% of your net income.

TAX TIP

It may be more beneficial for one spouse to claim the residency deduction and the additional residency amount, or it may be more beneficial for each spouse or common-law partner to claim their own residency deduction. The answer will depend on the income and marginal tax bracket of each spouse or common-law partner. A tax adviser can help you to make this determination.

Travel deduction

If you are an employee resident in a northern or intermediate zone, you may claim a travel deduction with respect to certain travel benefits provided to you and your family by your employer, to the extent that the value of the benefits is included in your income from employment. The amount of travel benefits provided by your employer is reported in box 32 or 33 of your T4 slip, or box 28 of your T4A slip.

This deduction applies with respect to all trips made by the employee or a member of the employee's household for the purpose of obtaining necessary medical services not available locally. If it is necessary for the patient to have an attendant, another member of the household may accompany the patient and the employer-paid cost of this will also be deductible.

The deduction also applies to a maximum of two trips per person made by the employee or a member of the employee's household (e.g., for vacations).

The maximum travel deduction you can claim for each eligible trip is the lowest of the following three amounts:

1. The taxable travel benefits you received from your employer;
2. The actual travel expenses paid for the trip (this includes fares for air, train or bus, vehicle expenses, meals, hotel or motel accommodations, camping fees, taxis and ferry tolls); or
3. The cost of the lowest return airfare available at the time of the trip between the airport closest to your residence and the nearest designated city (listed on Form T2222).

To calculate meal and vehicle expenses (for #2 above), you may choose the detailed or simplified method (see article 85).

The deduction for an employee of the northern zone is 100% of the least of the three amounts above. The deduction for an employee of the intermediate zone is 50% of this amount.

115 Special Rules for the Clergy

If you are a member of the clergy or a religious order or a regular minister of a religious denomination, you may be able to claim a deduction with respect to your residence. This deduction recognizes that your personal residence often serves as an office or meeting place for members of your congregation or parish. The amount of the deduction depends on whether your employer provides the residence or you provide your own residence.

Where your employer provides you with living accommodations, you can deduct the value of the accommodation to the extent that it is included in your employment income as a taxable benefit.

Where you provide your own living accommodations, you can claim a deduction equal to the least of the following three amounts:

1. your total remuneration from the office or employment;
2. one-third of that total remuneration or $10,000, whichever is greater; and
3. the rent paid for your residence, including utilities (or an amount equal to the fair rental value of your residence, if owned).

The calculation is adjusted if you are employed as a clergy for only part of the year or if other amounts are claimed as a deduction with respect to the same accommodation.

To claim the clergy residence deduction, you must file with your income tax return a prescribed form signed by your employer stating that you qualify to claim this deduction.

116 Taxation of Emergency Volunteers

This article will be of interest to you if you receive amounts from a government, municipality or other public authority for performing as a volunteer ambulance technician, firefighter or in some other capacity as an emergency worker.

The first $1,000 of remuneration received is exempt from tax. Only amounts over and above this $1,000 amount should be reported on your T4. For example, if you receive $2,500 in 2009 as a volunteer firefighter, your T4 should report only total remuneration of $1,500.

However, this $1,000 exemption is not available if you were employed by the same authority to perform the same or similar work other than as a volunteer.

117 Principal-Residence Rules

Your "principal residence" is generally any residential property owned and occupied by you or your spouse or common-law partner, your former spouse, or common-law partner or your child at any time in the year. It can be a house, condominium, cottage, mobile home, trailer or even a live-aboard boat, and it need not be located in Canada. Any gain on the sale of a principal residence is tax-free. However, if you sell your residence, you should be aware that some tax rules apply.

Just because you live in a house that you own does not automatically qualify it as a principal residence. For example, building contractors or house renovators who follow a pattern of living for a short period of time in a home they have built or renovated, and then selling it at a profit, may be subject to tax as ordinary business income on their gains.

Designating a principal residence

A home can be designated as your principal residence for each year in which you, your spouse or common-law partner and/or your children were residents in Canada and ordinarily lived in it for some time during the particular year. You are allowed to designate only one home as your principal residence for a particular year. If you are unable to designate your home as your principal residence for all the years you owned it, a portion of any gain on sale may be subject to tax as a capital gain. The portion of the gain subject to tax is based on a formula that takes into account the number of years you owned the home and the number of years it was designated as your principal residence.

Suppose you and your spouse own two residences, a home in the city and a cottage out of town. Only one of these homes can be designated as your family's principal residence each year. Before 1982, each spouse could designate a separate property as a principal residence for a particular year, provided the property was not jointly owned. However, for each year after 1981, the rules have tightened up and couples (and their unmarried minor children) cannot designate more than one home in total as their principal residence each year.

To help you make this designation, you should determine the fair market value of both homes as of December 31, 1981. Factors to consider will include the relative appreciation of each house and the expected timing of any sale.

Tax issues

If you made a capital gains election on a residential property such as a cottage (see article 145), the tax implications on the eventual disposition of the property will depend on a number of factors. These include the value of the property at the time of disposition, the number of years it was designated as a principal residence at the time of making the capital gains election and the years after 1994 it was designated as a principal residence. A property may still be designated as a principal residence on disposition even if it was not designated as such at the time of making the election. The rules in this area are quite complex and well worth a trip to your tax adviser's office.

TAX TIP

Be careful before designating a foreign-owned home as your principal residence. Even though the gain under Canadian rules is tax-free, you may incur a foreign tax liability when you sell your home.

Homes for rent

If you move out and rent your home, you can continue to treat the house as your principal residence for four additional years, or possibly more if you move as a consequence of a change of your place of employment with your employer. There are also rules that apply if you own property to earn rental income and subsequently convert the property to personal use. Basically, at the time of the change in use, you are deemed to have disposed of the property at its fair market value. If this value exceeds your original cost, you will have to report a capital gain. However, you can make a special election to defer recognizing this gain until you ultimately sell the home. This election is not available if you have claimed depreciation on the property for any year after 1984.

TAX TIP

Are you considering renting out your home or converting a rental property to personal use? Before doing so, you should visit your tax adviser to discuss the tax implications.

118 Selling Personal-Use Capital Property

Profits from the sale of almost all capital assets, with the exception of your principal residence, are subject to tax as a capital gain. Unfortunately, losses from the sale of most personal capital assets are not deductible.

What's involved

If you sell your boat or car at a loss, you cannot claim it as a capital loss. But if you sell it at a profit, half the gain is taxable (see article 144). With the exception of certain donations (see article 91), assets that have a cost of $1,000 or less and are sold for $1,000 or less are exempt from this rule. However, assets that cost less than $1,000 and are sold for more than $1,000 still face a tax bill on the difference between their sale price and the $1,000 cut-off point.

When a capital gains election was made on a personal-use property (see article 145), the amount designated in the election is generally the cost base of the asset. When the asset is sold, the difference between the sale price and the elected amount is a capital gain.

Losses from the sale of certain types of personal property, referred to as listed personal property, can be applied against gains from the sale of such property. Listed personal property includes coins, stamps, jewellery, rare books, paintings or sculptures, and similar works of art. Listed personal-property losses can be carried back for up to three years and forward for up to seven years, but they can be applied only against gains from the sale of similar property.

EXAMPLE/**Buying and selling**

> In 2000 you purchased a painting (which is listed personal property) at a cost of $2,000 and a boat (which is personal-use property) at a cost of $3,500. Nine years later, in 2009, you sold both items for $3,000 each. The sale of the painting will result in a capital gain of $1,000 ($3,000 – $2,000) to be reported on your 2009 tax return. The sale of the boat triggers a capital loss of $500 ($3,000 – $3,500), which cannot be claimed because it is personal-use property and not listed personal property.
>
> However, if the asset in question was a diamond necklace instead of a boat (assuming the same cost and sale price), the capital loss could be applied against the gain on the painting, resulting in a net capital gain of $500 being reported on your 2009 tax return.

119 Transfers and Loans to Family Members

All capital properties, such as shares in companies and real estate, are automatically transferred between spouses or common-law partners on a tax-free basis. If you want the transfer to take place at fair market value, you must file a special election requesting this treatment when you file your tax return for the year of the transfer. If such an election is filed, you will report a capital gain (assuming the property has appreciated in value), and the tax cost of the property to your spouse or common-law partner will increase accordingly.

Selling the property

When the property is eventually sold to a third party by your spouse or common-law partner, you will have to report any capital gain realized on the sale unless the following very specific requirements have been met. First of all, your spouse or common-law partner must have paid fair market value for the property at the time of the transfer. You must also have made the fair market value election (as noted above), and sufficient annual interest on any unpaid purchase price must have been paid in full no later than January 30 of the following year. Provided all these conditions have been met, any subsequent capital gain realized on a sale to a third party can be taxed in your spouse or common-law partner's hands. If any one of the conditions are not met, any capital gain (or loss) realized on the sale of the property will be taxed in your hands.

EXAMPLE/**Sharing the wealth**

A benevolent mood comes over you, and you decide to transfer your shares of XYZ Co. to your spouse. You acquired the shares in 1996 at a cost of $1,000 and they have a current fair market value of $6,000. For tax purposes, your spouse will be deemed to have acquired the shares from you at a cost of $1,000. Therefore, you will not recognize a capital gain or loss on the transfer. However, you will be taxed on any capital gain arising when your spouse disposes of the shares. The capital gain will be calculated using your original cost of $1,000.

Alternatively, by attaching a note to your tax return, you may elect to have the transfer to your spouse take place at fair market value. As a result of making this election, you will report a capital gain of $5,000 and your spouse will be deemed to have acquired the shares from you at a cost of $6,000.

Now assume you have made this election and your spouse subsequently sells the shares for $8,000. If your spouse did not pay you fair market value for the shares, the resulting capital gain of $2,000 is still taxable in your hands. However, if your spouse paid you $6,000 for the shares, say, by way of a loan from you, the $2,000 gain would be taxable in your spouse's hands—provided your spouse pays a reasonable rate of annual interest on the loan within the required time period.

Special rules apply in situations where the property has been transferred between spouses or common-law partners as part of a property settlement or where the couple is separated when the property is sold to a third party.

TAX TIP

With current interest rates at fairly low levels, you might want to consider an income-splitting loan to your spouse or common-law partner. The attribution rules will not apply if you are paid interest on the loan at the prescribed rate in effect at the time the loan is made. For example, the prescribed rate in effect for the third quarter of 2009 is 1%. This rate will remain in effect for as long as the loan is outstanding—even if rates increase in the future.

In implementing any income-splitting strategy, you have to be careful if you want to avoid the attribution rules. In situations where property is transferred to your spouse or common-law partner, attribution can apply to both income and capital gains. Contact your tax adviser to discuss the steps you need to take to accomplish this or other income-splitting strategies.

Transfers to other family members

A transfer of capital property to other family members is taxed just as if you sold the property at its fair market value. If the property has been transferred to a child, grandchild, niece or nephew, you must continue to report any income earned on such property after it has been transferred—such as interest or dividend income—until the child reaches 18 years of age. After 18, that individual must report the income. Capital gains, on the other hand, do not have to be attributed to you. This is a useful income-splitting tool.

TAX TIP

Unless the person receiving the property is your spouse or common-law partner, there is no requirement to attribute capital gains to you, the transferor. Consider buying in the names of your children capital property (such as equity-based mutual funds) with a low yield but high capital gains potential. The income will be attributed to you, but any future capital gains will be taxed in your children's hands.

TAX TIP

The deemed cost base of property received as a gift or inheritance is its fair market value at the time of transfer. However, if you charge a nominal amount for the transfer of property—for example, $10—you are deemed to receive fair market value for the property, but the recipient's cost base remains at $10. Therefore, it is better to gift property than to charge a nominal amount, since the recipient will receive the full increase in the cost base.

Interest-free loans to family members

Caution should be exercised if you provide low-interest or interest-free loans to family members, either to enable them to purchase income-producing assets or as consideration for the transfer of assets. If one of the main reasons for the loan is to reduce or avoid tax, you must report any income earned on the property, regardless of the age of the loan recipient. An outright gift to a child who is 18 years or older—or anyone other than a spouse or common-law partner—is not subject to this rule.

TAX TIP

Any involvement in the transfer of property or the lending of money to a spouse or common-law partner or other family members should have you consulting your tax adviser to ensure that the tax consequences of such transactions do not create a greater tax burden.

120 Registered Education Savings Plans (RESPs)

An RESP is a type of trust through which you can save for a child's education. If you make contributions to such a plan, the amounts are not tax deductible, but the major advantage is that earnings accumulate on a tax-deferred basis. Also, when the funds are finally issued to the child, only the accumulated income earned in the plan (such as dividends or interest) is considered the child's income and taxed at his or her lower rate.

Contributions

Prior to 2007, the annual contribution limit was $4,000 per beneficiary, subject to a lifetime limit of $42,000 per beneficiary. For contributions after 2006, the $4,000 annual limit is eliminated and the lifetime contribution limit is increased from $42,000 to $50,000.

Several plans include a transferability feature. This allows you to change the beneficiary of the plan to someone else or even to sell the plan should you conclude the designated child has no interest in post-secondary education.

Prior to 2008, contributions to an RESP could be made for 21 years, and the plan had to be terminated at the end of 25 years. In addition, no contributions could be made to a family plan for a beneficiary who was 21 years of age or older. The 2008 federal budget increased each of these limits by an additional 10 years.

The contribution and termination period is extended for beneficiaries who qualify for the disability tax credit (see article 90). The 2008 federal budget similarly extended each of these limits by an additional 10 years (to 35 years and 40 years, respectively).

TAX TIP

If a person with a disability is a beneficiary under a family plan, that individual's share of the family plan can be transferred into a single-beneficiary RESP to ensure access to the extended limits.

If all intended beneficiaries are not pursuing higher education by age 21, and the plan has been in place for at least 10 years, you can withdraw the income from the plan. If you have sufficient RRSP contribution room, you can transfer the RESP income to your RRSP (or a spousal RRSP). Any excess that cannot be transferred to an RRSP will be subject to a 20% penalty tax, in addition to regular income tax.

The total RESP income that you can transfer to an RRSP is subject to a lifetime limit of $50,000.

Canada Education Savings Grants

The Canada Education Savings Grant (CESG) program was introduced by the federal government as an incentive to aid with the rising costs of post-secondary education, as well as to encourage the use of RESPs. Paid directly to the plan trustee, the amount of the CESG is based on contributions made by the contributor. Prior to 2007, the amount contributed was equal to 20% of the first $2,000 of annual contributions for each child (up to $400 per year per child) for the benefit of children up to but not including age 18. For contributions after 2006, the maximum annual RESP contribution qualifying for the 20% CESG is increased to $2,500, thus increasing the maximum CESG per beneficiary from $400 to $500. If the contributor did not make a contribution to the RESP in one or more years, there are carry-forward rules that can double the CESG maximum (i.e., from $500 to $1,000 for 2007 and subsequent years). The maximum lifetime CESG limit per beneficiary is $7,200.

The grant is available for certain beneficiaries aged 16 and 17, and there are no restrictions for beneficiaries aged 15 and under in the year. In general, contributions for a child aged 16 or 17 will receive a grant only if there have been contributions of at least $100 per year in any four years before the year in which the beneficiary turned 16 or if total previous contributions for the child reached $2,000 before the year the beneficiary turned 16. This means that a new plan will not get the CESG for a beneficiary who is 16 or 17. These age restrictions are in place to encourage early RESP savings.

The maximum annual grant per child is increased for low- and mid-income families. The 20% matching rate is increased to 40% for families with incomes up to $38,832 and to 30% for families with incomes between $38,832 and $77,664. These enhanced rates apply to only the first $500 contributed to a child's RESP in a year. As a result, families with incomes of up to $38,832 qualify for a maximum annual grant of $600 and families with incomes between $38,832 and $77,664 qualify for a maximum annual grant of $550. For everyone else, the $500 annual maximum continues to apply.

EXAMPLE/**Calculating the maximum annual grant**

> Your family income for 2009 is $75,000. If you set up an RESP for your newborn son and make a $3,000 contribution in 2009, a CESG of $550 [(30% × $500) + (20% × $2,000)] will be paid to the plan trustee. Assuming your family income increases to $90,000 in 2010, the same contribution will result in a $500 grant being paid to the plan trustee.

When RESP funds are paid to a beneficiary, a formula will determine what portion of each payment is considered to be a taxable distribution.

An RESP will be required to repay CESG money in certain situations, such as when a beneficiary does not pursue higher education or the plan is terminated.

The Canada Learning Bond (CLB) program

Under the Canada Learning Bond (CLB) program, every child born after 2003 will qualify for assistance, provided the family is entitled to the National Child Benefit (NCB) supplement (generally, families with incomes under $38,832 for 2009). An initial $500 bond will be provided in the year of the child's birth, with subsequent annual instalments of $100 until age 15 in each year that the family is entitled to the NCB supplement. Children born after 2003 who do not initially qualify for the $500 CLB, but become entitled in a subsequent year (before the year in which the child turns 16), will get the $500 CLB at that time. The CLB will be paid into the child's RESP. An additional $25 will be paid with the initial $500 bond to assist with the cost of establishing the plan.

An application form must be completed and filed with a promoter to obtain the CLB. A promoter is any person or organization offering an RESP to the public.

TAX TIP

If you have had a child after 2003 and your family income is below $38,832 (for 2009), you should consider setting up an RESP for your child. The existence of the plan will ensure annual government contributions until the child reaches the age of 15, as long as your family income is below the income amount that qualifies for the lowest tax bracket (which increases annually). To enroll your child in an RESP you must obtain a Social Insurance Number (SIN) for the child.

121 Registered Disability Savings Plan (RDSP)

The RDSP was initially announced as part of the 2007 federal budget and is effective for 2008 and subsequent years. The intent of the plan is to improve the financial security of children with severe disabilities. To establish an RDSP for a particular person, that person must be eligible for the disability tax credit (DTC) (see article 90).

The plan operates similar to a RESP. Contributions to the plan are not deductible, but the income on the amounts contributed will accrue on a tax-deferred basis. When the amounts are finally paid out of the plan, only the investment income earned in the plan will be taxed in the beneficiary's hands. Payments will be required to commence by the end of the year in which the beneficiary reaches 60 years of age. Amounts paid out of an RDSP will not be taken into account for the purposes of calculating income-tested benefits.

Contributions to a RDSP will be limited to a lifetime maximum of $200,000 for each beneficiary, with no annual limits. Contributions will be permitted until the end of the year in which the beneficiary reaches 59 years of age.

TAX TIP

The $200,000 lifetime contribution limit is suitable for a large one-time donation. For example, if you sell your home or other capital property for significant proceeds, you might consider contributing some of the proceeds to a RDSP.

RDSP contributions will qualify for a Canada Disability Savings Grant (CDSG) at matching rates of 100%, 200% or 300%, depending on family net income and the amount contributed, subject to a lifetime limit of $70,000. An RDSP will be eligible to receive a CDSG until the end of the year in which the beneficiary reaches 49 years of age.

In addition, a Canada Disability Savings Bond (CDSB) of up to $1,000 will be paid annually to the RDSPs of low- and mid-income beneficiaries and families (subject to a lifetime limit of $20,000).

If the beneficiary ceases to qualify for the disability tax credit (or dies), there is a requirement to repay to the government all CDSGs and CDSBs (and related investment income) paid to the plan in the preceding 10 years. The remaining plan proceeds are then paid out to the beneficiary (or his or her estate) and the plan is collapsed.

In this regard, concern has been raised over the possibility that the beneficiary of a parent-initiated plan who continues to meet the DTC criteria might be able to force the premature collapse of the plan by rescinding his or her DTC certification. To address this concern, the rules provide that a mandatory collapse of the plan will be able to take place only where the beneficiary's condition has actually improved to the extent that the beneficiary would no longer qualify for the DTC. This does not affect a plan holder's ability to voluntarily collapse the plan.

In some provinces, parents use a "Henson Trust" to provide a certain level of financial support without having their children's provincial social assistance benefits clawed back. The provinces will have to agree to amend their social assistance legislation so RDSP monies received by a disabled person are not clawed back.

122 Splitting CPP Benefits with Your Spouse or Common-Law Partner

The Canada Pension Plan Act permits you to assign a portion of your retirement pension to your spouse or common-law partner.

For example, suppose you are entitled to $10,000 in annual CPP benefits, but your spouse or common-law partner is entitled to only $4,000. This assignment will generally result in each of you receiving $7,000 annually. If your spouse or common-law partner is in a lower tax bracket than you, shifting this income to his or her hands helps lower the total family tax bill. The number of months you have lived together is a factor in determining how the benefits are split.

If you both receive a CPP retirement pension, the assignment must be made for both retirement pensions. But if only one of you receives a retirement pension, the assignment can be made only if the other spouse or common-law partner has reached 60 years of age and is not a contributor to the CPP.

123 Income Splitting with Family Members

Income splitting is a tax-planning technique designed to shift income from a taxpayer paying a high rate of tax to another taxpayer within the family unit paying tax at a lower rate. Unfortunately, there are a number of legislative provisions—"attribution rules" and other anti-avoidance measures—designed to prevent saving taxes by shifting income between taxpayers.

Permitted arrangements

There are still a number of legitimate tax-planning arrangements that can be used to effectively redistribute income in a family unit:

- Have your business pay a reasonable salary to your spouse or common-law partner or children (see article 5).
- Make contributions to a spousal RRSP (see article 63).
- Invest child tax benefit payments in your child's name (see article 108).
- Share CPP payments (see article 122).

- Pension income splitting (see article 79).
- Have the higher-income spouse or common-law partner assume most or all of the personal household expenses, leaving the person with the lower income with as much disposable income as possible to invest.
- Transfer or sell assets to family members for fair market value consideration (see article 119).
- Gift to minor children capital assets that are appreciating in value so they can earn capital gains not subject to attribution (see article 119).
- Make a loan that splits income (see article 119).
- Use a management company. However, if the management company provides services to a professional who provides tax-exempt services under the GST, the taxable GST charge will present an absolute increase in cost that may outweigh the income-splitting benefits of the management company.
- Create testamentary trusts in your will to split income.
- Contribute to an RESP (see article 120).
- Give cash or other assets to your adult children (see article 119). Gifts of cash could enable them to maximize their deductible RRSP contributions.
- Have your spouse or common-law partner and/or adult children participate in an incorporated business by owning shares acquired with their own funds. This would allow company profits to be distributed to them in the form of dividends.
- Take advantage of the fact that income earned on income is not subject to the attribution rules. Although the initial income earned on property loaned to a non-arm's-length person may be attributed back to the person making the transfer, income earned on that income will not be attributed.

EXAMPLE/**Bypassing attribution**

If you purchased $10,000 in 4% bonds for your 10-year-old son in 2008, he would receive $400 of interest on the bond in 2009.

> If at that time he invests the interest in additional bonds at a rate of 5%, in 2010 your son will receive interest of $400 on the original bonds, plus $20 for the reinvested interest ($400 × 5%). Although the $400 received by your son in 2009 and 2010 is taxable in your hands, he reports the additional $20 he receives in 2010 as his income.

It's crucial that you confer with your tax adviser, who can review your personal situation and give you advice about which income-splitting strategies best fit your circumstances.

124 Income Splitting Using Family Trusts

In the past, family trusts were often used to provide a tax-effective way of splitting income with other family members. If properly structured, they could provide the following benefits:

- flexibility in the payment of dividends to different family members;
- multiple access to the qualified small-business capital gains deduction;
- accrual of other capital gains for the future benefit of family members;
- some creditor-proofing for cash currently accumulated in your company;
- a way to include family members in income distributions while deferring the decision on actual ownership for up to 21 years; and
- a structure to minimize taxes paid by your family unit.

Although there are now rules that eliminate many of the income-splitting benefits of family trusts and shareholdings by minors, all is not lost. Many of the above benefits are still available, though possibly not to the same extent as in the past.

The rules that prevent many of the income-splitting benefits with minors are referred to as the "kiddie tax." These rules assess tax at the top marginal rate on taxable dividends from a private corporation received by any child under the age of 18. It doesn't matter if the dividends are received directly or through a trust or other structure. The tax will also apply to income from property such as certain rental and financing income that is allocated to minor children. Income from property inherited from the minor's parent is excluded from this rule.

There can be ways to get around this rule by inserting a holding company between the operating company and the trust. Dividends from the operating company can be paid into the holding company on a tax-free basis and held there until the beneficiaries of the trust are no longer minors. Once the children turn 18—at which time dividends can begin to be paid out to them without the imposition of the "kiddie tax"—they can each receive a significant amount of dividend income each year and pay little or no tax (assuming they have no other income).

Based on your particular situation, other planning strategies may also be available.

TAX TIP

Although the "kiddie tax" rules may affect many trust structures previously set up, with proper planning some of the benefits of these structures may be retained. You should contact your tax adviser to review your situation and determine the best planning strategy.

125 Retroactive Lump-Sum Payments

If you have received a retroactive lump-sum payment, you may be eligible for a special tax calculation to provide tax relief. The special calculation will effectively recalculate your tax liability by assuming the lump-sum payment had been taxed in the year(s) to which it relates. It will be applied only where the calculation results in a decreased tax liability.

The following types of income qualify for this calculation:

- periodic superannuation or pension benefits;
- Employment Insurance benefits;
- spousal or child support amounts; and
- employment income payments received under a court judgement or arbitration award.

The lump-sum payment must be at least $3,000, excluding any interest amount included in the payment.

TAX TIP

If you have received a retroactive lump-sum payment, contact your tax adviser to determine whether you might benefit from requesting a recalculation of your tax return.

126 Some Income Is Tax-Free

Almost all types of income are subject to income tax. No surprise there. What *is* surprising is that there are a few exceptions.

If you are lucky enough to win a lottery in Canada, the amount you win is not taxable (but any income you receive from investing the money is taxable). Gains from casual gambling are not taxable. Proceeds from damage awards are generally tax-free and, under certain circumstances, income arising from damage awards for taxpayers under 21 years of age is also exempt until the taxpayer turns 21. Various defined payments to war veterans are also exempt.

Workers' Compensation benefits and welfare payments are also not directly subject to tax. However, they are a factor in determining eligibility for certain tax credits. The amounts must be included when calculating net income. To arrive at taxable income, an offsetting deduction is permitted.

If you are in receipt of pension income from a foreign country, you may be eligible to claim an offsetting deduction from income. This will depend on the terms of the tax treaty between Canada and that country.

In addition, for 2004 and subsequent taxation years, a portion of the income earned by Canadian Forces personnel and police serving on high-risk international missions is excluded from taxable employment income. The amount of the exclusion will be limited to the income of a non-commissioned member of the Canadian Forces.

127 Taxation of Non-Competition Payments

A 2003 Federal Court of Appeal case, *Manrell v. The Queen*, concluded that a taxpayer who received a non-competition payment on the sale of shares did not have to pay tax on the amount received. This was a very significant decision, since it opened the possibility for a portion of the proceeds on the sale of the shares of a business to be received tax-free.

The government did not like this outcome and moved quickly to put a stop to similar situations. Later that year, the Department of

Finance introduced rules that would generally treat an amount received or receivable for granting a restrictive covenant as ordinary income, subject to two main exceptions:

1. The taxpayer and the purchaser jointly elect to have the amount treated as eligible capital property; and
2. The taxpayer sells shares of a corporation or an interest in a partnership to an arm's-length party. In this case, the amount will be treated as additional proceeds of disposition for the taxpayer's shares or partnership interest to the extent that the non-competition agreement contributes to the value of the taxpayer's shares or partnership interest. If the covenant has value over and above this amount, it will be reported as income. The taxpayer and purchaser must also jointly elect to have this exception apply.

Although the legislation to implement these rules has not yet passed, it is generally proposed that they will apply to amounts received or receivable after October 7, 2003.

TAX TIP

If you are thinking of entering into a non-competition agreement on the sale of your shares or your business, you should consult your tax adviser to determine the tax consequences.

128 Taking Up Canadian Residence

Welcome to Canada. If you become a resident of Canada during 2009, a special set of income tax rules will apply. For instance, you are deemed to have disposed of and immediately reacquired each property you own (with the exception of taxable Canadian property) at proceeds equal to the fair market value on the date you take up residence. Accordingly, gains or losses accrued before becoming a Canadian resident are irrelevant for Canadian tax purposes when the property is later disposed of. You will calculate any future capital gain or loss in reference to the change from its fair market value at the date of immigration.

How much tax will you pay?

If you were employed or carried on a business in Canada prior to becoming a resident, you will be taxed in Canada on that income for the part of the year you were a non-resident of Canada. Once you become a resident of Canada, you are taxed in Canada on your worldwide income from the date you establish residency.

You are entitled to claim personal tax credits, but the amounts are generally reduced on a pro-rata basis according to the number of days in the year you are taxed on your worldwide income.

EXAMPLE/**What you can claim**

Suppose you are single, have no children and immigrated to Canada on June 1, 2009. During the first part of the year, you were employed in a foreign country. You would be entitled to claim a basic personal amount of $6,051 ($10,320 × 214 ÷ 365).

If you arrived from a country that has a tax treaty with Canada, any provision in the treaty that conflicts with the Canadian tax rules will override the Canadian rule.

TAX TIP

You may want to consider setting up a non-resident trust prior to becoming a resident of Canada. This trust is commonly referred to as an immigration trust. This strategy could be beneficial if you have significant investment income that will be subject to high rates of tax once you establish Canadian residency. By using a non-resident trust, foreign investment income can be sheltered from Canadian tax for a period of up to 60 months, provided income from the trust is not distributed to the Canadian resident who settled the trust.

Foreign pension plans

If you become a resident of Canada, you must consider the Canadian tax consequences if your employer continues to contribute to a foreign pension plan on your behalf. In general, provided you have not been a resident of Canada for more than 60 months in the preceding 72-month period, and you were a member of the foreign plan prior to establishing Canadian residence, contributions by your employer will not be subject to tax. However, membership in this type of foreign plan will diminish your ability to take advantage of Canadian tax-deferred savings plans, such as RRSPs, RPPs and DPSPs. Employer contributions outside these timelines may still be exempt from Canadian taxation, provided your employer files an election, you were a plan member prior to becoming a Canadian resident and you are not a member of an RPP or DPSP.

Distributions received from a foreign pension plan while you are a resident of Canada are generally taxable. However, the tax treaty between Canada and the foreign country may provide some relief.

129 Giving Up Canadian Residence

If you are thinking of leaving Canada, you should be aware of the tax rules in this area. In general, if you cease to be a resident of Canada, you will be deemed to have disposed of and reacquired your capital property at its fair market value on that date. You will be subject to tax on any taxable capital gain resulting from this deemed disposition.

These deemed disposition rules apply to all capital property unless specifically excluded. Such excluded property includes Canadian real estate, Canadian business property and certain other exclusions, such as retirement savings in RRSPs, stock options and interest in some trusts. Shares in a private company are not exempt from these rules. Therefore, if you own such shares, you must report a deemed disposition at fair market value. Professional assistance will likely be required to obtain this value.

Tax implications

You can either pay the tax on the deemed disposition when you file your tax return for the year of emigration or you can opt to post security in lieu of paying tax for any particular property. Taxpayers leaving Canada will generally have to post security by their balance-due date for the year of emigration. The CRA has the discretion to extend this deadline. The security will remain in place until the property is actually disposed of or until the taxpayer returns to Canada and "unwinds" the deemed disposition. As a relieving measure, security is not required with respect to the tax on the first $100,000 of capital gains that arise as a result of the deemed disposition rule.

If you subsequently dispose of property that has been excluded from the deemed disposition rules, you are generally required to file a Canadian income tax return and pay tax on any resulting gain. In some cases, a return is not required, but the proceeds of disposition will be subject to non-resident withholding tax (see article 133). In addition, when you actually dispose of capital property that has been subject to the deemed disposition rules and that is considered taxable Canadian property, you are required to file a Canadian income tax return. Additional Canadian tax may be payable on the gain accruing after you leave Canada.

"Taxable Canadian property" includes real property located in Canada, such as land and buildings, capital property used in carrying on business in Canada, shares of a private corporation resident in Canada and certain shares of public corporations.

TAX TIP

If you later sell the property while a non-resident of Canada and suffer a loss or have to pay foreign taxes on the gain, you may be able to recover some of the Canadian taxes paid on departure. Review these issues with your tax adviser prior to departure.

Reporting requirement

If you emigrate from Canada, you are required to report your property holdings to the CRA if you own "reportable property" with a total value of more than $25,000 at the date of departure from Canada. Exceptions will be provided for personal-use property with a value of less than $10,000. Other exceptions include cash (including bank deposits) and the value of pension plans, annuities, RRSPs, RRIFs, retirement compensation arrangements, employee benefit plans and deferred benefit plans.

Form T1161 must be filed regardless of whether you are subject to the departure tax. The requirement is also independent of the tax return requirement—you must file Form T1161 regardless of whether you are otherwise required to file a return for the year of emigration. To avoid late-filing penalties, this form must be filed on or before your filing due date for the year of emigration from Canada.

TAX TIP

The capital gains deduction is not available to a non-resident of Canada. If you have shares of a corporation that is a "qualified small-business corporation" (see article 146) or an interest in a farming or fishing operation (see articles 147 and 148), there may be opportunities to utilize the $750,000 capital gains deduction. Review this with your tax adviser, as extensive planning is required.

Special rules apply if you leave Canada for only a few years to work or study. The rules in this area are very complex. Therefore, if you are planning to leave Canada for any period of time, you should consult a tax specialist. In some cases, it might be beneficial to restructure your holdings prior to departure.

130 Temporary Assignments Outside Canada

Many assignments outside Canada are only temporary, ranging from a few weeks to several years. For income tax purposes, it is important that you determine your residency status during the period you are outside Canada. A resident of Canada is taxed on his or her worldwide income. Therefore, if you are a Canadian resident for income tax purposes, any income you earn during an assignment abroad will be subject to Canadian tax.

Residency defined

Residence is a question of fact and, surprisingly, the term "resident" is not defined in the Income Tax Act. The courts, however, have held that you are a resident of Canada for tax purposes if Canada is the place you regularly or customarily live.

In prior years, the CRA administratively took the position that, unless the circumstances indicated otherwise, you would likely be considered a non-resident if you were absent from Canada for two years or longer and you had severed your ties with Canada. A few years ago, the CRA revised its position to state that there is no particular length of stay abroad that necessarily results in an individual becoming a non-resident. In making a determination of residence status, all of the relevant facts in each case must be considered, including residential ties with Canada and length of time, object, intention and continuity with respect to stays in Canada and abroad.

Canada also has income tax treaties with a number of countries that contain tie-breaker rules to determine residency when you are considered to be a resident of both Canada and the other country.

TAX TIP

Depending on the circumstances, your residency status and the time of taking up residency may be difficult to ascertain. A discussion with your tax adviser is strongly recommended well in advance of any move into or out of Canada.

If you cease to be a resident of Canada for income tax purposes, special rules apply (see article 129).

131 Canadian Residents Working in the U.S.

If you are a resident of Canada but work in the U.S., the Canada–United States Tax Convention (1980) (the "treaty") provides special rules to determine how you are taxed. Under the Fifth Protocol to the treaty and effective for taxable years beginning after 2008, provided you are not a U.S. citizen, you will be exempt from U.S. taxation on employment income earned in the U.S. if either of the following conditions are met:

- the U.S. employment income does not exceed US$10,000; or
- you are present in the U.S. for less than 184 days in any 12-month period beginning or ending in the fiscal year concerned, and your remuneration is not paid by, or on behalf of, a person who is resident in the U.S. and is not borne by a permanent establishment in the U.S.

If you do not meet either of the above tests, you must pay U.S. federal and, if applicable, state income tax in the U.S. on your U.S.–source wages (income is sourced to the jurisdiction where the services are performed, not where you are paid from). You will also have to report this income on your Canadian tax return. However, you will generally be allowed to claim a foreign tax credit on your Canadian return for any tax you pay to the U.S. You should note that the individual U.S. states are not bound by the treaty. Therefore, even though you may be subject to an exemption from U.S. federal tax under the treaty, there is no guarantee that you will not be subject to a state's income tax. If you do any significant amount of work in the U.S., it's best to consult with your tax adviser to determine your Canadian and U.S. filing requirements.

If you are self-employed, the rules are different. U.S.–source self-employment income is not subject to U.S. tax if you do not have a fixed base in the U.S.

132 Canadian Tax Obligations for Non-Residents

A non-resident of Canada (see article 130 for residency) is subject to Canadian taxes, at graduated rates, on certain types of income from Canadian sources including:

- income/loss from employment in Canada;

- income/loss from a business carried on in Canada; and
- capital gains/losses from dispositions of taxable Canadian property which includes real estate in Canada and shares of a private corporation resident in Canada.

A non-resident of Canada is required to file an "Income Tax and Benefit Return for Non-Residents and Deemed Residents of Canada" to report the above sources of income. A non-resident who does not have a social insurance number is required to obtain an individual tax number (ITN). The ITN can be obtained by completing Form T1261, "Application for a Canada Revenue Agency Individual Tax Number (ITN) for Non-Residents."

A non-resident subject to Canadian tax on Canadian source employment income, business income or income from the disposition of taxable Canadian property is generally allowed to claim all deductions to arrive at net income from those sources that could be claimed by a Canadian resident. This would include eligible employment expenses and capital cost allowance. Non-residents may be allowed other general deductions, such as moving expenses and child care, but there are some restrictions. A non-resident can also claim certain non-refundable tax credits, such as donations, disability, tuition, the Canada employment amount, Canada pension plan and employment insurance tax credits. Other non-refundable credits, such as personal amounts and medical expenses, may be claimed only if 90% of the non-resident's worldwide income is reported on their Canadian return.

Non-residents of Canada are not required to file a Canadian tax return if their only income from Canada is passive income, such as dividends, interest and pensions. The only applicable tax is withheld at source by the payer when the investment or pension income is paid to the non-resident. The general rate of withholding tax under the Income Tax Act is 25%, but may be reduced to a lower rate pursuant to the tax treaty that Canada has with the non-resident's country. Effective January 1, 2008, there is no withholding tax on interest paid to all arm's-length non-residents regardless of their country of residence (see article 51), with certain exceptions. As well, pursuant to the Fifth Protocol of the Canada-US Income Tax Convention, as of January 1, 2009 the withholding tax on cross-border-related party interest payments between Canada and the U.S. is reduced to 4% and will be eliminated altogether in 2010, with certain exceptions.

In the vast majority of cases, the non-resident may be able to claim a foreign tax credit in their country of residence for Canadian taxes paid.

Starting in 2009, non-residents are exempt from filing Canadian income tax returns if all of the following criteria are satisfied:

- no tax is payable by the non-resident for the current taxation year or previous taxation year; and
- each taxable Canadian property disposed of by the non-resident in the year is either exempt from Canadian tax due to a tax treaty or a property with respect to the disposition of which the CRA has issued a clearance certificate to the non-resident (see article 133).

Previously, a non-resident had to file a Canadian tax return to report all dispositions of taxable Canadian property, even if there was no Canadian tax due to an exemption under a tax treaty.

TAX TIP

If you are a non-resident of Canada with Canadian-source income, you should consult a tax adviser to determine your tax obligations and ways to minimize your Canadian tax.

133 Disposition of Taxable Canadian Property by Non-Residents

As mentioned in article 132, a non-resident of Canada is liable to pay Canadian income tax on capital gains from dispositions of "taxable Canadian property," such as Canadian real estate and shares of Canadian private companies and on income or gains from dispositions of certain other property (unless exempt under a tax treaty). When a non-resident of Canada disposes of taxable Canadian property, the purchaser or the purchaser's representative is required to withhold tax from the purchase price and remit it to the CRA on account of the non-resident vendor's potential income tax liability. In general, the withholding tax rate is 25% on capital property and 50% for other property. The non-resident vendor may obtain from the Minister of National Revenue a "clearance certificate," verifying that the non-resident vendor has made arrangements for the payment of any resulting tax. This relieves the purchaser's obligation to withhold.

The 2008 budget included a number of changes to the disposition of taxable Canadian property (TCP) by a non-resident, effective for dispositions on or after January 1, 2009. Under these new rules, the purchaser of property from a non-resident vendor will not be required to withhold tax if:

- the purchaser concludes after reasonable inquiry that the vendor is resident in a country that has a tax treaty with Canada;
- at the time of the disposition, the property is treaty-protected property pursuant to the tax treaty between Canada and the country where the vendor is resident; and
- the purchaser sends to the CRA, no later than 30 days after the date of the acquisition, a notice setting out basic information about the transaction, the vendor and the purchaser.

The income or gain from a treaty-protected property is exempt from Canadian tax. Canada has tax treaties with many countries. The tax treaty Canada has with the country of residence of the vendor must be reviewed to determine if the property is treaty-protected property.

This change eases the administrative burden for taxpayers by allowing an exception for withholding tax in a situation in which there will ultimately be no Canadian tax liability due to an exemption under a tax treaty. However, the onus is on the purchaser to confirm the vendor's country of residence, as well as the fact that the property disposed of is treaty protected.

134 U.S. Citizens Resident in Canada

The U.S. taxes its citizens and green-card holders (collectively U.S. persons) on their worldwide income, regardless of whether they live in the U.S. As a result, if you are a U.S. citizen living in Canada, you are required to file both a Canadian and a U.S. income tax return.

Watch out for tax liabilities

Although there are several mechanisms in place to prevent double taxation, the many differences between the two tax systems can still lead to unexpected tax liabilities—for example, capital gains or losses on the sale of capital property, exempt municipal bonds and many others. For this reason, you should always obtain professional tax advice if you are a U.S. citizen residing in Canada.

Filing your returns

For Canadian tax purposes, each taxpayer must file a separate return. For U.S. tax purposes, you have the option of filing a joint return with your spouse. If your spouse has little or no income, but you are paying tax to the U.S., filing a joint election will generally be beneficial.

If your spouse is not a U.S. citizen, you can still file a joint return, but the rules are a little more complicated. First of all, you must file an election to treat your non-resident spouse as a U.S. resident. Once this election is made, your spouse must file a U.S. income tax return each year until the election is revoked. Once revoked, the election cannot be reinstated. During the years in which the election is in force, you and your spouse may decide annually whether to elect to file a joint return. This decision can change from year to year. A discussion with your tax adviser is recommended.

If you are a U.S. citizen, you are required to file a U.S. tax return even if you owe no U.S. tax. Several years ago, the Internal Revenue Service (IRS) launched a "non-filer program" in an attempt to bring back into the U.S. tax system taxpayers who have not been filing returns. Substantial resources have been devoted to finding non-filers who are likely to owe a significant amount of tax.

If you have not been filing a U.S. return, you should get professional advice. As well as filing a tax return, you may also be required to disclose a substantial amount of other financial information to the U.S. government. Recent U.S. legislation has significantly increased penalties for non-compliance.

If you are a U.S. citizen living in Canada, you have an automatic extension to June 15 to file your U.S. tax return. Interest will be charged on any unpaid tax from April 15, but no late-filing penalties will be assessed if you file by June 15. You can also receive an automatic extension to October 15 if you file an application and pay at least 90% of your final tax liability. Late-filing penalties are assessed only if there is a balance due on your return. Therefore, if there is no balance due, you should not be subject to any late-filing penalties.

Ownership of registered savings plans by U.S. persons

If you are a U.S. citizen, permanent resident card (green-card) holder or U.S. resident, and you hold an interest in a Canadian RRSP or RRIF, you should contact your tax adviser to determine your filing obligations under these rules. In general, you must make a special election under the Canada–U.S. tax treaty to defer the U.S. taxation of income earned in the RRSP until such time as a distribution is made from the plan. IRS Form 8891 must be filed as part of this election. The filing requirements are more complex in situations where you have received a distribution from the plan during the year.

135 U.S. Social Security Payments

U.S. social security benefits received by residents of Canada are subject to tax only in Canada. The U.S. will not tax these benefits.

The full amount of the benefit received will be included in net income, but 15% of that amount will be deductible in calculating taxable income. As a result, only 85% of the benefits received in a year will be subject to tax. But the full amount is included in net income for purposes of assessing various clawbacks and other net income-based calculations: the OAS clawback (see article 80) and the age credit (see article 101).

136 U.S. Real Estate Owned by Canadian Residents

Canadian residents who receive rent from U.S. real estate are normally subject to a withholding tax of 30% of the gross amount of any rent paid. As an alternative, you can elect to pay tax on a net-income basis. In this case, you must file a U.S. tax return at the end of the year, reporting your net rental income. By making this election with the IRS and providing appropriate information to the tenant, the 30% withholding tax is not required. Once you make this election, it is permanent and can be revoked only in limited circumstances.

Many people assume that because their expenses always exceed their rental income, there is no need to file a U.S. tax return or to have tax withheld at source. If tax is not withheld at source, however, a tax return must be filed within 19 1/2 months of the year-end if you want to claim expenses.

In addition, unlike Canadian tax rules, depreciation is a mandatory deduction in the U.S. If you don't file a return, you are still deemed to have claimed depreciation and would be subject to recapture.

Failure to file also reduces your ability to carry forward passive activity losses, since the IRS has no record of them. As a result, on a subsequent sale of the property, you would have an income inclusion in the form of recapture with no offsetting loss carry-forward.

TAX TIP

Professional advice is the best remedy if you receive rental income from U.S. real property and have not filed a U.S. tax return because your expenses exceed your rental income. The IRS has strict rules regarding the timely filing of such returns. If the returns are not filed within 19 1/2 months of the year-end, these rules provide that you will not be entitled to claim any deductions and tax will be assessed on the gross income. A 2006 tax court case (*Swallow Holding, Ltd.*) ruled that the IRS did not have the authority to disallow expenses on a late-filed return on the basis that the IRS interpretation of the statute was contrary to the plain meaning of the statute as intended by Congress. The IRS has not yet accepted the Tax Court's decision.

Selling your U.S. property

If you are selling your U.S. real property, then expect to have 10% withheld from your gross proceeds as a withholding tax against your actual U.S. income tax liability. There are certain exceptions to this rule. For example, this withholding will not apply if the property is sold for less than US$300,000 and the purchaser intends to use the property as a residence. Also, you can apply to the IRS to have the withholding tax reduced if the expected tax liability on the sale will be less than 10% of the sale price.

Regardless of the amount of withholding tax, the gain on the sale of any U.S. property is still taxable in the U.S. and a U.S. tax return must be filed. The 10% withholding, if applicable, will be applied against the tax balance owing in the U.S.

The U.S. tax that is paid generates a foreign tax credit that can be used to reduce the Canadian tax payable on the sale. If you have owned the property continuously since before September 27, 1980, for personal use only, there is a provision in the Canada–U.S. tax treaty that can be used to reduce the gain. In such cases, professional advice should be sought.

137 Withholding Tax on Income from U.S. Sources

If you are not a U.S. citizen, and you receive certain types of income from U.S. sources—such as interest, dividends, rents, royalties or annuities—you are required to complete Form W-8BEN to benefit from the reduced rates of withholding tax under the income tax treaty. If this form is not remitted to the payer of the income, the payer is required to withhold up to 30% on any reportable distributions. For example, under the Canada–U.S. tax treaty, an individual residing in Canada is entitled to a 15% rate of withholding tax on dividend income from U.S. sources. But if Form W-8BEN is not filed with the payer, 30% must be withheld.

138 U.S. Estate Tax

If you die owning certain U.S. property, your estate could be subject to U.S. estate tax. Rather than taxing just the accrued gain during the period of ownership, estate tax applies to the fair market value of the U.S. property at the time of your death. U.S. citizens are subject to estate tax on their worldwide estates. However, Canadian residents who are not U.S. citizens are taxed only on certain U.S. properties, such as U.S. real property, shares of U.S. companies, tangible personal property located in the U.S. and debts issued by U.S. residents, including the U.S. government.

But there is good news. Regardless of your U.S. holdings, you are not subject to U.S. estate tax if the value of your worldwide gross estate is less than US$3.5 million. Both houses of the U.S. Congress continue to debate the issue of the U.S. estate tax and a number of proposals have been put forth from both houses. However, no one proposal has yet been passed in the Senate or the House of Representatives. Absent any further developments, the estate tax will be repealed in 2010 and will be reintroduced in 2011 with a US$1 million exclusion.

For purposes of calculating the available exclusion for non-U.S. citizens, the applicable credit ($1,455,800 for 2009) is prorated, based on the percentage of a Canadian resident's worldwide estate value that is subject to the estate tax. For example, assume Mr. Smith owned the following assets when he died in 2009:

U.S. real estate	US$500,000
Canadian assets	US$5,500,000
Total estate value	US$6,000,000
Prorated credit:	($500,000 ÷ $6,000,000) × $1,455,800 = $121,317

In this example, the estate tax on a $500,000 U.S. estate is $155,800 reduced by the $121,317 exclusion. The amount of estate tax owing is US$34,483. If Mr. Smith was married and left the U.S. real estate to his surviving spouse, he could claim an additional marital credit of $121,317 to bring his U.S. estate tax liability to zero. If any U.S. estate tax remains, after applying all available credits, the balance may be claimed as a foreign tax credit on your Canadian tax return. The ability to claim the foreign tax credit is very fact-specific so you should seek professional tax advice.

TAX TIP

Do you own or are you about to acquire property situated in the United States? If so, consult your tax adviser to review your exposure to U.S. federal estate tax. Planning strategies are available to defer, reduce or eliminate this potential liability.

TAX TIP

If you are the beneficiary of the estate of a U.S. resident, you should seek professional tax advice. Without planning, cross-border estates often experience double taxation, since the tax systems of Canada and the U.S. are not necessarily coordinated.

139 U.S. Residency Regulations

Many Canadians who regularly spend winters in the U.S. may find that they are required to fill out a special declaration—the Closer Connection Exemption Statement—to be exempt from paying U.S. taxes.

Are you exempt?

To determine whether you are one of the Canadians who should file this declaration, you must add up the number of days (or part days) you spent in the U.S. in 2009, one-third of the days in 2008 and one-sixth of the days in 2007. If this calculation adds up to 183 days or more, you may be considered a U.S. resident for tax purposes under U.S. domestic tax law.

However, you can qualify for the "closer connection" exemption if you meet the following provisions:

- You have not applied for a U.S. permanent resident card (green card).

- You were present in the U.S. for fewer than 183 days in 2009.
- You have maintained a permanent place of residence in Canada throughout 2009.
- You can claim a closer connection to Canada.
- You file the special declaration by June 15, 2010.

The "closer connection" form (Form 8840) cannot be filed late. If you miss the June 15 deadline, you must file Form 1040NR and make a treaty election to avoid U.S. taxation. Also, green-card holders are not entitled to file this declaration. If you hold a green card, or if you spent more than 182 days in the U.S. in the current year, you will have to rely on the tie-breaker rules in the Canada–U.S. tax treaty to avoid U.S. resident status. In such cases, you will be required to file a treaty-based U.S. tax return if you are relying on the treaty to exempt you from U.S. tax. As a cautionary note, the U.S. Citizenship and Immigration Service has issued a warning to green-card holders that they may jeopardize their green-card status if they use treaty provisions to be taxed as a non-resident of the U.S.

TAX TIP

Over the past several years, the U.S. has issued numerous rules and regulations of concern to Canadians with interests in that country. If you spend a considerable amount of time in the U.S. each year, contact your tax adviser to ensure you are complying with these rules.

140 Succession and Estate Planning

Estate planning is a difficult subject to deal with briefly. It is simply not possible to advise people on such matters without considerable reference to other areas of taxation and to personal and financial circumstances and objectives.

Generally speaking, succession and estate planning focuses on planning for the transition of wealth. That being said, as an ongoing process, estate planning means different things to different people. From a tax-planning perspective, one of the main objectives is to maximize the value of the estate for its beneficiaries by minimizing applicable taxes. Key elements of a tax-effective estate-planning strategy include arranging your financial affairs during your lifetime to minimize income taxes and estate administration fees upon your death, as well as ensuring that the estate will have sufficient liquidity to pay income taxes and other liabilities arising on death.

On death, a taxpayer is deemed to have disposed of all his or her capital property at fair market value in the moment immediately before his or her death, with an exception relating to property passing to a spouse or common-law partner or to certain trusts created for the benefit of a spouse or common-law partner. This deemed disposition is the mechanism that triggers the potential income tax liability.

Estate planning can include elements such as:

- transferring assets to family members during one's lifetime;
- capping the value of growth assets at their current values by transferring future asset appreciation to other family members (estate freezing);
- probate planning;
- planned giving;
- preparation of a will; and
- acquisition of life insurance to fund a future income tax liability.

The introduction of the eligible-dividend rules (see article 153) has had a significant impact on estate-planning considerations (for both planning objectives to be achieved during your lifetime and post-mortem planning). Results will vary by province (see Table 2 on page 287), but the intent is that the cost of redeeming shares (using eligible dividends) should approximate the capital gains rate. Since most planning that was completed prior to the introduction of these rules was done on the basis that capital gains were taxed more favourably than dividends, such planning will now warrant another look where eligible dividends are available.

Asset transfers

If you have decided that you have more assets than you need, you can reduce your estate probate and executor fees, and possibly income taxes upon death, if you transfer assets during your lifetime. If these assets have increased in value since acquisition, however, the transfer could cause an income tax liability. You should carefully assess which assets to transfer, and to whom, and how to avoid triggering a tax liability.

TAX TIP

If you are fortunate enough to have assets that can provide an income larger than lifetime needs, gifting some of the assets to beneficiaries during your lifetime is a logical way to reduce taxes. Complicated rules apply to income and capital gains on gifts to spouses or common-law partners and children under 18 (see article 119).

Freezing/refreezing your estate

Estate freezing is a popular method of limiting death taxes. It consists primarily of transferring to a younger generation the growth potential of assets such as real estate or shares of corporations. By doing so, the asset value to the transferor is frozen at its value at the date of transfer. Accordingly, the amount of potential capital gain on death is also frozen. This will allow you to estimate your potential tax liability on death and better plan for the payment of income taxes.

You can usually accomplish an estate freeze through a transfer of assets to a corporation or an internal reorganization of capital. The mechanics can vary, but the transfer must be professionally planned to avoid the many punitive provisions of the Income Tax Act.

But what if the value of the frozen assets actually decreases after the date of the freeze? For example, assume you have an investment company that was frozen in the past few years while businesses and markets were still in bull mode, but now, due to the recent market turmoil, the value of the company is less than it was on the date of the estate freeze. This presents an excellent tax-planning opportunity. The previously frozen assets can be "refrozen" at the lower current value, and the future increase in value can accrue to other (generally younger) family members. If you have already undertaken an estate freeze, you should consider if now is the time to do a refreeze.

Alter-ego and joint-partner trusts

To avoid probate fees, will substitutes—such as inter vivos trusts—have been used to transfer assets to beneficiaries. However, a gift of assets to a non-spousal trust that names other persons as beneficiaries usually results in a disposition of those assets at fair market value for income tax purposes. This can result in the payment of significant tax at the time of the transfer.

If you are 65 years of age or older, alter-ego and joint-partner trusts can be used to avoid having to dispose of the assets at fair market value. One of the advantages of these types of trusts is that assets can be transferred to them on a tax-deferred basis, thereby avoiding triggering any tax on accrued gains. However, there will be a deemed disposition of all property in the trust on the day you or (where applicable) your spouse or common-law partner dies, whichever is later.

Another advantage of these trusts is that they can avoid the application of wills variation legislation in those provinces that have this legislation.

One main disadvantage of these types of trusts is the CRA's position that assets in the trust cannot pass to a continuing testamentary trust after death, thereby preventing the use of a testamentary trust's graduated tax rates on income earned on the assets after death.

If you establish an alter-ego or joint-partner trust, you (or you and your spouse or common-law partner) must be entitled to receive all of the trust's income prior to death, and no other person can obtain the use of any of the trust's income or capital before your death (or that of your surviving spouse or common-law partner in the case of a joint-partner trust).

TAX TIP

If you own assets with an accrued gain, and live in a jurisdiction with high probate rates, talk to your financial adviser about the advisability of setting up an alter-ego or joint-partner trust. These types of trusts are also often used in interprovincial planning.

Planned giving

The value of your estate—and, as a consequence, income taxes and estate administration fees—can be reduced by making charitable donations during your lifetime (see article 91).The added benefit is that you also earn income tax credits during your life rather than on your death. Over the past few years, several rules have been introduced to encourage the private funding of charitable organizations. For example:

- The general annual limit on charitable donations as a percentage of net income has risen from 20% to 75%.
- The limit on gifts by individuals in the year of death and prior year has risen to 100% of net income.

- The capital gains inclusion rate is reduced to zero where certain types of appreciated capital property are donated to a registered charity—for example, donations of publicly listed securities (see article 91).

Through effective "planned giving," you can balance your personal financial goals and your charitable interests while realizing significant tax benefits. Other benefits may include the reduction of probate fees and other estate costs.

Following are some of the more common planned-giving opportunities.

Gifts of life insurance

Life insurance can be used to provide a relatively large endowment to a registered charity on your death, while requiring comparatively modest cash outflows during your lifetime. The gift can be in the form of a new or an existing whole-life insurance policy. In situations where an existing policy is donated, it is the CRA's current administrative position that the charitable organization can issue a receipt for the fair market value of the life insurance policy at the time it is gifted to the charity. For the charity to acquire an interest in the policy, however, there must be an absolute and unconditional assignment of all rights, title and interest in the policy. The amount you would report as your proceeds of disposition would be the policy's cash surrender value at the time of the donation. Based on the circumstances, a life insurance policy can have a fair market value that is significantly greater than its cash surrender value.

Charitable annuities

Some charities have the legal right to issue annuities. In this case, you make a contribution of capital to the charity. In return, the charity agrees to make periodic payments to you either for a specified period or for life. Those charities that cannot issue annuities themselves may acquire the annuity from a third party.

A few years ago, the CRA changed its position on how this type of gift should be valued for purposes of issuing a charitable donation receipt. For charitable annuities issued after December 20, 2002, the amount of the gift will equal the amount contributed by the donor in excess of the amount that would be paid at that time to a third party to acquire an annuity to fund the same stream of guaranteed payments. In addition, a portion of the annuity payments received by the donor will be taxable. The old administrative position will continue to apply to annuities issued before December 21, 2002. This position provided that no portion of any annuity payment was taxable in the hands of the donor.

Charitable remainder trusts

The most common form of a charitable remainder trust is an irrevocable trust that holds property that you want to contribute to a specified charity. The real attractiveness of this type of vehicle is the ability to make the gift on an inter vivos basis while guaranteeing you the right to enjoy the use of the property or the revenue from investments during your lifetime. You receive an immediate tax receipt for the present value of the remainder interest in the property. For example, you might consider donating the remainder interest in your personal residence. No tax results on the disposition of a personal residence (see article 117), and the donation receipt can be used to shelter tax other sources of income while you are still alive.

The main disadvantage of these trusts is that once the donation is made, you cannot change your mind and take the property back.

Use of private foundations

Private foundations have the advantage of providing you with an immediate donation receipt for the amount contributed to the foundation, while at the same time allowing you to retain control of the funds and delay the distribution of capital to qualifying charities (subject to special rules). For gifts made after March 18, 2007, there is no capital gains tax on donations of publicly listed shares to a private foundation. This now parallels the rules that exist for gifts to public foundations (see article 91).

Planned giving does not have to be as complex as the above strategies might imply. It may simply involve reviewing your charitable objectives with a view to accelerating your intended donations now to maximize tax savings.

Since many of the planned-giving strategies involve the disposition of capital, you may also have to report income or a capital gain as the result of making a gift. As the name suggests, planned giving consists of planning and giving. "Planning" refers to a careful consideration of estate planning, financial planning and tax planning as part of making the gift. Your tax adviser can help you develop a planned-giving strategy that is most appropriate to your individual situation.

TAX TIP

Planning to make significant charitable donations in your will? It may not be your best option. If you make them during your lifetime, you will reduce the value of your estate for probate purposes, reduce your executor fees and realize tax savings earlier.

Preparing a will

Both you and your spouse or common-law partner should have wills. This is probably one of the most critical elements of your estate-planning strategy, as dying intestate (without a will) can defeat almost all the estate-planning arrangements you have put into place.

TAX TIP

A periodic review of your will is part of prudent estate planning. It should ensure that your assets will be dealt with in the most tax-effective manner and that your will complies with current laws, such as provincial family law acts.

Life insurance

Just as you can't avoid death, it is not possible to avoid taxes when you die. If your estate has enough liquid assets, the payment of income taxes may not be much of a problem. But if a major portion of your estate consists of shares of private companies or real estate, it may not be possible to satisfy your tax bill on death without selling off the assets.

Funding potential income taxes through the purchase of life insurance can be an effective estate-planning tool. If sufficient insurance proceeds are available and the policies are properly structured, any income tax arising on the deemed dispositions of assets on your death can be paid without resorting to the sale of your assets.

In recent years, the investment aspect of some life insurance policies has become more attractive. One of the major reasons for this is the favourable tax treatment provided for "exempt" policies. Any investment income earned in such a policy and any amounts paid out on the death of the insured are exempt from tax. The tax shelter aspect of an exempt policy has several potential uses—particularly after other tax shelter opportunities such as RRSPs have been exhausted. This type of a policy is often used in conjunction with a shareholder buy-sell agreement. You may also be able to access the tax-sheltered earnings through taxable draws on the cash surrender value of the policy or by pledging the policy as collateral for a loan.

To be exempt, a policy must satisfy certain complex rules. As with any other tax shelter, an investment in an exempt policy should be assessed on its merits.

TAX TIP

If you have decided to acquire life insurance to fund any income taxes that may arise from the deemed disposition of shares of a private corporation, plan carefully to determine whether you or your company should own the policy. Both options have different advantages. Consultation with your tax and insurance advisers is a must.

Succession planning

More than 90% of businesses in North America are family owned. However, it's estimated that only 30% survive into the second generation.

If you are the owner-manager of a private company, succession planning is one additional aspect of estate planning. The survival of your business may depend on it! In doing so, you will have to consider:

- providing for continuation of the business;
- balancing business, family and personal well-being;
- choosing a successor;
- training a successor;
- transferring ownership and control of the business;
- ensuring adequate retirement income; and
- minimizing income taxes on capital gains.

In developing a succession strategy, you have to determine in advance when you plan to retire, your financial objectives during retirement and how the family business will contribute to those requirements. Your professional adviser can assist you in addressing these issues and making sure that the transition process goes as smoothly as possible.

141 Deceased Taxpayers

Coming to grips with death, particularly of someone close, is never easy. Nevertheless, the deceased's family and legal representative have to ensure that legal formalities are complied with and deadlines met.

Executor's responsibilities

A deceased's legal representative is the person named in the will (executor) or a person appointed to handle the estate if there is no will or if an executor has not been named in the will (administrator).

From a tax perspective, the main responsibilities of the legal representative are as follows:

- File all tax returns for the deceased.
- Make sure all taxes are paid.
- Obtain clearance certificate or authorization from the tax authorities to distribute the assets of the deceased.
- Let the beneficiaries know which of the amounts they receive from the estate are taxable.

Government authorities and financial institutions should be notified as soon as possible of the date of death. The deceased's social insurance number and date of birth must be provided if:

- the person was receiving OAS benefits;
- the person was receiving CPP or QPP benefits;
- the person was receiving the GST/HST or QST credit;
- the person or his/her spouse was receiving the CCTB;
- the person was a child with respect to whom the CCTB was being paid; or
- the person was receiving benefits under a RRIF or RRSP.

Instalments

No instalments have to be paid for a deceased person for the period after the date of death. Nevertheless, the legal representative should ensure that any amounts due prior to the date of death were in fact paid.

Canada Pension Plan and Old Age Security payments

The CPP and OAS pensions are paid for the month during which the taxpayer died and have to be reported in the tax return of the deceased. Any cheques received for months following the month of death have to be returned to the federal government.

GST/HST credit

GST/HST credit payments are issued in July, October, January and April. If a single individual dies before one of these months, any payment must be returned to the government. If a person dies during the month the payment is made, the estate will be entitled to it.

If the deceased had a spouse, the surviving spouse may be eligible for the GST/HST credit. The spouse should contact the CRA and request any remaining credit for the year and file a tax return for the preceding year (if this has not already been done).

Canada Child Tax Benefit (CCTB)

If the deceased leaves a surviving spouse who is the father or mother of a child with respect to whom the deceased was receiving the CCTB (see article 108), the surviving spouse should contact the tax authorities to have the benefits transferred to her or him. If, on the other hand, the surviving spouse was the recipient of these benefits, he or she can ask the tax authorities to recalculate the benefits taking only his or her income into consideration.

If the person now responsible for the care of the child is someone other than the father or mother, this person has to submit a written request to the tax authorities to be recognized as eligible to receive these payments.

If the deceased was an eligible child, the benefit entitlement ceases the month following the death. Any amounts received in that or subsequent months have to be returned.

Tax filing obligations of the legal representative

As a legal representative, one of your main responsibilities is to ensure that the deceased's taxes are paid. This may necessitate obtaining tax information that is available from the respective tax authorities. To have access to this information, you will have to present a copy of the death certificate, the deceased's social insurance number, and a certified copy of the will or other document to show that you are the legal representative of the deceased person.

You must also file, where applicable, tax returns for the year of death and any prior years for which the deceased had not filed a tax return. In addition, for the year of death, you may be able to elect to file more than one return for certain types of income. These are referred to as the final return and optional returns. By filing more than one return, income taxes on the deceased's income may be reduced or even eliminated in certain cases.

The deadlines for filing returns may vary depending on whether it is a final return, an optional return or a return for a year prior to death.

In general, for the final return, you must comply with the filing dates for tax returns (April 30 of the following year or June 15 for taxpayers carrying on a business). However, you have up to six months from the date of death if this is later. For example, if a person dies on December 20, 2009, you have until June 20, 2010, to file the final return. On the other hand, if the taxpayer died on May 10, 2009, the filing deadline would be April 30, 2010.

Taxes must be paid no later than the filing due date for the returns, unless the filing date is June 15 (for taxpayers carrying on a business), in which case the payment date will be April 30. If a return is filed late, a late-filing penalty and interest are charged.

There may be as many as three other separate types of returns for a deceased taxpayer:

1. a "rights or things" return (see "Income," following);
2. a return reporting business income;
3. a return arising from a testamentary trust.

The filing dates for optional returns and the payment of any balances owing are the same as those for a final return, except for the "rights or things" return, where the filing date and the date for the payment of any balance owing is one year following the date of death or 90 days after the date a Notice of Assessment or Notice of Reassessment is mailed with respect to the final return for the year of death (if this is a later date).

Income

The final and optional returns of a deceased taxpayer have to report all income for the period from January 1 of the year of death to the date of death. Income earned after that date should generally be reported in the estate's return.

All periodic amounts earned prior to death—such as salary, interest, rent and most annuities—must be reported in the final return, even if the deceased did not receive them before he or she died. This rule does not apply if the amounts were not payable prior to death or if such annuities were considered as having matured at the time of death. If this is the case, certain income of this nature can be reported in an optional return.

"Rights or things" are income amounts that the deceased was entitled to receive before he or she died but that had not yet been paid. The main rights or things are:

- employment income (salaries, commissions, vacation pay) owing by the employer but not payable at the time of death for a pay period that ended before the date of death, as well as retroactive payments paid pursuant to a collective agreement signed before the date of death;
- uncashed matured bond coupons;
- accumulated unpaid bond interest;
- unpaid dividends declared before the person died;
- OAS, EI and CPP benefits not yet received for a period ended before the date of death or for the month of death;
- work-in-progress if the deceased carried on a business and had elected to exclude work-in-progress when calculating income;
- retroactive payment of a disability annuity or EI benefit paid after the date of death, but to which the deceased was entitled prior to that date; and

- pension plan, RRSP or RRIF payments for the month of death that had not been received at the date of death.

If you elect to file an optional return, all rights and things have to be reported therein except those transferred to beneficiaries. Rights or things transferred to a beneficiary before the filing deadline for an optional return have to be reported by the beneficiary.

If the deceased was a beneficiary of a testamentary trust in the year he or she died, the fiscal year of the trust was not the calendar year, and the deceased died after the end of the trust's year, income from the trust from the end of the trust's year to the date of death can be taxed in an optional return.

If the deceased carried on business as a partner or sole proprietor and the fiscal year of the business was not the calendar year, the legal representative can elect to report the business income earned between the end of the fiscal year and the date of death in an optional return. As the fiscal year of an individual who carries on business normally corresponds to the calendar year, this measure applies only when the deceased used the optional method for reporting self-employment income (see article 2).

Capital properties

In general, deceased persons are deemed to dispose of all of their capital property at fair market value immediately before death.

There is an exception to this rule for capital properties left to a spouse or common-law partner or a qualifying spouse trust. In this case, any capital gain or loss is deferred until the property is disposed of by the spouse or common-law partner or the spousal trust. The legal representative can still elect to have the transfer take place at fair market value. For example, you might want to make this election if the deceased owned shares in a qualified small-business corporation (see article 146), owned qualified farm or fishing property (see articles 147 and 148), or had capital losses that had not yet been utilized.

Funeral and estate administration expenses

Funeral and estate administration expenses are personal expenses and are not deductible in calculating the income of the deceased or the estate.

142 Taxation of First Nations

Most First Nations individuals also have to pay income tax every year. But there are some exceptions.

The primary exception is found in subsection 87(1) of the Indian Act. In general, this section provides that the interest of an Indian or a band in a reserve or surrendered lands, and the personal property of a status Indian or band situated on a reserve are exempt from tax. The exemption applies to only individuals and bands, and not to other entities such as corporations or trusts. It also applies only to personal property situated on a reserve.

Exactly how broad this exemption can be has been the subject of much debate and numerous court cases.

Taxation of employment income

Most of the case law in this area has dealt with the application of the exemption to employment income.

Being a status Indian and living on a reserve is not enough to exempt your employment income from tax. Since the 1992 Supreme Court of Canada decision in *Williams*, there must also be sufficient connecting factors between the employment income and the reserve for the income to be considered "situated on a reserve" and eligible for the tax exemption.

In many cases, this is not an easy assessment. If the most significant factors connect the property to a location on a reserve, the income will be tax-exempt. In 1994, the CRA developed the following guidelines to assist in determining if your income is "situated on a reserve" and potentially exempt from taxation:

- If at least 90% of your employment duties are performed on a reserve, all of the income from that employment will normally be exempt from tax. In this case, it is not necessary for you or your employer to reside on a reserve. If less than 90% of your duties are performed on a reserve, the exemption can be prorated;
- If you and your employer both reside on a reserve, all of your income from that employment will normally be exempt from tax;
- If more than 50% of your employment duties are performed on a reserve and either you or your employer resides on a

reserve, all of your income from that employment will normally be exempt from tax; and

- If your employer resides on a reserve and is either an Indian band or other organization controlled by one or more Bands, and your employment duties are in connection with your employers' non-commercial activities carried on exclusively for the social, cultural, educational or economic benefit of Indians who, for the most part, live on the reserve, all of your income from employment will normally be exempt from tax.

One particular taxpayer attempted to broaden the above exemption. In *Shilling v. The Queen*, the taxpayer did not live on a reserve but was employed by Native Leasing Services located on the Six Nations reserve near Brantford, Ontario. The leasing company provided her services to a downtown Toronto health agency that provided services to the city's Aboriginal street people. Shilling argued that because she was technically employed by a company located on a reserve, her salary should not be subject to tax. Although she initially won her case, the decision was eventually overturned by the Federal Court of Appeal. The Supreme Court refused to hear her appeal.

The courts continue to support the "connecting factors" test established in *Williams*, and the guidelines noted above continue to represent a reasonable interpretation of the law.

Taxation of investment income

It used to be the CRA's position that interest income earned by an Indian on an account maintained at a branch situated on a reserve was exempt from tax. However, based on the *Williams* case (commented on above), the proper approach to use in determining whether income is situated on a reserve is to evaluate the various connecting factors that would tie the property to the reserve. The location of the savings account alone is not sufficient to connect the income to the reserve.

One significant court case in this regard was the 1998 case of *Recalma v. The Queen*. In this case, the Federal Court of Appeal agreed with the Tax Court that investment income earned by an Indian living on a reserve from investments purchased from a bank on a reserve was taxable. Although several factors were considered in arriving at this decision, the Courts gave particular weight to the location of the issuer's income-generating activity from which the investment was made. Since the income from the investments started with companies located off the reserve, the income was taxable.

Based on this decision, the CRA now maintains that, among other factors, for investment income to be exempt it would have to be from a financial institution located on the reserve that generates its income exclusively from investments and loans to Indians who reside on a reserve. Given the extreme difficulty in satisfying all of the connecting factors, investment income earned by an Indian is generally taxable.

Taxation of business income

As has been noted, only individuals can benefit from the tax exemption in the Indian Act. Therefore, to qualify for tax-exempt status, you must carry on the business as a sole proprietor or in partnership. In determining whether your business income is connected to the reserve, the CRA will look at a number of factors:

1. Where is the business office located?
2. Where do the employees report for work?
3. Where are the records kept?
4. Where are the inventory and fixed assets located?
5. Where do the transactions with customers and suppliers take place?

In considering whether there are sufficient connecting factors to tie the business income to the reserve, the Courts have given considerable weight to the location where the work is performed and where the income is earned. In addition, it is easier to support tax-exempt status if the business is integral to the life of the reserve, rather than being part of the "commercial mainstream."

As a separate legal entity, corporations cannot rely on this exemption even if all of the shareholders reside on a reserve and the head office of the corporation is located on a reserve.

The location of the corporation can be relevant, however, where payments are made to you in the form of wages. Based on the guidelines noted above, the employment income may or may not be exempt from taxation. If the employment income would qualify for tax-exempt status, business income that would otherwise be taxable at the corporate level can be converted to tax-exempt employment income. Keep in mind that to be deductible by the corporation, the salary must be reasonable in the circumstances.

TAX TIP

Since corporations do not qualify for the exemption, Indian-owned businesses operated on the reserve should, in most cases, be structured as a sole proprietorship or partnership.

Corporate and other structures

There are certain situations where a corporate form of ownership might be used. As a regular rule, a corporation is taxable on its income unless it is otherwise exempt from taxation under a specific provision of the Income Tax Act. There are two main income tax exemptions from taxation:

1. Paragraph 149(1)(d) of the Income Tax Act exempts municipal corporations from taxation. A company is a municipal corporation if it is owned 90% or more by a Canadian municipality.

2. Paragraph 149(1)(c) of the Income Tax Act exempts a public body that performs a function of government in Canada.

Corporations whose shares are owned by an Indian band may be able to qualify for tax-exempt status under one of these exemptions. For a corporation whose shares are owned by an Indian band to qualify under the first exemption, the band must be considered a Canadian municipality and no more than 9.99% of its income can be earned outside the geographical boundaries of the band. To qualify under the second exemption, it will be a question of fact whether a band performs a function of government. Historically, the CRA has recognized a band as a public body performing a function of the government in Canada, where it has passed by-laws under both Sections 81 and 83 of the *Indian Act*.

TAX TIP

A band can apply to the CRA Charities division for a determination as to whether it is a public body performing a function of the government. The request should include a band profile, as well as comments on the band's community involvement or functions of government activities performed.

As First Nations become more involved in business activities that may or may not be located on reserve lands, limited partnership (LP) structures are becoming increasingly popular. The LP carries on the business operations. The general partner is a corporate entity owned by the First Nations and the limited partners are the same First Nations. In many cases, as a means of protecting the operating assets from liability risks, the assets are held in a separate company and then leased to the LP.

This structure is beneficial from an income tax perspective as it provides a means by which a separate legal entity exists to operate a business, but still allows for each of the First Nation partners to maintain their tax-exempt status with respect to the income earned in the business. This structure is also appealing from an operational perspective as it provides a means by which control of the business and related profits can be removed from the chief and council of the various First Nations. As elections occur and changes are made to the band councils, the management of the business will not be affected.

Taxation of trusts

Trusts are often used by bands to receive the proceeds from a land-claim settlement. These are often referred to as settlement trusts. As noted above, a trust is not exempt from taxation. However, if all the trust income can be allocated to tax-exempt Indian beneficiaries of the trust, the trust pays no tax. Income received by an Indian from the trust will be exempt from taxation, provided it would have been exempt had the Indian received the income directly.

Income that is not allocated is subject to tax at the top marginal rate for individuals (see Table 2, page 287).

What about GST?

The CRA has developed a number of policies on how the Indian Act exemption applies to GST.

Generally, an Indian, Indian band and an Indian-band-empowered entity will not have to pay GST on the purchase of property, provided the vendor of the goods arranges for the delivery of the items to a reserve. The vendor is required to maintain supporting evidence to prove that the goods were actually delivered to a reserve. The vendor also has to maintain evidence that the purchaser was an Indian or an Indian band. If the purchaser is an Indian, the

CRA accepts as adequate evidence a notation of the Indian registry number on the invoice or the band name and family number. If the purchaser is a band or a band-empowered entity, a certificate must be provided and retained by the vendor that the property is being acquired for band management activities. A "band management activity" is generally an activity that is not commercial in nature. If the activity at issue would normally allow the band or the entity to recover any GST incurred by way of claiming an input tax credit, it will not be considered a band management activity. If the goods are not delivered to a reserve by the vendor or a carrier hired by the vendor, then GST will apply.

For a service to be purchased without GST by an Indian individual, the entire service must be provided on the reserve. For example, a haircut provided on a reserve will not attract tax whereas the same haircut provided off the reserve will attract tax.

Services acquired on or off a reserve by an Indian band or band-empowered entity for band management activities are not subject to GST. Despite this, Indian bands and band-empowered entities do pay GST on off-reserve purchases of transportation, short-term accommodation, meals and entertainment. The GST incurred on these items may be recoverable by filing a rebate with the CRA provided certain conditions are met.

The above exemptions generally do not apply to corporations owned by Indians or bands. The only exception is corporations that are considered to be band-empowered entities. Such corporations must be owned or controlled by a band, tribal council or group of bands. The entity must also be situated on a reserve.

A detailed summary of the application of GST to Indians can be found by reviewing CRA Technical Information Bulletin B-039R3, *GST/HST Administrative Policy—Application of the GST/HST to Indians.*

S E C T I O N 3

Investors

IN THIS SECTION

143 Rental Properties
144 What About Capital Gains?
145 Lifetime Capital Gains Deduction
146 Qualified Small-Business Corporations Capital Gains Deduction
147 Qualified Farm Property Capital Gains Deduction
148 Qualified Fishing Property Capital Gains Deduction
149 Capital Gains Deferral for Investments in Small Businesses
150 Capital Gains Reserves
151 Capital Loss Rules
152 Business Investment Losses
153 Taxation of Dividends
154 Transfer of Dividend Income Between Spouses
155 Taxation of Interest Income
156 Mutual Funds
157 Income Trusts and Real Estate Investment Trusts (REITs)
158 Investment Holding Companies
159 Cumulative Net Investment Loss (CNIL) Rules
160 Deductibility of Interest Expense
161 Resource Sector as a Tax Shelter
162 Mineral Exploration Tax Credit
163 Limited Partnerships
164 CRA Warning—Tax Shelters
165 Taxation of Personal Trusts
166 Foreign Taxes on Investment Income
167 Foreign Reporting Requirements
168 Alternative Minimum Tax

In this section, we discuss rental properties, capital gains and the capital gains deduction, business investment losses and capital loss rules. We also look at investment vehicles such as Canada Savings Bonds, mutual funds, segregated funds, income trusts and real estate investment trusts. The deductibility of interest expense is also addressed, as well as the reasons for the different tax rates that apply to interest and dividend income. We discuss the different types of dividends you can receive, as well as their tax treatment. If you have earned investment income from foreign sources, you can find out your tax obligations while also learning more about your foreign reporting obligations. To round out the section, we've provided numerous tax tips that highlight some of the strategies you can use to your advantage as you build your portfolio.

143 Rental Properties

If you owned a rental property in 2009, any net income or loss must be reported on your 2009 income tax return. Rental income is usually reported on a calendar-year basis because the earnings are classified as property income, not as business income. Any income or loss from a rental property you own outside Canada must also be included in your return.

What can I deduct?

All reasonable expenses incurred in operating the property can be deducted. This can include the cost of insurance, property taxes, mortgage interest, electricity, heat, repairs and even advertising for tenants. If you borrowed money to make the down payment on the rental property, interest on that loan is also deductible. In certain circumstances, you may also be able to claim depreciation. However, you should be careful if you expect your expenses will consistently exceed your income from the property. If there is no reasonable expectation of making a profit from the investment, there is the possibility that your losses may be denied (see additional comments below).

TAX TIP

Keep accurate records of all expenses relating to your rental property. Retain all receipts; make a small note on each one indicating what the money was spent on and why. It will help your adviser determine quickly if it's a valid expense and eligible for deduction or depreciation.

Joint owner or partner?

If you have acquired a partial interest in a rental property, it is important to know whether it is in a partnership or in a joint venture. If you don't know which it is, consult your tax adviser.

With an interest in a partnership, you must report your share of its net profit or loss on your personal tax return. Depreciation is calculated at the partnership level, not by each individual partner.

As a joint owner, you have to report your share of the revenue and expenses related to the property. Next, you calculate depreciation based on the cost of your share of the property. Your depreciation claim is independent of the depreciation that may be claimed by the other joint owners.

What can I depreciate?

In general, depreciation on a rental property cannot be used to either create or increase your rental loss. When more than one rental property is owned, all net rental income (or loss) is combined to determine the total income or loss for the year.

Depreciation may be claimed on the property only to the extent of any net income from the rental of these properties before depreciation. Net income for purposes of determining the amount of depreciation that may be claimed includes recaptured depreciation on another rental property.

TAX TIP

If capital costs are required, try to time them for the end of the year instead of the first of the following year—this will speed up your tax-depreciation expense. In other words, you will be able to start writing off the cost immediately instead of having to wait another 12 months.

What happens if I sell?

Two different types of income may arise on the sale of your rental property. If you sell your property for more than its original cost, you have to report a capital gain to the extent that the proceeds exceed that cost. If the property was purchased before February 1994, some or all of this gain may have been eligible for the capital gains deduction. To take advantage of this, however, you should have made a special election when you filed your 1994 return (see article 145).

You may also have to pay tax on income that represents previously claimed depreciation. If proceeds from the sale exceed the undepreciated capital cost (UCC) of the property, the excess, up to the original cost, is taxed as recaptured depreciation in the year of sale.

Therefore, if the proceeds are more than the original cost, there will be full recapture and a capital gain. In some cases, where the property was destroyed or expropriated and another property was purchased, the gain and/or recapture may be deferred.

EXAMPLE/**The UCC factor**

> You purchased a building in 1996 at a cost of $400,000 and the UCC at the end of 2008 was $340,000. If you sell the building in 2009 for proceeds of $1,200,000, you will have to report recapture of $60,000 and a capital gain of $800,000.

If you did not receive the full proceeds of the sale in the year of the sale, you may be able to claim a capital gains reserve (see article 150). However, you cannot claim any reserve against the recaptured depreciation.

Anything else?

You may have a terminal loss if the proceeds from the sale are less than the UCC of the property, and this loss may be deductible from your other sources of income.

In the past, the tax agency often disallowed such losses, as well as net rental losses, on the basis the taxpayer had "no reasonable expectation of profit." Numerous tax cases have dealt with this issue. One significant court case in this regard was *Ludco Enterprises Ltd. v. The Queen.* This case dealt with the meaning of "income" for purposes of justifying that an expense had been incurred to earn income. In *Ludco*, the Supreme Court determined that the term "income" refers to income generally, not just net income. In almost all "reasonable expectation of profit" (REOP) cases dealing with rental properties, it has been the deduction for interest that has created the losses. Other Supreme Court decisions have found that the REOP test should not be an issue where it is evident that a loss does not have a personal or non-business element.

Based on the results of these cases, the Department of Finance introduced reasonable-expectation-of-profit rules (see article 160). These rules are still in draft form and it's not known if they will ever be finalized in their current form. However, if they are enacted as proposed, careful planning will be required to support the deductibility of losses. You should also exercise caution before acquiring any new investment where the reasonable expectation of profit may be in doubt.

Terminal loss restrictions

There are special rules that may reduce a terminal loss for tax purposes. If the building was sold together with the underlying land, the transaction is treated as if you sold two separate items. If the portion of the sale price attributed to the building is less than its undepreciated cost, you may be required to increase the portion allocated to the building and reduce the portion allocated to the land. This will result in a reduced terminal loss on the building.

These rules apply to only depreciable buildings and do not apply to a real estate developer who is holding real estate as inventory.

144 What About Capital Gains?

A capital gain occurs when you sell a capital property for more than its original cost. In general, half the gain is included in your income for the year. The other half is not subject to tax. Certain dispositions resulting in a capital gain are not subject to any tax (see article 91).

When is a gain a capital gain?

In most circumstances, there is no set rule that determines whether a particular gain should be treated as a capital gain. Most individuals who invest in the stock market can treat their gains and losses as capital gains or losses. However, if you spend considerable time playing the market and/or borrow money to make your purchases, your profits or losses may be taxed in full as business income.

Similarly, if you bought a property intentionally to resell at a profit, the entire gain would be taxable, rather than just half the gain. For example, taxpayers who purchase property for immediate resale—"flipping"—are subject to tax on the full gain, even though they may have spent little time on the venture and may have sold only one or two properties. In some cases, there is no clear-cut answer. If in doubt, consult your tax adviser.

TAX TIP

Most taxpayers are eligible to elect capital gains treatment from the disposition of qualifying Canadian securities by filing Form T123. Once you make the election, however, all subsequent gains and losses from the disposition of qualifying securities will be recorded as capital gains and losses. Be sure you understand the implications of making this election before you file the form.

Identical properties

Subject to the special rules for stock option shares (see the following subsection), when you acquire securities that are exactly the same—for example, Class A common shares of XYC Corp.—the shares are pooled for purposes of determining your cost when you sell a portion of the shares.

EXAMPLE: **Calculating the cost base**

Assume you buy 100 shares today for $20 each (total cost $2,000) and 50 shares next month for $26 each (total cost $1,300). Your cost per share for tax purposes is $22 (150 shares at a total cost of $3,300). If you then sell 75 shares for $30 each, your capital gain is $600 [($30 – $22) × 75 shares].

There are special rules if you own identical properties, some of which were acquired before 1972. In this case, two separate pools will determine the cost of the properties sold: one comprising the pre-1972 properties and the other for properties acquired after 1971. On a disposition, you will be deemed to have sold the pre-1972 properties before those acquired after 1971.

Sale of stock option shares

The cost base of shares acquired through stock option plans equals the sum of the option price plus the amount of the taxable employment benefit. The amount of a deferred stock option benefit (see article 42) is added to the cost base of the stock option share at the time the share is acquired, even though the amount is not taxed until the share is disposed of.

But what happens if you acquire shares under a company stock option plan and you already own other identical shares in the company, or if you exercise more than one stock option at the same time? If you sell only some of the shares, how do you calculate the tax cost of the shares sold? The rules in this area are extremely complex. Special rules deem the order in which the shares are disposed of. In addition, in certain cases, a special designation may be available that permits you to designate the new stock option shares as the shares being sold, provided they are sold within 30 days of exercising the option.

TAX TIP

Before selling or otherwise disposing of shares acquired under a stock option plan, consult your tax adviser to determine the tax consequences and whether you qualify for the special designation.

145 Lifetime Capital Gains Deduction

In 1985, every Canadian became eligible for a limited lifetime capital gains deduction. In 1994, it was eliminated for dispositions of property after February 22, 1994, except for gains realized on the disposition of qualified small-business corporation shares (see article 146) and qualified farm property (see article 147). In 2006, the capital gains deduction was extended to dispositions of qualified fishing property (see article 148).

$100,000 capital gains deduction

When the $100,000 capital gains deduction for other property was eliminated in 1994, everyone was permitted to make a special one-time-only capital gains election. In most cases, this election had to be made on your 1994 tax return. The election allowed you to opt to have a deemed disposition of any capital property you owned on February 22, 1994, at any amount up to its fair market value on that day.

In most cases, the amount you elected as a deemed disposition became your new cost base. The election was made by filing Form T664 with your 1994 income tax return.

TAX TIP

If you still own property for which a capital gains election was made, you should continue to monitor the revised cost base to ensure it is taken into consideration on a subsequent sale of the property.

146 Qualified Small-Business Corporations Capital Gains Deduction

Shares of a qualified small-business corporation (QSBC) continue to qualify for an enhanced capital gains deduction. For dispositions prior to March 19, 2007, the maximum lifetime capital gains deduction was $500,000. However, for dispositions after March 18, 2007, the maximum lifetime deduction increased to $750,000. For eligibility as a QSBC, a company must be a Canadian-controlled private corporation and at least 90% of its assets must be used in an active business in Canada. There are additional conditions that must be met for up to two years before the sale. Further complications may arise where there are investments in related companies.

Each individual is entitled to a lifetime cumulative capital gains deduction of $750,000. As a result, the maximum capital gains deduction available on the disposition of QSBC shares will be reduced by the amount of QSBC or other capital gains deductions previously claimed on any property.

EXAMPLE/**Capital gains deduction at work**

> Let's assume that on your 1994 tax return you elected to have a deemed disposition of shares of public companies and claimed a capital gains deduction of $100,000 (see article 145). In July 2009, you realize an $800,000 capital gain on the sale of shares of a qualified small-business corporation. You are entitled to only a $650,000 capital gains deduction in 2009 because you used $100,000 of your $750,000 lifetime capital gains deduction in 1994. However, if you had previously claimed only a $60,000 capital gains deduction, you would be entitled to a $690,000 capital gains deduction in 2009.

The amount of capital gain that is eligible for the capital gains deduction may be affected by the balance in your CNIL account (see article 159) and if you have ever claimed an ABIL (see article 152).

Although the $750,000 deduction continues to be available, it may be appropriate to consider various tax-planning techniques that can be used to obtain the deduction. The end result of most of these planning strategies will be to increase the cost base of your shares for purposes of a future sale or deemed disposition. Professional tax advice on these matters is essential.

TAX TIP

For a company to qualify as a QSBC at the time of a future sale, it may be necessary to take steps now to remove from the company non-active business assets, such as excess cash or portfolio investments. This can be as easy as having the company use its excess cash to pay off debts or pay dividends to its shareholders, or it may involve a corporate reorganization to transfer the non-active assets into a separate company.

Election for private companies going public

Shares of a public corporation do not qualify for the enhanced capital gains deduction. However, if you own shares in a small-business corporation that is about to go public, you can make an election to be treated as having disposed of all the shares of a class of the capital stock of the small-business corporation immediately before it becomes a public corporation. The amount you can elect as the deemed proceeds of disposition can be anywhere between the cost and fair market value of the shares. The shares are deemed to be reacquired for the same amount. By doing so, you increase the adjusted cost base of the shares, and reduce the amount of any future gain on those shares when they are ultimately disposed of.

147 Qualified Farm Property Capital Gains Deduction

Qualified farm property is also eligible for the enhanced $750,000 capital gains deduction. Similar to the disposition of QSBC shares, the capital gains deduction available on the disposition of qualified farm property will be reduced by the amount of capital gains deductions claimed on other property. The amount of gain eligible for this deduction may be affected by the balance in your CNIL account (see article 159), and if you have ever claimed an ABIL (see article 152).

What qualifies?

In general, if you acquired certain property before June 18, 1987, and it was used in the business of farming by you or a member of your family, it will be qualified farm property, provided the property was used for farming in the year you sell it or in any five previous years during which you or a member of your family owned it.

If you acquired the property after June 17, 1987, you must normally have owned it for at least two years, been engaged in farming on a regular and continuous basis, and earned more gross income from farming than from other sources. Similar rules also apply to allow the deduction to be claimed for gains realized on the sale of shares of a family farm corporation and on an interest in a family farm partnership.

However, if you made a capital gains election (see article 145) on property that would otherwise be considered qualified farm property, the qualifying tests may be different than outlined above. Discuss this with your tax adviser.

TAX TIP

Professional advice from your tax adviser is recommended to determine if you are eligible for the enhanced capital gains deduction on the disposition of your farm property or property that was formerly used in farming.

148 Qualified Fishing Property Capital Gains Deduction

Qualified fishing property is also eligible for the enhanced $750,000 capital gains deduction. Similar to the rules for farm property and small-business shares, the available capital gains deduction will be reduced by the amount of capital gains deductions claimed on other property. In addition, the amount of gain eligible for this deduction may be affected by the balance in your CNIL account (see article 159) and if you have ever claimed an ABIL (see article 152).

What qualifies?

Only dispositions of qualified fishing property that take place after May 1, 2006, qualify for this deduction. Qualified fishing property includes real property, fishing vessels and eligible capital property used principally in a fishing business carried on in Canada in which the individual, or the individual's spouse or common-law partner, parent, child or grandchild, was actively engaged on a regular and continuous basis. It also includes shares of the capital stock of family fishing corporations and interests in family fishing partnerships. The definitions are generally similar to those used for purposes of the enhanced capital gains deduction for farmers.

149 Capital Gains Deferral for Investments in Small Businesses

To increase the availability of equity capital for small-business corporations, individuals can defer tax on the capital gain if the proceeds from the disposition of a qualified small-business investment are reinvested in another eligible small-business investment. Eligible investments are newly issued common shares in a small-business corporation with assets not exceeding $50 million after the investment.

To qualify, the proceeds must be reinvested in the eligible small business within 120 days after the end of the year.

The cost base of the new investment is reduced by the capital gain deferred.

EXAMPLE/**Deferring the capital gain**

On April 30, 2009, you sell shares of an eligible small-business investment for $200,000 and realize a capital gain of $160,000. On July 1, 2009, you invest $180,000 of the proceeds to acquire common shares of another eligible business investment. The capital gain that can be deferred is $144,000 [($180,000 ÷ $200,000) × $160,000].

Capital gain for 2009	$160,000
Minus deferred gain	($144,000)
Net gain for 2009	$16,000
Cost of new investment	
Amount invested	$180,000
Minus deferred gain	($144,000)
Revised cost base	$36,000

If you sell this new investment for $320,000 in 2012, you will report a capital gain of $284,000 ($320,000 – $36,000) at that time.

150 Capital Gains Reserves

When you sell capital property, such as real estate or shares in a corporation, and the proceeds from the sale will not all be receivable in the year of sale, you can defer a portion of the capital gain by claiming a reserve.

The rules provide that at least one-fifth of your taxable capital gain must be reported in the year of sale and each of the four following years. An exception is provided if you transfer certain farm property, fishing property or shares in a small-business corporation to your children. In these cases, you can claim a reserve over a maximum 10-year period. Reserves deducted from income in one year must be added to income in the subsequent year.

TAX TIP

Claiming a reserve is optional—any amount up to the maximum allowed can be claimed. To make a claim, you must file Form T2017 with your income tax return.

Special rules

Capital gains reserves included in income will be eligible for the capital gains deduction if the property is a share of a qualified small-business corporation, a qualified farm property or a qualified fishing property (see articles 146, 147 and 148). Special rules ensure that reserves are adjusted for changes in the capital gains inclusion rate.

Should you decide to report all of the capital gain and claim the offsetting capital gains deduction even though a reserve is available, take care to ensure you are not caught by the alternative minimum tax (AMT) (see article 168) or the CNIL rules (see article 159).

TAX TIP

In structuring the sale of property, make sure you have sufficient funds to pay the taxes required. If proceeds are deferred over a long period, the tax may be due before the proceeds are received. Suppose you sell real estate for a significant capital gain in 2009 and the proceeds are due over the next 10 years. The taxes arising on the capital gain must be paid in full by 2013, even though all proceeds will not be received until 2018.

151 Capital Loss Rules

Generally, capital losses are deductible only against capital gains. However, there are cases where unused allowable capital losses realized prior to May 23, 1985, can be claimed against other sources of income at the rate of $2,000 per year. After that date, capital losses can be claimed only against capital gains. Capital losses can be carried back for up to three years and forward indefinitely.

TAX TIP

Many investors have reported recent capital losses. If you realized a capital loss in the past few years, but realized a capital gain in any of the three prior years, determine if it's to your advantage to carry back the loss to offset the gain. This will depend on your marginal tax bracket in the year of the gain as well as your expected future tax bracket and your ability to use the loss in the future. In most cases, it makes sense to benefit from the loss as soon as possible.

There are also special rules that will deny a capital loss in certain situations. For example, if you transfer a property with an accrued loss to an "affiliated person," the loss will be denied. In general, you are affiliated with yourself and your spouse or common-law partner and with a corporation that you control, or you and your spouse or common-law partner control—but not with your children.

TAX TIP

It may be possible to use these loss-denial rules to transfer accrued losses to affiliated persons with accrued gains. Contact your tax adviser if this situation applies to you.

Similar rules will deny the loss if you sell investments with an accrued loss and the property or an identical property is acquired by you or your spouse or common-law partner within the period beginning 30 days before and ending 30 days after the disposition, and it is still owned 30 days after the disposition.

Rules are also in effect to adjust prior years' capital loss carry-forwards for changes in the capital gains inclusion rate.

Unused capital losses from prior years may be claimed in the year of death or the immediately preceding year. Available capital losses must first be used to reduce capital gains in those years. Any remaining capital losses may then be deducted from other sources of income, subject to a restriction based on the total capital gains deduction that has been claimed over the years. As these special rules on the deductibility of capital losses for deceased persons are quite complex, consult your tax adviser for further details.

TAX TIP

If you realized a capital gain in the current year, consider selling investments with accrued losses before the end of the year. Keep in mind that transactions involving publicly traded securities take place on the settlement date, which is generally three days after the trading date in the case of Canadian stock exchanges.

TAX TIP

Don't sell your losers to your RRSP. Losses arising on the sale of capital property to an RRSP will be denied. You would be better off selling the investment to an unrelated party and making a cash contribution to your plan. These stop-loss rules will also apply if you sell investments at a loss and your self-administered RRSP subsequently acquires the same or identical shares within 30 days before or after the disposition.

152 Business Investment Losses

If you realize a capital loss on the disposition of shares or debt of a small-business corporation, you may be eligible to treat the loss as a business investment loss. Half this loss can be applied against your income from other sources (not just capital gains).

Meeting the conditions

Specific conditions must be met before a capital loss can be classified as a business investment loss. First, the shares or debt must be of a small-business corporation. Consult your tax adviser to determine if the corporation qualifies. Second, if the loss results from an actual sale, you must have sold the shares or debt to a taxpayer who is not related to you. Third, if the debt is established to be a bad debt, you may recognize the loss even though a sale has not taken place (regardless of whether you are related to the corporation).

Similarly, if shares of a small-business corporation are worthless, any capital loss incurred may qualify as a business investment loss. Your loss will be recognized, if you so elect, by filing a statement with your tax return and if the following criteria are met:

- At the end of the year in which the loss is claimed, the company has to be insolvent and not carrying on any business (including a business carried on by any company it controls).

- The fair market value of the share must be nil, and it must be reasonable to assume the company will not start carrying on a business and will be dissolved or wound up.

If you claim the loss and the company (or another company that it controls) begins to carry on a business within two years from the end of the year in which the loss was claimed, you have to report a corresponding capital gain in the year the business commences.

Restrictions on ABILs

Following the introduction of the lifetime capital gains deduction, rules were introduced to prevent you from claiming the deduction as well as benefiting from an ABIL. As a result, you will not be able to claim the capital gains deduction to the extent of ABILs claimed in 1985 or later.

It's a similar situation if you have claimed the capital gains deduction on a disposition or as a result of the capital gains election and you realize what would otherwise be an ABIL in a subsequent year. The loss will be treated as a regular capital loss to the extent of your previously claimed capital gains deduction.

TAX TIP

If you have loaned money to a small-business corporation and the debt is not collectible, consider whether you have incurred an ABIL. It is important that you determine the time at which the amount becomes uncollectible.

153 Taxation of Dividends

When you receive a dividend from a Canadian corporation, the amount you report on your return is not the amount you received—it's more. But this actually works to your advantage. The rules are further complicated by the fact that there are now two separate tax rates that can be applied to taxable dividends, depending on whether it is an "eligible" dividend or other dividend (hereafter referred to as an "ineligible" dividend). Capital dividends, on the other hand, are not subject to tax at all (see article 28).

Eligible-dividend rules

These rules apply to certain dividends paid after 2005 by corporations resident in Canada to individual shareholders resident in

Canada. To qualify as an eligible dividend, the dividend must be designated as such at the time it is paid. These rules are discussed more fully below.

How the new rules affect individuals

The tax treatment of dividend income received by an individual (which includes a trust) depends on whether the dividend has been designated as an eligible dividend by the corporation that paid it. Dividends designated as eligible dividends are subject to a dividend gross-up of 45% and a federal dividend tax credit equal to 27.5% of the actual dividend.

Taxable dividends from Canadian resident corporations that are not designated as eligible dividends are ineligible (or regular) dividends. These dividends are subject to a 25% dividend gross-up and a federal dividend tax credit equal to 16.667% of the actual dividend. The provinces all have their own dividend tax credit rates (see Table 2, page 287 for a comparison of the top marginal eligible and ineligible dividend rates by province).

EXAMPLE/**Taxation of eligible dividends**

> You receive a $1,000 dividend from BCE Inc. in 2009 that is designated as an eligible dividend. You will include $1,450 in your income and receive a deduction from your federal income tax equal to $275 (i.e., 27.5% × $1,000). Your provincial tax liability will be based on the dividend tax credit rate for your province of residence.

EXAMPLE/**Taxation of ineligible dividends**

> You receive a $1,000 dividend from your corporation (a CCPC) and the dividend is not designated as an eligible dividend. You will include $1,250 in your income (25% gross-up) and $166.67 (i.e., 16.667% of $1,000) will be deducted from your federal taxes payable as a dividend tax credit. Again, each province has a similar mechanism to offset provincial income taxes.

As a result of the dividend gross-up and tax credit mechanism, dividends are taxed more favourably than most other types of income (except for capital gains). In some provinces, eligible dividends are taxed at an even lower rate than capital gains (see Table 2, page 287).

Dividends received from a foreign corporation are not subject to the gross-up and dividend tax credit mechanisms. Therefore, you will pay a higher rate of tax on dividends from a foreign corporation.

How the eligible dividend rules affect corporations

A corporation's ability to pay an eligible dividend depends on its status. A Canadian-controlled private corporation (CCPC) can pay an eligible dividend only to the extent that it has a balance in its "general rate income pool" (GRIP) at the end of the taxation year in which the dividend is paid. Although the actual formula is quite complex, the GRIP generally reflects taxable income that has not benefited from preferential tax rates, such as the small-business rate, or from refundable dividend tax treatment afforded to investment income earned by a Canadian-controlled private corporation. There is an exception for public company dividends that have been designated as eligible dividends. Such dividends retain their status as eligible dividends when they pass through a private corporation.

A non-CCPC that is resident in Canada can pay eligible dividends without restriction, unless it has a balance in its "low rate income pool" (LRIP) at the time the dividend is paid. The LRIP is generally made up of taxable income that has benefited from the small-business deduction, either in the hands of the dividend-paying non-CCPC itself (at a time when it was a CCPC) or in the hands of a CCPC that paid an ineligible dividend to the non-CCPC. Many non-CCPCs will never have an LRIP, and thus will be able to designate all of their dividends as eligible dividends. However, if a non-CCPC does have an LRIP balance, it must reduce the LRIP through the payment of ineligible dividends before it can pay an eligible dividend.

A special rule may give an existing CCPC a starting GRIP balance at January 1, 2006. In general, this rule provides for an addition to the GRIP that is intended to approximate the after-tax corporate earnings for the 2001 to 2005 taxation years that have not benefited from preferential tax treatment (such as the small-business deduction—see article 27) and that have not been paid out by the corporation as taxable dividends during those taxation years. For example, a CCPC earning active business income that has not always bonused down to the small-business limit may have a GRIP balance as at January 1, 2006. A CCPC that is a pure investment corporation (i.e., has earned income from passive investments) or that has always bonused down to the small-business limit will not have an addition to GRIP under this provision.

TAX TIP

If you are the owner-manager of a CCPC and you want to pay a dividend from the company, consult with your tax adviser to determine if it should be designated as an eligible dividend. If you wait until after the dividend is paid, it is too late to designate it as an eligible dividend.

As noted above, for a taxable dividend to be an eligible dividend, it must be designated as such by the corporation paying the taxable dividend. The rules provide that this designation must be made in writing at the time the dividend is paid. For the 2006 year, the CRA indicated that an eligible-dividend designation would be valid if it was identified as such on the T3 or T5 slip for the 2006 tax year. However, for 2007 and subsequent years, more formal notice is required at the time the dividend is paid. For private corporations, proper notice will include (1) a letter to the shareholders; (2) a notation on dividend cheque stubs; or (3) in cases where all shareholders are directors, a notation in the corporate minutes. The notification procedure for public corporations is more simplified. Before or at the time the dividend is paid, the corporation needs only to make a designation stating that all dividends are eligible dividends unless indicated otherwise. This designation can generally be found on the corporation's website (under Investor Services).

If a corporation makes a designation for eligible dividends that exceeds its capacity, the corporation will be subject to a penalty tax. However, there are special rules that may allow the corporation to retroactively undo all or part of an excessive designation by making an election to treat the excess eligible dividend as being a taxable dividend.

TAX TIP

If you have no other sources of income, you can receive a significant amount of Canadian dividend income and pay little or no tax. The amount will vary depending on your province of residence at the end of the year and whether the dividend is an eligible or an ineligible dividend. Note, however, that Alternative Minimum Tax (see article 168) may apply—in particular, on the receipt of eligible dividends.

TAX TIP

If you are a shareholder of a Canadian-controlled private corporation (CCPC), you should contact your tax adviser to determine if any planning or restructuring needs to be undertaken to benefit from the eligible dividend rules.

Foreign spinoffs

If you receive shares of a foreign corporation from another foreign corporation as part of a "spinoff" transaction, you may have to report foreign-source dividend income.

However, if the transaction was not a taxable transaction in the U.S., you may be able to make a special election that will allow you to avoid being taxed on the foreign-source dividend. You can elect to take advantage of the deferral by including a letter with your tax return for the year in which the distribution occurs. This return must be paper-filed with the CRA. Also, under the taxpayer relief provisions (see article 177), a taxpayer is allowed to late-file certain prescribed tax elections. The foreign spinoff election can be late-filed under this provision.

To qualify for the deferral, shares must be distributed by an actively held and widely traded U.S. public corporation. In addition, U.S. tax law must provide for a tax deferral to the distributing corporation and its U.S. resident shareholders.

If the election is made, there is a cost-base adjustment to the original and spinoff shares based on their relative fair market values, as illustrated in the following example.

EXAMPLE/**Cost base adjustment**

Assume you own one original common share of AB Inc. (resident in the U.S.). AB Inc. distributes a spinoff share of CD Inc. (also resident in the U.S.) on a per-share basis to the holders of the common shares of AB Inc.

The cost amount of your original share in AB Inc. is $10 immediately before the distribution, and its fair market value immediately after the distribution is $70. The fair market value of your CD Inc. spinoff share is $30 immediately after the distribution. The cost base of the original share ($10) must be reallocated to the original and spinoff shares as follows:

Original share	$10 × ($70 ÷ $100) = $7
Spinoff share	$10 × ($30 ÷ $100) = $3

Any gain or loss on a later sale of the original or spinoff shares would be the difference between the $7 or $3 calculated above and the net sale proceeds.

TAX TIP

If you receive or have received shares of a foreign corporation as part of a share restructuring, you might qualify for a tax deferral or tax refund under these rules. You should contact your tax adviser to determine if you qualify and to assist you in making the special election.

154 Transfer of Dividend Income Between Spouses

If your spouse or common-law partner has little or no income except for taxable dividends from Canadian corporations, you may reduce your family's tax bill by including his or her dividends in your income.

This can be accomplished only if, by doing so, you are able to increase the claim you make for your spouse or common-law partner as a dependant. In effect, you delete the dividends from his or her income and include them in yours, entitling you to claim the dividend tax credit. The election must apply to all your spouse or common-law partner's dividends from taxable Canadian corporations—you cannot pick and choose to maximize tax savings.

155 Taxation of Interest Income

With the exception of certain investments made before 1990, you are required to report interest on investments on an annual basis, regardless of when the interest is actually paid. Similar rules apply to certain life insurance policies and annuity contracts. For investments purchased before 1990, you have the option of reporting interest income on either an annual or three-year accrual basis. Once you opt to report annually, however, you must continue to use that method of reporting in subsequent years.

You are also required to calculate the interest on debt where the value of, and/or the return on, the investment is adjusted for inflation and/or deflation. If you own such a security, you will have to report an amount annually as interest income.

TAX TIP

Do you own investments that earn significant interest income? There may be valid reasons for you to consider transferring them to a holding company—for example, income splitting and estate planning. Proper planning is needed to ensure that the effects of the income attribution rules are minimized. Your tax adviser can assist you with this and best assess if it's worth your while.

Canada Savings Bonds

There are two different types of Canada Savings Bonds (CSBs): regular and compound interest. With regular bonds, you will receive and report the interest each year. Compound bonds, however, are something else entirely. If you own compound bonds, you will not receive the interest until the bond matures or is cashed in. Nevertheless, the interest must still be reported annually. The government will provide you with an information slip indicating the amount of income to be reported.

TAX TIP

When you purchase Canada Savings Bonds with a loan that is repaid through a payroll deduction plan, any interest you pay on the loan is tax deductible.

Treasury bills

In general, the difference between the purchase cost and the selling price of Treasury bills is deemed to be interest. A capital gain is realized only if market interest rates drop and the Treasury bills are sold before maturity. In such situations, the capital gain equals the selling price minus the purchase cost plus accrued interest up to the date of disposition. Conversely, a capital loss will arise if interest rates increase and the Treasury bills are sold before maturity.

156 Mutual Funds

Mutual funds are pools of assets that are invested by professional managers, either in general investments or in a particular sector.

Some mutual funds pay dividends but may designate all or a portion of the dividends as capital gains dividends to reflect capital gains earned by the mutual fund. Such dividends are treated as capital gains and, for income tax purposes, are generally subject to the usual treatment of capital gains.

If you sell or redeem mutual fund units, you have to recognize a capital gain or loss, depending on the circumstances. As mutual fund units are identical properties, a new tax cost calculation has to be made each time other units are purchased or distributions are reinvested.

Most mutual funds allocate their income to registered owners as of December 31 of the particular year. Therefore, if you invest in a fund at the end of the year, you may receive an income information slip showing income that has to be reported for tax purposes even if you have owned the fund units for only a few days.

Special rules apply if a capital gains election was made on a mutual fund (see article 145). The elected capital gain did not increase the cost base of the mutual fund. Instead, a special tax account, called an exempt capital gains balance, was created. The balance in this account could have been used to offset future capital gains designated by the fund, as well as any gain on an actual disposition of the mutual fund units. Any balance remaining in this tax account at the end of 2004 should have been added to the cost base of the fund.

EXAMPLE/**Capital gains in action**

Let's say you made a $12,000 capital gains election in 1994 on your XYZ mutual fund. From 1995 to 2004, the fund allocated to you a total of $9,500 in capital gains.

Assuming you used the $12,000 exempt capital gains balance created in 1994 to offset these gains, you would have had a remaining balance of $2,500 in the pool at the end of 2004. This amount would be added to increase the cost base of any remaining units you held in the mutual fund. For example, if you had still owned 600 units with a cost base of $8,000 at the end of 2004, the cost of the units for tax purposes would have increased to $10,500 (or $17.50 per unit). This will have the effect of reducing any capital gain or increasing any capital loss on a future disposition of the units.

TAX TIP

If you made a capital gains election on a mutual fund that you have since disposed of, you should review your tax return to determine if there was any remaining exempt capital gains balance at the time of disposition. Any unused balance in the account at that time should have been added to the adjusted cost base of those interests or shares. If this was not done, you should request an adjustment to the capital gain or capital loss that was reported. Such an adjustment can be made for any of the 10 preceding calendar years (see article 177). Discuss the potential adjustment and tax savings with your tax adviser.

Segregated funds

Segregated funds are actually insurance contracts with two components: an investment that produces the return and an insurance contract that covers the risk. Like mutual funds, these funds are managed by investment professionals and cover a wide variety of asset categories. However, they also provide some benefits that are not available in a mutual fund. For example, segregated funds guarantee either 75% or 100% of your principal. A small part of the fund's assets goes to ensure there will be enough cash to pay that guarantee. They also offer protection from creditors if certain conditions are met. This can be a benefit if you are a sole proprietor or in partnership and want to save for your retirement without putting those funds at risk. Finally, like all insurance contracts, they allow you to name a beneficiary. This means that after your death, the fund proceeds can be paid to the beneficiary without having to go through probate.

157 Income Trusts and Real Estate Investment Trusts (REITs)

Every year, in addition to a share of the income earned, this type of trust distributes part of the capital to its unitholders. For this reason, the amount distributed to you is not the same as the amount on which you have to pay tax. Each capital distribution reduces the tax cost of the units, which generally results in a capital gain when the units are sold.

EXAMPLE/**Cost reduction**

You hold income trust units with a value of $10 each and an annual distribution of $1 per unit. This distribution is made up of

> taxable income of $0.20 and a non-taxable return on capital of $0.80, which reduces the tax cost of the investment. In five years of distributions, each unit will yield $1 of taxable income and $4 in non-taxable return of capital. The tax cost of the holding is now $6 ($10 – $4). If you sell your units for the purchase price of $10, you will have a capital gain of $4 ($10 – $6).

Over the past few years, these types of investments have increased in popularity. Since the income is flowed through to the unitholders, such that the trust pays no tax, they are more tax effective than corporate investments, which incur two levels of taxation—one at the corporate level, and again when the income is distributed to the shareholders. In an attempt to bring the taxation of corporations more in line with income trusts and other flow-through entities, the "eligible-dividend rules" (see article 153) were introduced to reduce the effective personal tax rate on large-corporation dividends. However, it was felt that these rules still did not go far enough to eliminate the tax advantage of income trusts, particularly in the case of non-resident investors and tax-exempt entities (such as pension plans).

As a result, the government introduced additional rules to essentially tax publicly traded income trusts and limited partnerships otherwise known as specified investment flow-through (SIFT) trusts or partnerships as though they were corporations. The main change was the introduction of a new distribution tax on certain income distributions from an income trust. This rate, which is intended to approximate the combined federal and provincial tax rate that applies to corporations, comprises two components: (1) a factor that is tied to the general federal corporate tax rate (19% for 2009); and (2) a provincial component, originally set at a 13% notional provincial tax rate that would apply across all provinces. This notional rate created problems for income trusts in provinces with a general provincial tax rate lower than 13%, and planning opportunities for provinces with a higher provincial rate. As a result, beginning with the 2009 tax year, the 13% rate will be replaced by the general provincial corporate income tax rate for the province in which the trust carries out its business. Similar rules will apply to publicly traded limited partnerships. Based on current and proposed rate reductions, the federal component of the distribution tax is 19% for 2009, 18% for 2010, 16.5% for 2011 and 15% for 2012 and subsequent taxation years.

For income trusts and limited partnerships that began to be publicly traded after October 2006, these rules are effective for the 2007 and subsequent taxation years. For existing trusts and limited partnerships that were publicly traded before November 1, 2006, the rules will not apply until the entity's 2011 taxation year. There are special rules that clarify how much an existing income trust can grow over the four-year period without forfeiting its "grandfathered" status.

In general, real estate investment trusts (REITs) that hold real properties situated in Canada are excluded from these new rules and will not be subject to the special distribution tax.

Draft legislation released in 2008 included new tax rules that will allow a SIFT trust or partnership to convert to a corporate structure on a tax-free or tax-deferred basis, at both the unitholder and entity levels. Subject to meeting a number of conditions, unit holders will be able to transfer their units to a taxable Canadian corporation on a tax-deferred basis automatically (as opposed to filing an election) in exchange for shares of that corporation. While these continue to be draft proposals, if enacted, they will likely have a significant impact on investors who would otherwise be subject to the SIFT tax on distributions from such entities.

158 Investment Holding Companies

The tax system contains special rules that are intended to eliminate any preference for earning income in a corporation as opposed to personally. Some of these are designed to ensure that the after-tax return on income realized through a corporation and subsequently distributed to the shareholder is roughly the same as if the shareholder had received the income from the investments directly (see article 26). One of the main objectives behind the introduction of the eligible dividend rules (see article 153) was to improve this system of integration.

Nevertheless, there may still be some situations where you might want to use a company to hold your investments. For example, individuals eligible for OAS benefits whose personal income (excluding investment income) is $66,335 or less (see article 80) may come out ahead by holding their investments in a corporation. Investment holding corporations can also be used to implement an estate freeze (see article 140).

Every situation is unique and requires a separate analysis. Your tax adviser can assist you in determining whether this strategy is suitable for your particular situation.

TAX TIP

A regular review of your tax situation, including an annual look at your portfolio, is the best way to determine the most advantageous structure in light of any tax rate adjustments, new legislation and changes to your business.

TAX TIP

The eligible dividend rules (see article 153) may affect a decision to hold your investments in a corporation. If you already have an investment holding company, you should contact your tax adviser to determine if any restructuring might be needed.

159 Cumulative Net Investment Loss (CNIL) Rules

The cumulative net investment loss (CNIL) rules are intended to prevent individuals from reducing their income by claiming investment losses, such as rental losses, interest expense and other carrying charges, and subsequently recouping the losses by selling the underlying investment and then not paying any tax on the resulting gain by using the capital gains deduction. With the elimination of the $100,000 capital gains deduction on other property, your CNIL is relevant only if you have a gain from the disposition of qualified farming or fishing property or a share of a qualified small-business corporation.

What is a CNIL?

Your CNIL account is the cumulative excess of your investment expenses over your investment income. Investment expenses include losses from rental property, non-active partnership losses (such as tax shelters), interest on money borrowed for investments and 50% of resource-related deductions.

Investment income includes all income from property (including rental income, interest income and dividends), non-active partnership income and 50% of the recovery of resource-related deductions. Investment income does not include taxable capital gains, although capital gains that cannot be sheltered by the capital gains deduction reduce the impact of the CNIL account.

Since the CNIL account is a cumulative account (for 1988 and subsequent years), it is recommended that you keep a running total each year even if you are not claiming a capital gains deduction in the year. In general, you will be able to claim the capital gains deduction only to the extent that your taxable capital gain for the given year exceeds the amount of your CNIL.

TAX TIP

If you are an owner-manager of a corporation and have a CNIL problem, you should consider receiving enough interest or dividend income from your corporation to eliminate the balance in your CNIL account.

160 Deductibility of Interest Expense

Interest expense is deductible for income tax purposes if the borrowed funds are used to earn income and certain other conditions are met. Over the years, the CRA has allowed interest as a deduction even though it may not be deductible from a strictly technical point of view—for instance, if a company borrows funds to pay a dividend rather than using its own funds. However, following the 1987 Supreme Court decision in the *Bronfman Trust* case, considerable uncertainty developed as to whether interest would continue to be deductible under these circumstances.

When is interest deductible?

To try to resolve this problem, the government introduced draft legislation in 1991 on the deductibility of interest expense. This legislation proposed to deal with numerous situations where the deductibility of interest might be unclear—for example, where borrowed money is used on behalf of corporations and partnerships to distribute retained earnings or capital.

This legislation was never passed and the CRA continued to assess based on the following criteria: Interest will generally be deductible if the funds are borrowed to pay dividends or redeem shares, provided the amount of the dividend or redemption does not exceed the accumulated profits of the company. In addition, funds borrowed by individual shareholders to loan to their corporation at no or low interest will continue to be deductible, provided the company uses the funds to earn income, no unfair advantage is derived and the company is unable to obtain the same terms of financing from a third party without the guarantee of the individual.

Recent court cases

Over the past few years, several Supreme Court cases have addressed the issue of the deductibility of interest.

In *The Queen v. Singleton*, the taxpayer (a partner in a law firm) withdrew funds from his capital account in the firm to finance the purchase of a house. The same day, he borrowed money to replace the funds in his capital account. The Minister of Revenue attempted to deny the interest deduction on the grounds that the borrowed money was used to finance the house, not as a business investment. The Supreme Court determined that the interest on the borrowed funds was deductible. A direct link could be drawn between the borrowed money and an eligible use—i.e., the taxpayer had used the borrowed funds for the purpose of refinancing his partnership capital account with debt.

Lipson v. The Queen was another case in which the taxpayers entered into a series of transactions designed to make their mortgage interest deductible. Mrs. Lipson borrowed money from a bank to buy shares in her husband's investment company. The husband then used the money received from his wife to buy the family home. The next day, the taxpayers used the family home as collateral for a loan which was then used to repay the money that the wife had borrowed from the bank. The end result of the series of transactions was that the dividend income from the shares acquired by the wife was attributed back to the husband. However, the amount attributed was net of the interest expense paid on the secured loan. In 2006, the Tax Court of Canada found that the general anti-avoidance rule (GAAR) applied to a series of transactions designed to make mortgage interest deductible. The Federal Court of Appeal agreed with the Tax Court's decision. The taxpayers appealed to the Supreme Court. Tax planners eagerly awaited the decision in this case, since it had caused them to reconsider Singleton-like strategies undertaken to make mortgage interest deductible. Early in 2009, the Supreme Court finally rendered its decision in this case. Although the Supreme Court found that the interest deductibility rules in the Act had not been misused or abused, it nevertheless found that the GAAR applied to the series of transactions. The series became problematic when Mr. Lipson and his wife tried to use the attribution rules to allow Mr. Lipson to apply his wife's interest deduction to offset his own income.

Therefore, Singleton-like financing arrangements are not abusive.

You can arrange your affairs such that capital is used to purchase personal assets and borrowed funds are used to purchase income-producing assets to deduct the interest on the borrowed funds for tax purposes. The series of transactions in *Lipson* amounted to abusive tax avoidance only when the plan coupled interest deductibility with the attribution rules. The use of the attribution rules permitted the husband to deduct the interest expense to reduce the tax payable on the dividend income from the shares and other income, something he could not have done if his wife was dealing with him at arm's length. It was this result from the series of transactions that constituted abusive tax avoidance. The end result was that the interest continued to be deductible, but in the wife's hands.

Ludco Enterprises Ltd. v. The Queen was another significant Supreme Court case dealing with the deductibility of interest. Here, the taxpayers borrowed funds to acquire common shares in offshore corporations. In the eight years they held the shares, the shareholders received approximately $600,000 in dividends and incurred approximately $6 million in interest charges. After several years, the taxpayers disposed of their shares and reported substantial capital gains.

Although the deductibility of interest with respect to funds used to acquire common shares is generally not an issue, the taxpayers were not allowed to deduct their interest expense. The government took the position that the borrowed funds had not been used to earn income from a business or property and that the taxpayers had no reasonable expectation of profit from the dividend payments. The real purpose of the investment was to realize a capital gain on their investment. This case raised concerns about interest deductibility with respect to borrowings for common shares and other growth investments.

Significantly, the Supreme Court determined that the interest was deductible on the basis that it had been incurred to earn "income." In determining what was meant by the term "income," the court found that income referred to gross income—in other words, income before expenses. As long as one of the purposes of borrowing was to earn income from property (the dividend income), the interest deduction should be allowed. It did not matter that the interest expense incurred exceeded the amount of income received.

In *Stewart v. The Queen*, a taxpayer acquired four condominiums, each for $1,000 down with the balance fully financed. The real estate generated significant losses—mainly due to the interest deduction—

that the taxpayer sought to deduct from his other sources of income. Although the minister had attempted to disallow the losses on the basis that the taxpayer had no reasonable expectation of profit from his investment, the Supreme Court referred to the decision in the *Ludco* case and concluded that the question of the deductibility of expenses is entirely separate from the determination of whether a source of income exists. A clear analogy was drawn between the facts in *Ludco* and the facts in *Stewart*. Since the taxpayer had used borrowed money to engage in a bona fide investment from which he had a reasonable expectation of income, the interest should be deductible and the losses allowed.

In light of these decisions (with the exception of the *Lipson* case, which came later), the CRA reviewed all its interpretive and administrative positions on interest deductibility and concluded that it would assess taxpayers based on the decisions in the above cases. But this isn't the end of the story. In October 2003, the Department of Finance introduced draft legislation that would effectively disallow losses from a business or property where it is not reasonable to expect that the taxpayer will realize a cumulative net profit over the whole period that the taxpayer carries on (and is likely to carry on) the business or holds (and is likely to hold) the income-producing property. The rules also provide that capital gains and losses are specifically excluded from the determination of cumulative profit for this purpose.

Since the Department of Finance introduced these rules, concern has been expressed that the proposals could limit the deduction for interest for common-share investments. Although the Department of Finance has consistently said the proposals are not intended to target the deductibility of interest on funds borrowed to invest in common shares, and the CRA has agreed that it would generally not challenge the deductibility of interest on such investments, tax practitioners still feel a need for legislative assurance that backs up this stated administrative position. As part of the 2005 federal budget, the Department of Finance announced that it intended to make changes to the draft rules to address some of the concerns that have been raised about these proposals. As of June 30, 2009, there has been no further word on the status of these proposed measures. No indication has been given as to when (or if) we can expect to see revised legislation or its effective date.

Check before borrowing

As new legislation could be introduced at any time, and current assessing practices are always subject to change, you should check with your tax adviser to determine the CRA's position if you are borrowing funds and want to deduct the interest.

If you no longer own the income-producing property, there are also rules that may permit a continued deduction for interest expense. It is not clear how the new "reasonable expectation of profit" (REOP) rules will affect these "loss of source" rules, although the Department of Finance has indicated that they are intended to override the REOP rules. Due to the complexity of the rules, professional tax advice is recommended.

TAX TIP

When you borrow, try to borrow for investment or business purposes before you borrow for personal reasons. Conversely, when repaying debt, consider repaying loans on which interest is non-deductible before you repay those on which the interest is deductible. After all, why would you prematurely eliminate an arrangement that provides a measure of tax relief?

161 Resource Sector as a Tax Shelter

Most investors do not invest directly in the resource sector. Instead, they obtain tax write-offs or tax credits by investing in limited partnerships created for that purpose or in shares (flow-through shares) whereby the companies pass on the deductions to the shareholders, who claim them on their own tax returns.

There are various types of resource expenses you can claim and each one is subject to special rules regarding the amount that can be claimed as a deduction. As with any other investment, your deliberations on investing in the resource sector should consider its overall investment potential rather than just focusing on the write-offs. Your financial adviser can assist you in making this assessment.

162 Mineral Exploration Tax Credit

Canadian corporations that are principally engaged in the exploration and development of mineral or other natural resources can renounce certain expenses incurred in mining exploration activities and flow them out to shareholders (individuals or partnerships). The shareholders can then deduct these items on their own tax returns.

The renounced amounts are typically reported on a T101 or T5013A slip.

If you invest in these "flow-through" shares, you may also qualify for a mineral exploration tax credit equal to 15% of the flow-through mining expenditures for the year. The tax credit is calculated on Form T2038, *Investment Tax Credit*. If the amount of the tax credit cannot be fully utilized in the current year because the amount of the credit exceeds your federal tax liability, the unused credit may be carried forward for up to 20 years.

In its 2009 budget, the federal government announced that eligibility for this tax credit has recently been extended to flow-through share agreements entered into on or before March 31, 2010. Therefore, the credit is available for expenditures that are incurred by mining corporations before 2011, or in 2011 pursuant to the "look-back" rules.

163 Limited Partnerships

Another type of tax shelter involves the purchase of an interest in a limited partnership. In this type of arrangement, you share the profits or loss of the business with the other partners and report as your income or loss a percentage of the partnership's income or loss. However, your liability with respect to the partnership's debts is limited. In general, you can lose only up to your original investment.

Restrictions

Although a limited partnership may be an attractive investment if the partnership business is expected to have losses in its initial years but to eventually show a profit, special rules prevent you from writing off more than the amount you have invested in the partnership.

The write-off you can claim is further restricted if the purchase of an interest is financed with certain types of "limited recourse" financing. This can include arrangements involving loans that you have little or no risk of repaying. Certain partnerships also have to prorate expenditures that would otherwise be deductible in the current year over a longer term. In addition, if the adjusted cost base of your interest in a limited partnership becomes negative, you will have to report a capital gain equal to the negative amount. These and other changes have substantially reduced the attractiveness of limited partnerships as tax shelters.

Some limited partnerships have been scrutinized by the CRA.

Investors should be aware that if the limited partnership is found to have no reasonable expectation of profit, the losses might be disallowed (see article 160).

As you would with any other investment, you should thoroughly evaluate the investment potential of a tax shelter. It does not make any economic sense to invest in a shelter if there is little chance of either earning a return on your investment or recovering the amount you have at risk.

The AMT (see article 168) and CNIL rules (see article 159), as well as restrictions on the deductibility of limited partnership losses, make it imperative that you pursue expert tax advice about your situation before making an investment.

164 CRA Warning—Tax Shelters

The CRA has recently issued a warning indicating that they plan to audit all tax-shelter gifting arrangements.

Many promoters state that they have obtained an advance income tax ruling from the CRA. While the Rulings Directorate will rule on certain aspects of proposed transactions, it will not rule on issues such as the existence of a business, reasonable expectation of profit and the fair market value of a property or service. Therefore, if you are considering investing in a tax shelter, you should be aware that an advance ruling is not a guarantee of the proposed deductions and you should exercise caution if the anticipated net return during the initial years arises primarily from projected income tax refunds.

You should also be aware that a tax shelter identification number is used only for identification purposes. It does not mean that the tax shelter transactions have been approved by the CRA as being legitimate. Tax shelter promoters are required to include a statement to this effect on the tax shelter documents.

There are three common types of tax shelter arrangements involving charities that the CRA views as abusive (although variations of these and other new arrangements are always being promoted):

1. **Buy low, donate high:** You acquire property for $3,000, then transfer the property to a charity and receive a $10,000 receipt.
2. **Gifting trust arrangements:** You pay $3,000 cash to a charity and receive property from a trust with a purported fair market value of $7,000, which is also transferred to a charity, and receive a donation receipt of $10,000.

3. **Leveraged cash donations:** You purportedly borrow $8,000, add another $2,000 (in cash), and receive a $10,000 donation receipt. The $8,000 loan is never actually repaid. This is facilitated by paying a third party a much lesser amount (around $1,000) to repay the loan in full. As a result, the total cash donated is about 30% of the amount reported on the donation receipt.

New arrangements claiming to be different from those listed above are always being marketed. However, you should be cautious of all arrangements that promise a donation receipt in excess of the cash donated. It is the CRA's position that proposed legislation, effective since 2003, will apply to reduce the donation credit to no more than the actual cash payment.

There is the added risk of losing the benefit associated with the actual cash donation. To qualify for a donation credit, a gift must be made voluntarily with no expectation to receive anything in return. In most of the charitable donation arrangements being looked at by the CRA, it would be difficult to argue that the donation would have been made were it not for the expected tax savings.

165 Taxation of Personal Trusts

A trust is an arrangement under which a trustee holds property for the benefit of one or more beneficiaries. It can be created through your will at any time, including on death. Trusts are taxed as separate taxpayers. A trust created on death is taxed at the same rate as an individual, while other trusts are taxed at the highest marginal individual rate of tax (from 39% to just over 48%, depending on the province in which the trust is taxed).

Flexibility in taxation

The income of the trust will be subject to tax, but there is flexibility in the determination of exactly who gets taxed. If the trust agreement requires the income to be paid to beneficiaries, the general rule is that the beneficiaries will pay the tax. However, it is possible to make an election to have some or all of the income taxed in the trust. Alternatively, the trust agreement may provide that the income stays in the trust for a set period of time. In this case, the general rule is that the trust will pay the tax.

TAX TIP

Consider revising your will to create separate testamentary trusts for each of your beneficiaries. This will help them save tax on income they will earn on money you plan to leave them in your will.

The preferred-beneficiary election allows the trustee and the beneficiary to retain the income in the trust while having that income taxed in the hands of the beneficiary. This election is available only if the beneficiary is entitled to claim a tax credit because of a mental or physical impairment, and applies only to the beneficiary's share of the trust income.

TAX TIP

Consider creating a trust to hold investments for the benefit of a child or parent with a physical or mental disability. The income can be retained in the trust and may be taxed at a lower rate on the preferred-beneficiary's tax return. This can effectively reduce taxes while allowing the trustee to control the investments.

The 21-year rule

Along with the introduction of the tax on capital gains in 1972 came the 21-year rule that prevents the indefinite deferral of tax on accrued gains on property held in trusts. Under this rule, most trusts are deemed to dispose of all their property every 21 years for proceeds equal to the fair market value of the property.

TAX TIP

If you are the trustee of a trust that will soon be subject to the 21-year rule, you should contact your tax adviser to determine what strategies are available to avoid or defer the tax on the deemed disposition. If the trust document permits, it might be advantageous to transfer out of the trust to the capital beneficiaries the capital property with the accrued gains. If there are no accrued gains on the property, the 21-year rule is not an issue and the property can remain in the trust.

166 Foreign Taxes on Investment Income

As a resident of Canada, you are subject to Canadian income taxes on your worldwide income, even if it was earned in another country. If the amount of foreign income received is net of foreign taxes withheld, you must gross-up the amount received by the amount of income taxes withheld. For example, if you received a foreign dividend payment in the amount of $170 ($200 in foreign dividends minus $30 in withholding tax), you must include the full $200 in your income. The foreign income is to be converted into Canadian dollars by using the average rate of exchange for 2009 or the actual exchange rate in effect when you received the income. The $30 in withholding tax can be claimed as a foreign tax credit with certain restrictions.

Foreign tax credits

You can claim a foreign tax credit for taxes withheld by the foreign country. In most cases, if the amount of foreign taxes withheld exceeds 15% of such income, the excess cannot be claimed as a foreign tax credit. You may be able to deduct the excess tax paid as an expense against that foreign income. The foreign tax credit is calculated on a per-country basis, and separate calculations are required for business and non-business income tax.

TAX TIP

Foreign investments should generally not be held in a TFSA (see article 78). Since a TFSA is not taxable on income earned within the account, there is no ability to claim a foreign tax credit against Canadian tax payable for the amount of tax withheld.

167 Foreign Reporting Requirements

A significant amount of misinformation continues to circulate in the public domain with respect to offshore tax planning. To the uninformed taxpayer, it is difficult to distinguish between legitimate and not-so-legitimate offshore planning strategies. Many of the illegitimate strategies rely on the fact that the taxpayer's interest in the offshore entity is unknown to the Canadian tax authorities. In an effort to identify such strategies, the government has introduced various foreign-reporting requirements.

What to report

Reporting may be required if a taxpayer has transferred or loaned funds or property to a foreign-based trust; has received funds or property from, or is indebted to, a foreign-based trust; has a foreign affiliate; or owns foreign property having a total cost of more than $100,000. Failure to disclose the required information may result in substantial penalties.

Loans and transfers to foreign trusts

If a taxpayer has transferred or loaned funds or property to a foreign-based trust at any time before the end of the trust's tax year, Form T1141 must be filed by the due date for the taxpayer's return for the particular year that includes the end of the trust's year before which a transfer was made or during which the non-resident trust was indebted to the taxpayer. For example, a corporation with a March 31 year-end transfers property to a foreign-based trust on June 30, 2008. The year-end of the trust is December 31. Since the March 31, 2009, year-end of the corporation includes the December 31, 2008, year-end of the trust (the year-end of the trust during which the transfer was made) Form T1141 must be filed by September 30, 2009, which is the filing due date for the corporation's 2009 tax return.

Distributions by and loans from foreign trusts

If a taxpayer has received funds or property from, or is indebted to, a foreign-based trust, Form T1142 must be filed by the due date of the taxpayer's tax return for the particular year during which a distribution was received or during which the taxpayer was indebted to the foreign-based trust. In the case of a partnership, the form must be filed by the due date for the partnership information return, regardless of whether such a return is required to be filed. For example, an individual receives a distribution of funds from a trust on June 30, 2009. Form T1142 must be filed by the due date of the individual's 2009 tax return—either April 30, 2010, or June 15, 2010.

Interest in foreign affiliates

Taxpayers who own shares of foreign affiliates are also required to file an information return annually. The information return—Form T1134A or T1134B, as appropriate—must be filed no later than 15 months after the end of the taxpayer's taxation year for which it is required to be filed. For example, a corporation with a December 31, 2009 year-end is required to file this information return no later than March 31, 2011.

Foreign property holdings

Taxpayers with interests in certain foreign property (such as shares, bank accounts, real property, etc.) with a cost in excess of $100,000 must report and provide details on such holdings on Form T1135. This form must be filed by the due date for filing the income tax return for the particular year.

Certain foreign property, such as personal-use property and property that is used in carrying on an active business, is excluded from this reporting requirement. A trust governed by an RRSP is also exempt from this reporting requirement.

For example, an individual owns a rental property in the U.S. with a cost of C$150,000. Form T1135 must be filed by the due date of the individual's 2009 tax return—either April 30, 2010, or June 15, 2010.

TAX TIP

Does your portfolio include foreign investments? If so, then it's time to consult your tax adviser to review your filing requirements. In some cases, the information you are required to report will not be readily available and you will need time to accumulate it. Failure to comply with these requirements can result in penalties.

Foreign investment entities (FIEs) and non-resident trusts (NRTs)

For several years now, proposed legislation has been outstanding on the taxation of foreign investment entities and non-resident trusts. These rules are generally designed to ensure that income earned indirectly by Canadian taxpayers through foreign intermediaries is not taxed at a more favourable rate than it would be if the income were earned without the involvement of those intermediaries. These new rules are very complex and far-reaching.

The foreign investment entity rules require Canadian taxpayers to include an amount in their taxable income to reflect the accrued income or gain in the value of certain foreign entities. These rules apply to individuals, corporations and trusts. The non-resident trust rules will tax certain foreign trusts in the same manner as Canadian resident trusts.

When they were originally proposed, these rules were to be effective for taxation years beginning after 2002. The most recent proposals note that these measures will generally take effect for taxation years that begin after 2006 (with an ability to elect an earlier application of the rules).

In its 2009 budget, the federal government announced that it would be reviewing the proposed rules in light of several submissions that it has received. As a result, it is possible that further changes will be made to these rules before they are finalized.

TAX TIP

If you think you might own an investment in a foreign investment entity or have an interest in a non-resident trust, you should contact your tax adviser to determine the tax consequences.

168 Alternative Minimum Tax (AMT)

The purpose of the alternative minimum tax (AMT) is to restrict the tax benefits derived from various tax preference items, such as approved tax shelters, capital gains, investment tax credits and certain losses. It either imposes an overall limit on the total of these identified deductions, credits, and exclusions, or reduces the tax savings derived from these items.

You should not have to pay AMT unless your tax preference holdings exceed a $40,000 exemption. Even then, depending on your circumstances, the total of such items may significantly exceed this limit before AMT is triggered. In many cases, no AMT will be due. Additionally, it does not apply in the year of death.

The AMT calculation

The AMT is calculated as 15% of the amount by which your "adjusted taxable income" exceeds the exemption of $40,000. Your adjusted taxable income is your taxable income determined for ordinary tax purposes, adjusted to add back certain deductions (tax preference items) that are not allowed as deductions for determining AMT.

If your AMT exceeds the amount of your regular federal taxes payable, the AMT becomes the amount of federal tax used to determine your tax liability. From this amount, you subtract the tax credits (i.e., personal tax credit, spousal amount, etc.) that are allowable for AMT purposes and make all other necessary tax calculations (i.e., surtaxes, other credits and provincial taxes). You can also be subject to provincial AMT.

Relief in future years

If you have to pay AMT, you will pay more tax than that required under the regular rules. However, you are entitled to a credit for the excess in future years when your regular tax liability exceeds your AMT for that year. The carry-forward period is up to seven years.

SECTION 4

Everyone

IN THIS SECTION

169 Understand the Rules Before You Act
170 The CRA's Policy and What's Really Law
171 T4s, T5s and Other Information Slips
172 EFILE, NETFILE and TELE-FILE
173 Notice of Assessment and Your Return
174 My Account—Personal Tax Information for Individuals
175 My Business Account—Corporate Tax Information for Businesses
176 Represent a Client—Third-Party Access to Client Information
177 Taxpayer Relief Provisions
178 The CRA's Collection Procedures
179 Income Tax Refunds
180 Income Tax Instalments
181 Books and Records
182 Be Aware of Penalties and Interest
183 Penalties on Late Payroll Remittances

This final section of *Smart Tax Tips* deals with topics that are relevant to most taxpayers—a business owner, aspiring entrepreneur, employee, homemaker, retiree or anyone else who has to file an income tax return—especially if there are taxes owing.

There are 15 items here for you to consider. Some of them provide a bit of insight into how the tax agency works, what it expects you to do and what it will do if you can't comply. We also explain the CRA's collection procedures, the penalties and interest you can expect and what you can do to help mitigate the situation.

This section also presents articles discussing how you can file your tax return electronically via EFILE, TELEFILE or NETFILE, as well as other filing options that are available to some taxpayers.

169 Understand the Rules Before You Act

Are you considering a financial transaction that is not part of your ordinary routine? If so, it's important to understand the tax rules that apply to your proposed action. For the most part, taxation in Canada is quite complex, creating challenges for even the most knowledgeable person. Often, you will discover there is more than one way to accomplish a particular goal. However, the tax impact may be radically different depending on how you structure the transaction.

TAX TIP

In most cases, the opportunities available to save or defer income taxes arise at the preliminary stage, before you have completed the proposed transaction. How a transaction is structured may also affect the GST/HST payable. If you wait until you have completed the arrangement to have your tax adviser review the situation, it's usually too late. The best way to benefit from the rules is to conduct your tax planning well in advance.

170 The CRA's Policy and What's Really Law

In most cases, amendments to the Income Tax Act are presented to the House of Commons as part of a budget. The Department of Finance, under the direction of the Minister of Finance, prepares these amendments. After an amendment becomes law, the Canada Revenue Agency (CRA) administers it.

Over the years, due to the uncertainty in many areas of tax law, the CRA has developed a number of administrative rules in an effort to deal with practical problems that always seem to arise. In some cases, the administrative rules may not even agree with the law.

In tax planning, you should know whether your plan complies with the tax law or depends on the agency's stated policy. The CRA is not bound by its stated policy, and the courts do not necessarily consider this policy in making their decisions.

171 T4s, T5s and Other Information Slips

Any employment, pension and most investment income you receive in 2009 is reported on information slips prepared by the person or organization that paid you. In general, these slips must be mailed or delivered to you by February 28, 2010. If you are a beneficiary of a trust, your T3 information slip could be delayed until the end of March, depending on the year-end of the trust. Partnerships in which all members are individuals are required to file a partnership information return and issue the required information slips to the partners by March 31, 2010 (see article 3).

Regardless of whether you receive the appropriate slip, you must declare all your income. Be sure to check the amounts reported on the slips to ensure that they are correct, as mistakes on these documents are not uncommon. If there is an error, you can obtain an amended slip. If you are filing your tax return on paper, do not file it until all the necessary receipts and slips are in your hands. Otherwise, processing delays could result. Nevertheless, you should do everything possible to ensure that you do not file late.

If you are filing your return electronically (EFILE) or using TELEFILE or NETFILE (see article 172), all information slips and other supporting documentation, such as charitable donation receipts, must be retained in case the CRA requests confirmation of the amount claimed. Your return may be reassessed if you cannot provide a copy of the relevant slip.

172 EFILE, NETFILE and TELEFILE

EFILE for individuals

Electronic filing (EFILE) allows authorized service providers (registered tax professionals) to electronically send personal income tax returns directly to the CRA. Since the returns are received and verified almost instantly, refunds can often be issued within a couple of weeks of submitting your return. Although almost all Canadians are eligible to use this system, there are certain returns that cannot be

EFILED, such as returns for non-residents, taxpayers who have an address outside Canada, and taxpayers who have to pay income tax to more than one province or territory. Beginning in 2008 and subsequent tax years, the T1 pre-bankrupt return and the Final T1 for a deceased taxpayer can now be EFILED. For deceased taxpayers, Part F of form T183, *Information Return for Electronic Filing of an Individual's Income Tax and Benefit Return* must be signed by the legal representative for the deceased.

NETFILE and TELEFILE for individuals

Certain individuals are able to file their personal income tax return directly to the CRA using the Internet—this is known as NETFILE. If you qualify to use this option, you need a four-digit web access code (WAC) that will be noted on the computer-generated label that is included in the T1 personal income tax package you receive from the CRA. This code changes each year, and you can use it only to file your own tax return. If you did not receive your NETFILE access code or cannot find it, you can either get it online or by calling the CRA at 1-800-714-7257. To file your return on the Internet, you must use a NETFILE-certified tax preparation software program or web application that supports this function.

There is also a telephone-based system for filing individual tax returns called TELEFILE. Under this system, you can transmit income tax information over the telephone toll-free at 1-800-959-1110. All you need to use the service is a touch-tone telephone, your social insurance number (SIN), your personalized access code (a four-digit number) and your completed tax return. Only certain taxpayers are eligible to use TELEFILE. The system accepts the most common types of income tax information, such as employment income, pension income, interest income, registered pension plan contributions and charitable donations. More complex tax information, such as self-employment income, capital gains and rental income, are not accepted by the system. In addition, first-time filers are not eligible to use TELEFILE. If you are eligible to use this system, you will receive information about TELEFILE, as well as your personalized access code, with your T1 personal income tax package.

TELEFILE does not eliminate the need to complete a copy of the tax return. To use this system, you must enter data from a completed income tax return using your telephone keypad. On completion of the automated telephone interview, the CRA will issue a confirmation number. A Notice of Assessment is usually sent out within two weeks.

Neither NETFILE nor TELEFILE requires you to file the supporting documentation used to prepare the return, unless requested to do so.

GST/HST NETFILE/TELEFILE

Selected businesses can now use the GST/HST NETFILE filing service to file their GST/HST returns directly to the CRA over the Internet. Your business is eligible to use this service if:

- it has at least a one-year GST/HST filing history with the CRA;
- an access code is printed on its GST/HST return;
- the name, business number, reporting period and address printed on the GST/HST return are correct;
- the return being filed results in a nil balance or a refund of $10,000 or less;
- it is not filing a rebate application form with the return; and
- the return being filed does not include an amount on line 111.

To file your GST/HST return using TELEFILE, the same eligibility requirements as listed above must be met. Your GST/HST information can then be submitted through a touch-tone phone.

More information about GST/HST NETFILE and TELEFILE can be found on the CRA's website.

Internet filing for T4s, T5s and other information returns

Businesses can now file several different information returns over the Internet, including T4s and T5s. The option to Internet-file T4s and T5s is available to those businesses that file up to 50 slips and use authorized tax preparation software. For slips filed after 2009 (this would include 2009 T4 and T5 slips filed in 2010), businesses that file more than 50 slips related to a particular type of information return must file electronically in extensible mark-up language (XML) by Internet file transfer or on electronic media (DVD or CD). To use this service, you need your business's individualized web access code, which will be different each year.

Corporation Internet filing

This filing option allows corporations that meet the eligibility criteria to use a web access code to file their income tax returns directly to the CRA through the Internet. Instead of using a web access code to file returns, tax professionals who file corporations' income tax returns for their clients can register and transmit using an EFILE online number and password.

Certain corporations cannot use this filing option. For example, a corporation that has any of the following characteristics must still paper-file the corporate tax return:

- The corporation is a non-resident of Canada.
- The corporation is involved in scientific research and experimental development (SR&ED) activities.
- The corporation is an insurance company.
- The corporation is filing an amended return or a return for any year prior to the 2002 taxation year.
- There have been changes to the corporation's name, head office or mailing address, or direct deposit information (including new requests).

For taxation years that end after 2009, corporations with annual gross revenues in excess of $1 million will be required to file their income tax returns in electronic format. There will be certain exceptions from this mandatory electronic filing requirement. To date, the CRA has confirmed that insurance corporations will be exempt, and it's expected that others, such as non-resident corporations and corporations filing in a functional currency, will be exempt as well.

To ensure compliance with the mandatory electronic filing changes, new penalties will be introduced for filing a corporate tax return in an incorrect format, commencing with returns required to be filed after 2010.

173 Notice of Assessment and Your Return

Shortly after you file your 2009 return, you should receive a Notice of Assessment from the CRA. When you receive it, compare it to the taxes payable as reported on your return. If there is any discrepancy, try to determine the reason.

If you do not understand why the amounts are different or you disagree with the assessment, consult your tax adviser or ask the CRA to provide further details. Do not automatically assume you made the error. The assessment may be based on a misunderstanding of the facts, or the tax department quite possibly may have made an error in processing your return.

Reassessments and Notices of Objection

As a matter of policy, the CRA will reassess returns if the adjustment relates to a calculation error or a misunderstanding of the facts. If your dispute is based on a different interpretation of the law, you may have to file a Notice of Objection.

Individual taxpayers can initiate the appeal process by outlining the objection on Form T400A or by setting out the facts and reasons for their objection in a letter to the chief of appeals at their local district taxation office.

Generally, a Notice of Objection must be filed within 90 days of the mailing date of the Notice of Assessment. However, individuals and testamentary trusts are granted a longer period to object to their assessment. They must object within one year from either the filing due date of the return or 90 days after the day of mailing the Notice of Assessment, whichever is later. Consult your tax adviser if you believe a reassessment or an objection is warranted.

174 My Account—Personal Tax Information for Individuals

The CRA has an online service that will allow you to access your own tax and benefit account information over the Internet. You need a Government of Canada epass to access this service. To obtain an epass, you must provide certain information, such as your date of birth, SIN, the amount reported as total income (line 150) on your tax return and your postal code. You will also need a CRA security code to access this service. This code is an eight-digit number that will appear on your Notice of Assessment.

More information on this service can be found on the CRA's website.

175 My Business Account—Corporate Tax Information for Businesses

The CRA also has an online service that allows business owners, partners, directors and officers to access corporate account information over the Internet. The services available on My Business Account include the following:

- Internet file transfer to transmit information slips, such as T4s, T4As, T4A-NRs, T4RIFs and T4RSPs;
- automobile benefits online calculator;
- corporation income tax return transmittal;
- viewing of returns status (corporation and payroll); and
- viewing of account balance and transaction (GST/HST, corporation and payroll).

A government of Canada epass and a CRA security code are required to access this service. More information about this service can be found on the CRA's website.

176 Represent a Client—Third-Party Access to Client Information

This service is designed for use by your representative, such as the person or business that prepares your tax return. Once authorized, your representative can go online to access your personal tax information, such as carry-forward amounts, your tax instalments, RRSP contribution room, etc.

Your representative must get an epass to use this service (this is the same as the process above for My Account). You will have to authorize your representative to use this service before he or she will be given access to your personal tax information. This authorization can be provided for an individual by submitting to the CRA Form T1013 (Authorizing or Cancelling a Representative). You can also authorize your representative online by using the My Account service.

A business can also authorize a representative online using the My Business Account service or by submitting to the CRA Form RC59 (Business Consent Form).

More information on this service can be found on the CRA's website.

177 Taxpayer Relief Provisions

The CRA has rules to improve the fairness of the tax system when personal misfortune or circumstances beyond your control make you unable to meet your filing or payment deadlines or comply with certain rules. For example, interest and penalties may be waived if you can show that you were prevented from filing on time due to extraordinary circumstances such as illness, death, or natural disaster. Penalties and interest may also be waived if they arose primarily because of actions of the CRA, such as disruption in services or erroneous information from the tax department in the form of incorrect written answers, errors in published information, or undue delays in resolving an objection or an appeal or in completing an audit. Interest may also be waived in whole or in part if a taxpayer is unable to pay due to financial hardship. Penalties will not generally be waived due to financial hardship.

Individuals and testamentary trusts can also use these rules to apply for a refund for any taxation year that ends in the 10 preceding calendar years, which includes years which would otherwise be barred by statute. Still other provisions permit you to amend or late-file certain prescribed tax elections.

To request this relief, you must write a letter to the CRA indicating why you think the taxpayer relief provisions should apply to your particular situation. You will have to submit receipts or other backup information to support your claim. Relief is not automatic, and the rules are not intended to permit retroactive tax planning. However, the CRA will generally permit the requested amendment where their guidelines have been met. Your tax adviser can assist you in determining whether you are likely to qualify, as well as in making the application.

TAX TIP

If you think you may be entitled to a refund for any year after 1999, you should request an adjustment of your tax return under the taxpayer relief provisions. For example, you may find that you failed to claim the disability tax credit (see article 90) in previous years even though you were entitled to do so. By writing a letter to the department and including any supporting documents, you can request a refund.

178 The CRA's Collection Procedures

If you cannot afford to pay taxes owing, you should know about the CRA's collection procedures. Without a doubt, you should still file your return on time even if you are unable to pay the outstanding taxes. Filing late will incur a 5% penalty on the taxes owing, which is automatically added to the amount you owe. Another 1% is added for each additional complete month the return is late, to a maximum of 12 months. Interest also accrues on the unpaid taxes. And if this is not your first late-filing offence, and a demand has been issued for you to file a return, you could be subject to a 10% penalty plus 2% per month for up to 20 months on the second late-filed return. If you wilfully attempted to evade payment of income taxes by failing to file your return, additional penalties could apply.

What to expect

Your Notice of Assessment will show the amount of taxes owing, including penalties and interest, and will state that no further interest will be charged if the entire amount is paid within 20 days. If a payment is not made within 20 days, the CRA will issue a request that the amount be paid. In most cases, the CRA cannot begin legal proceedings to collect until 90 days after the day on which the Notice of Assessment was mailed. There are further delays if you file a Notice of Objection or otherwise indicate that you are objecting to the assessment. Nevertheless, interest is charged that compounds daily and accumulates on the amount due from April 30 to the date of payment.

Subject to the restrictions relating to the disputed amounts, the CRA can seize funds from your bank account or require your employer to pay a portion of your salary directly toward your taxes owing.

Try to work out a payment schedule

The CRA will make every effort to contact you before beginning formal legal proceedings, but it would be prudent for you to immediately contact the CRA if you are unable to pay the full amount. Depending on your circumstances, a schedule of payments over a period of time will normally be accepted.

Changes to the limitation period for collection of tax debts

The CRA has long held that there was no limitation period to the collection of amounts owing by taxpayers under the Income Tax Act.

This position was cast in doubt by the 2003 Supreme Court decision in the case of *Markevich v. The Queen*. In this case, the CRA attempted in 1998 to collect a tax debt that had been outstanding and inactive since 1986. The court concluded that the taxpayer was not required to pay the tax debt since the collection of the federal income tax debt was subject to the six-year limitation period set out in the Crown Liability and Proceedings Act (CLPA).

In response to this decision, the Department of Finance has introduced a 10-year limitation period for the collection of income tax debts. All federal tax debts and any other amounts that became payable before March 4, 2004, but remained unpaid at that date, are subject to a 10-year limitation period to start as of March 4, 2004. For debts that become payable after this date, the limitation period is 10 years. This 10-year limitation period also applies to requests for refunds filed under the taxpayer relief provisions (see article 177).

179 Income Tax Refunds

You are eligible for an income tax refund if the amount of income taxes withheld from you or paid by you during the year exceeds the actual taxes you owe. Although you may look forward to receiving a tax refund, it is not always good planning to get one. If you get a refund, that means the government has been holding your money and not paying you interest on it for many months.

TAX TIP

If you expect to receive a refund after filing your return—for example, for support payments or other deductions—you can apply to the CRA to obtain permission to have your source withholdings reduced. In some cases, the TD1 form you file with your employer can be amended to provide for the reduced withholdings.

TAX TIP

You can now transfer certain lump-sum payments to your RRSP without withholding. Previously, unless a waiver from the CRA was obtained, employers were required to withhold on the entire amount of such payments exceeding $10,000. Under these rules, you can now transfer the payment without withholding if you can show reasonable grounds that the payment is deductible. For example, a copy of your Notice of Assessment may show unused RRSP contribution room.

Losing interest

Although you won't be penalized for filing a return late when you are owed a refund, interest does not begin to accrue on the refund amount until you file the return. For individual tax returns, interest on tax refunds does not start to accrue until 30 days after the balance-due date (April 30) or 30 days after the actual filing date or the date the overpayment arose, whichever is later.

If you have made an error and you actually owe money, late-filing penalties and interest will apply on the balance owing. Therefore, regardless of whether you owe money or are receiving a refund, you should always file your return on time.

180 Income Tax Instalments

Instalments for individuals

Historically, if you owe taxes each year when filing your return, there is a good chance you will be required to prepay your tax through quarterly instalments. Failing to remit the instalments on time can be costly. The CRA charges interest on the deficient amounts as if you owed the money and, if this interest charge adds up to more than $1,000, a charge of 50% of the interest in excess of $1,000 is added (or 25% of the instalment interest on the instalment payments if no instalment was made during the year, if greater). This can become quite expensive and should be avoided if possible.

Instalments are due on March 15, June 15, September 15 and December 15, and the rules used to determine when an individual is required to remit instalments cause difficulties for many taxpayers. That's why it's so important to understand the requirement to remit the instalments and the options available to do so.

Instalments are required if the difference between your combined federal and provincial tax and the amount of tax actually withheld at source was greater than $3,000 in 2006, 2007 or 2008 and will be greater than $3,000 in 2009. This last test requires an estimate in advance of the actual calculation of 2009 tax.

Once it is determined that you are required to make instalment payments in 2009, you can choose from three options to calculate the amount of your instalment. Under the first two options, you can base your instalments on your 2008 tax or on your estimate of your 2009 tax. If you choose the latter option, be careful. Underestimating your

2009 tax means the CRA will charge you interest based on the higher instalment required.

With the third option, the CRA calculates the amount of your instalment and sends you the calculation as a reminder. The government initiated this option to eliminate some of the uncertainty in this area. Unfortunately, the calculation notices look very much like requests to pay and have created confusion for many taxpayers. This third method uses your 2007 tax as the base for the first two instalments. For the last two instalments, the amounts are based on your 2008 tax, minus whatever was required for the first two instalments. The final result will be total instalments equal to your 2008 instalment base.

The major advantage in paying the amounts shown on the CRA notices is that you will not be charged any instalment interest if you pay on time. The CRA sends the instalment reminders in batches of two—in February for the March and June instalments, and in August for the September and December instalments.

TAX TIP

If you discover during the year that you should have been making higher instalments, it is possible to catch up, because the CRA will credit interest on overpayments and apply that against interest deficiencies. For instance, if you remit $5,000 on March 15 and then discover just before the June 15 deadline that you should be remitting $6,000 each quarter, it would be prudent for you to remit $8,000 on June 15, $5,000 on September 15 and $6,000 on December 15. The end result will be that you were $1,000 short for the three months from March 15 to June 15 and $1,000 over for the next three months. The interest calculations for these two periods will offset one another, assuming the prescribed interest rate does not change over that period.

You can now use a pre-authorized payment plan to make your quarterly personal instalments. To do this, complete Form T1162A, attach a cheque marked "void" and return it to the CRA. This will authorize the CRA to automatically debit your bank account for a predetermined amount on a specified date.

Instalments for corporations

In general, your corporation is not required to make instalments if its total tax liability for the current or preceding taxation year is $3,000 or less. In this case, the amount owing is paid on the balance-due day for the taxation year.

Once it is determined that your corporation is required to make monthly instalment payments, the instalment amount can be determined in one of three ways. Under the first two options, you can base your corporation's instalments on its "instalment base" for the immediately preceding year or on your estimate of its tax liability for the current year. Again, if you choose the latter option, be careful. If you underestimate the amounts, the CRA will charge non-deductible interest on the underpayments.

Under the third option, the first two instalments can be calculated as 1/12 of the corporation's instalment base for its second-last taxation year, and the next 10 instalments can be based on the corporation's instalment base for the immediately preceding taxation year after deducting the first two instalments.

Each instalment is due on the last day of each month of the taxation year.

A Canadian-controlled private corporation that meets all of the following criteria will be able to make quarterly instalments:

- the taxable income of the corporation and all associated corporations for either the current or previous year does not exceed the amount that qualifies for the small-business deduction (see article 27);
- the corporation qualified for the small-business deduction in either the current or previous year;
- the taxable capital employed in Canada of the corporation and all associated corporations does not exceed $10 million in either the current or previous year; and
- the corporation has no compliance irregularities during the preceding 12 months.

As for quarterly instalments, there will be three available methods for determining the quarterly instalment amounts. Under the first two options, you can make four instalments equal to one-quarter of the tax payable for the previous taxation year or one-quarter of the estimated tax payable for the current year.

Under the third option, the first instalment can be calculated as one-quarter of the corporation's tax payable for the second preceding year. The remaining three instalments will be equal to one-third of the amount by which the tax payable for the previous taxation year exceeds the first instalment made for the current taxation year.

Each instalment will be due on the last day of each quarter of the corporation's taxation year.

TAX TIP

Although the third option appears the most complex, it has the advantage of allowing two months (or one quarter) after the year-end for the accumulation of information needed to determine the previous years' instalment base. For this reason, it is commonly used.

There are special rules in situations where a corporation has undergone a corporate reorganization or where the instalment base year was less than 365 days.

181 Books and Records

Individual taxpayers should keep their tax records for at least four years—approximately the period during which the CRA can reassess a return—and preferably longer.

If you operate a business, you must keep your business records for a minimum of six years from the end of the last tax year to which they relate. For non-incorporated businesses, permanent books and records must be kept for six years after the last day of the taxation year in which the business ceased. For corporations, permanent records must be kept for two years after dissolution. Permanent books and records include the general ledger and special contracts and agreements, as well as all incorporation documentation. If a return is filed late, the books and records must be kept for six years from the day the return is filed.

Note that the minimum retention period is generally determined by the last tax year for which a record may be required for purposes of the Income Tax Act, not the year in which the transaction occurred and the record was created. For example, records supporting the acquisition and capital cost of investments and other capital property should be maintained until the day that is six years from the end of the last tax year in which such an acquisition could enter into any calculation for income tax purposes.

Books and records can be destroyed at an earlier time only if you obtain written permission from the tax department. To get such permission, you can use Form T137, *Request for Destruction of Records*, or you can apply in writing to the director of your local tax services office. A written request, signed by the person concerned or an authorized representative, should provide the following information:

- a clear identification of books, records, or other documents to be destroyed;
- the tax years for which the request applies;
- details of any special circumstances that would justify destroying the books and records at an earlier time than that normally permitted; and
- any other pertinent information.

182 Be Aware of Penalties and Interest

The concept of increased penalties for repeat offenders is now firmly entrenched in the Income Tax Act.

The penalty for filing a return late is 5% of the unpaid taxes plus an additional 1% for each complete month the return is late, up to a maximum of 12 months—a maximum penalty of 17%.

Additionally, if you have been assessed this penalty for any of the three previous years and the CRA issues a demand to file the current year's return, it's a good idea to comply. The penalty for a repeat offence will be 10% of the unpaid taxes plus an additional 2% per month for a period up to 20 months—a maximum penalty of 50%.

Similarly, if you fail to report an amount for a given year and then fail to report another amount in any of the three subsequent years, a special penalty will apply that is equal to 10% of the amount you failed to report for the second time.

And don't forget the additional penalties imposed for failing to remit the appropriate amount of income tax instalments (see article 180).

There is a penalty for late filing information returns even though no taxes are owing. The penalty is the greater of $100 and $25 per day to a maximum of 100 days, or $2,500. Information returns include foreign reporting forms (T106, T1134A, T1134BT1141, T1142, and T1135) and non-profit organization returns (T1044).

Generally, the CRA's administrative policy is to charge the penalty in all cases, even for first-time late filers.

There are also penalties for failing to provide your SIN (social insurance number) or your BN (business number) or for failing to include the SIN or BN on an information slip you have prepared. Partnerships and tax shelters are also subject to penalties for failure to file the required information returns.

Even bigger penalties

If you knowingly, or in circumstances amounting to gross negligence, make false statements or omit information from a return, a penalty may be imposed that is equal to whichever is the greater of $100 or 50% of the tax avoided or benefit improperly claimed. And if the CRA finds that a false statement or omission amounts to tax evasion, a fine of 50% to 200% of the tax evaded may be imposed.

The interest rate charged on amounts owing to the CRA is 2% higher than the rate the CRA pays on refunds. The increased rate applies to all amounts owing to the CRA, including unpaid taxes, instalments and source deductions.

Voluntary disclosures

It is the CRA's policy not to impose penalties when a voluntary disclosure is made. If a taxpayer has never filed tax returns and the returns are then voluntarily filed, the taxpayer will be required to pay only the tax owing—with interest—on the reported incomes. If a taxpayer has given incomplete information in a return and subsequently submits the missing information, the taxpayer will be required to pay only the tax owing on the adjusted income, with interest.

To make a voluntary disclosure, you have to initiate the process. A disclosure is not considered voluntary if it arises when the CRA has begun an audit or a request for information has been issued. Contact your tax adviser regarding initial contact with the tax department and the information to be provided.

Ministerial discretion to waive interest and penalties

In some cases, interest and penalties may have arisen through no fault of your own. To deal with such inequities, there are rules that give the minister the discretion to waive or cancel interest or penalties (see article 177).

Civil penalties for misrepresentation by third parties

It's not only taxpayers who have to deal with the prospect of penalties—tax preparers and other persons are now faced with their possible imposition.

Third parties can be subject to two different penalties: one for advising or participating in a false filing (preparer penalty) and the other for participation in a tax shelter or other tax-planning arrangement that includes a false statement or omission that may be used for tax purposes by another person (planner penalty).

For participating in a false filing, the penalty is whichever is the greater amount of $1,000 or 50% of the tax sought to be avoided (subject to a maximum of $100,000, plus the person's gross compensation). For misrepresentations in a tax-planning or valuation activity, the planner penalty is the greater of $1,000 or the person's "gross entitlements" with respect to the arrangement. Gross entitlements are defined as all amounts a person is entitled to receive or obtain with respect to the activity.

The penalties will apply in situations where a person knowingly makes (or participates in the making of) a false statement or omission that is used for tax purposes by another person, or where the person would have known had it not been for circumstances amounting to "culpable conduct." This is defined as conduct equivalent to intentional acting, that shows indifference to whether the tax law is complied with or that shows a wilful, reckless or wanton disregard of the law.

183 Penalties on Late Payroll Remittances

In 2003, the CRA created a pilot project for payroll remittances that replaced the 10% fixed penalty for late remittances with the following graduated penalty amounts, based on the number of days that the required remittance is late:

- 3%—one to three days late;
- 5%—four or five days late;
- 7%—six or seven days late; and
- 10%—more than seven days late.

Due to the success of the pilot project, the 2008 budget enacted the graduated penalty regime. This graduated penalty regime also applies to large remitters that fail to remit their withholdings directly to financial institutions (a requirement since 1992).

TAX CALENDAR

Payment and Filing Due Dates

Type of Return	Balance Due Date[1]	Filing Due Date
Individual income tax returns		
Federal & provincial[2]		
general	April 30	April 30
self-employed[3]	April 30	June 15
deceased	April 30[4]	April 30/June 15[5]
Corporate income tax returns	**End of**	**End of**
Federal, Alberta, Ontario & Quebec	2 months after y/e*[6]	6 months after y/e
Trust (estate) income tax returns		
Federal	90 days after y/e	90 days after y/e
Quebec	90 days after y/e	90 days after y/e
Information returns		
Partnership	N/A	March 31[7]
Tax shelter	N/A	Last day of February
Transactions with related non-residents	N/A	6 months after y/e
Foreign holdings		
Transfers/loans to non-resident trusts	N/A	Filing due date of taxpayer's income tax return for the year[8]
Distributions from non-resident trusts	N/A	Filing due date of taxpayer's income tax return or partnership's information return[9]
Interests in foreign affiliates	N/A	15 months after y/e
Specified foreign property	N/A	Filing due date of taxpayer's income tax return or partnership's information return
Information slips		
T4, T5	N/A	Last day of February[10]
T3	N/A	90 days after y/e[11]

* Note: y/e means year-end

Notes

1. The date indicates the due date for the final payment of taxes for the year. Instalment payments may be required throughout the year. Individuals, if required, make quarterly tax instalments (i.e., March 15, June 15, September 15 and December 15). Corporations, if required, generally remit taxes monthly.
2. Currently, Quebec is the only province that files a separate individual tax return.
3. The filing deadline applies to an individual who carried on business (other than a tax shelter investment) in the year. The same deadline also applies to such an individual's spouse or common-law partner.
4. For deaths occurring before November 1 of the year. For deaths occurring during November and December of the year, tax is payable six months after the date of death. When the death occurs between January 1 and April 30, the tax payable for the prior year is due six months after the date of death. Quarterly instalments of tax are not required after the date of death.
5. For deaths occurring before November 1 of the year, the return is due by the normal filing date, either April 30 or June 15. For deaths during the period beginning November 1 of the year and ending April 30 of the following year (or June 15 if the filing extension would have applied), the return is due by the later of six months after the date of death or the normal filing date.
6. End of third month following the year-end if the corporation is a Canadian-controlled private corporation throughout the taxation year and:

   Federal: the small-business deduction is claimed in the current or preceding year, and the aggregate of taxable income of the corporation and all associated corporations for the immediately preceding year was equal to or less than the small-business limit for the year.

   Ontario: the corporation has taxable income for the preceding year that did not exceed the Ontario small-business limit for the year.

   Alberta: the corporation claimed the Alberta small-business deduction in either the current or the immediately preceding year and had taxable income of not more than $500,000 in either the current or the immediately preceding year. The three-month deadline is also available if the tax for the year is not more than $2,000.

7. If all members are individuals throughout the fiscal year. If all members are corporations throughout the fiscal year, the deadline is the last day of the fifth month following the fiscal year-end. For partnerships with mixed members, it is the earlier of these two dates. If the partnership discontinues its business or activity, the deadline is the earlier of 90 days after the discontinuance and the date the return would otherwise be required.
8. Where a taxpayer has transferred or loaned funds or property to a foreign-based trust at any time, the information return (T1141) must be filed by the due date of the taxpayer's return for the particular year that includes the end of the trust's year before which a transfer was made or during which the non-resident trust was indebted to the taxpayer.
9. Where a taxpayer or partnership has received funds or property from, or is indebted to, a foreign-based trust, the information return (T1142) must be filed by the due date of the taxpayer's return for the particular year during which the distribution was received or the taxpayer was indebted to the foreign trust. In the case of a partnership, the information return must be filed by the due date of the partnership information return, regardless of whether one is required.
10. Where the business activity is discontinued, the filing deadline is 30 days thereafter.
11. In addition to issuing T3 slips, a public trust (a mutual fund trust whose units are listed on a designated stock exchange) has to post financial information concerning distributions and allocations of income and capital to the website of CDS Innovations Inc. no later than 60 days after the trust's tax year-end.

TABLES

Table 1/Federal and Provincial Personal Income Tax Rates and Credits for 2009

	Federal	Newfoundland
Range of 1st bracket	$0 to $40,726	$0 to $31,061
Rate	15.00%	7.70%
Range of 2nd bracket	$40,727 to $81,452	$31,062 to $62,121
Rate	22.00%	12.80%
Range of 3rd bracket	$81,453 to $126,264	$62,122 and over
Rate	26.00%	15.50%
Range of 4th bracket	$126,265 and over	N/A
Rate	29.00%	N/A
Range of 5th bracket	N/A	N/A
Rate	N/A	N/A
1st Tier Surtax criteria	N/A	N/A
Rate	N/A	N/A
2nd Tier Surtax criteria	N/A	N/A
Rate	N/A	N/A
Basic Personal Amount	$10,320	$7,778
Age Amount	$6,408	$3,655
Pension Income Amount	$2,000	$1,000
Education full time/month	$400	$200
Education part time/month	$120	$60
Textbook full time/month	$65	N/A
Textbook part time/month	$20	N/A
Disability Amount	$7,196	$5,249
Spouse Amount	$10,320	$6,356
Eligible Dependent Amount	$10,320	$6,356
Child Amount <18 years	$2,089	N/A
Child Amount <6 years	N/A	N/A
Adoption Amount	$10,909	$10,497
Caregiver Amount	$4,198	$2,470
Infirm Dependent >18 years	$4,198	$2,470

	Nova Scotia	PEI
Range of 1st bracket	$0 to $29,590	$0 to $31,984
Rate	8.79%	9.80%
Range of 2nd bracket	$29,591 to $59,180	$31,985 to $63,969
Rate	14.95%	13.80%
Range of 3rd bracket	$59,181 to $93,000	$63,970 and over
Rate	16.67%	16.70%

	Nova Scotia	PEI
Range of 4th bracket	$93,001 and over	N/A
Rate	17.50%	N/A
Range of 5th bracket	N/A	N/A
Rate	N/A	N/A
1st Tier Surtax criteria	prov. tax in excess of $10,000	prov. tax in excess of $12,500
Rate	10.00% on excess	10.00% on excess
2nd Tier Surtax criteria	N/A	N/A
Rate	N/A	N/A
Basic Personal Amount	$7,981	$7,708
Age Amount	$3,897	$3,764
Pension Income Amount	$1,104	$1,000
Education full time/month	$200	$400
Education part time/month	$60	$120
Textbook full time/month	N/A	N/A
Textbook part time/month	N/A	N/A
Disability Amount	$4,738	$6,890
Spouse Amount	$6,778	$6,546
Eligible Dependent Amount	$6,778	$6,294
Child Amount <18 years	N/A	N/A
Child Amount <6 years	$1,200	$1,200
Adoption Amount	N/A	N/A
Caregiver Amount	$4,610	$2,446
Infirm Dependent >18 years	$2,633	$2,446

	New Brunswick	Quebec
Range of 1st bracket	$0 to $35,707	$0 to $38,385
Rate	9.65%	16.00%
Range of 2nd bracket	$35,708 to $71,415	$38,386 to $76,770
Rate	14.50%	20.00%
Range of 3rd bracket	$71,416 to $116,105	$76,771 and over
Rate	16.00%	24.00%
Range of 4th bracket	$116,106 and over	N/A
Rate	17.00%	N/A
Range of 5th bracket	N/A	N/A
Rate	N/A	N/A
1st Tier Surtax criteria	N/A	N/A
Rate	N/A	N/A
2nd Tier Surtax criteria	N/A	N/A
Rate	N/A	N/A
Basic Personal Amount	$8,605	Quebec
Age Amount	$4,202	credit
Pension Income Amount	$1,000	calculation

	New Brunswick	Quebec
Education full time/month	$400	differs from the other provinces.
Education part time/month	$120	
Textbook full time/month	N/A	
Textbook part time/month	N/A	
Disability Amount	$6,966	
Spouse Amount	$7,307	
Eligible Dependent Amount	$7,307	
Child Amount <18 years	N/A	
Child Amount <6 years	N/A	N/A
Adoption Amount	N/A	
Caregiver Amount	$4,064	
Infirm Dependent >18 years	$4,064	

	Ontario	Manitoba
Range of 1st bracket	$0 to $36,848	$0 to $31,000
Rate	6.05%	10.80%
Range of 2nd bracket	$36,849 to $73,698	$31,001 to $67,000
Rate	9.15%	12.75%
Range of 3rd bracket	$73,699 and over	$67,001 and over
Rate	11.16%	17.40%
Range of 4th bracket	N/A	N/A
Rate	N/A	N/A
Range of 5th bracket	N/A	N/A
Rate	N/A	N/A
1st Tier Surtax criteria	prov. tax in excess of $4,257	N/A
Rate	20.00% on excess	N/A
2nd Tier Surtax criteria	prov. tax in excess of $5,370	N/A
Rate	36.00% on excess	N/A
Basic Personal Amount	$8,881	$8,134
Age Amount	$4,336	$3,728
Pension Income Amount	$1,228	$1,000
Education full time/month	$478	$400
Education part time/month	$143	$120
Textbook full time/month	N/A	N/A
Textbook part time/month	N/A	N/A
Disability Amount	$7,175	$6,180
Spouse Amount	$7,541	$8,134
Eligible Dependent Amount	$7,541	$8,134
Child Amount <18 years	N/A	N/A
Child Amount <6 years	N/A	N/A
Adoption Amount	$10,835	$10,000
Caregiver Amount	$4,186	$3,605
Infirm Dependent >18 years	$4,186	$3,605

	Saskatchewan	Alberta
Range of 1st bracket	$0 to 40,113	
Rate	11.00%	
Range of 2nd bracket	$40,114 to $114,610	all income
Rate	13.00%	10.00%
Range of 3rd bracket	$114,611 and over	
Rate	15.00%	
Range of 4th bracket	N/A	
Rate	N/A	
Range of 5th bracket	N/A	
Rate	N/A	
1st Tier Surtax criteria	N/A	
Rate	N/A	
2nd Tier Surtax criteria	N/A	
Rate	N/A	
Basic Personal Amount	$13,269	$16,775
Age Amount	$4,340	$4,675
Pension Income Amount	$1,000	$1,292
Education full time/month	$400	$652
Education part time/month	$120	$196
Textbook full time/month	N/A	N/A
Textbook part time/month	N/A	N/A
Disability Amount	$8,395	$12,940
Spouse Amount	$13,269	$16,775
Eligible Dependent Amount	$13,269	$16,775
Child Amount <18 years	N/A	N/A
Child Amount <6 years	N/A	N/A
Adoption Amount	N/A	$11,473
Caregiver Amount	$8,395	$9,711
Infirm Dependent >18 years	$8,395	$9,710

	British Columbia	Yukon
Range of 1st bracket	$0 to $35,716	$0 to $40,726
Rate	5.06%	7.04%
Range of 2nd bracket	$35,717 to $71,433	$40,727 to $81,452
Rate	7.70%	9.68%
Range of 3rd bracket	$71,434 to $82,014	$81,453 to $126,264
Rate	10.50%	11.44%
Range of 4th bracket	$82,015 to $99,588	$126,265 and over
Rate	12.29%	12.76%
Range of 5th bracket	Over $99,589	N/A
Rate	14.70%	N/A
1st Tier Surtax criteria	N/A	terr. tax in excess of $6,000
Rate	N/A	5.00% on excess
2nd Tier Surtax criteria	N/A	N/A
Rate		

	British Columbia	Yukon
Basic Personal Amount	$9,373	$10,320
Age Amount	$4,203	$6,408
Pension Income Amount	$1,000	$2,000
Education full time/month	$200	$400
Education part time/month	$60	$120
Textbook full time/month	N/A	$65
Textbook part time/month	N/A	$20
Disability Amount	$7,030	$7,196
Spouse Amount	$8,026	$10,320
Eligible Dependent Amount	$8,026	$10,320
Child Amount <18 years	N/A	N/A
Child Amount <6 years	N/A	N/A
Adoption Amount	$10,909	$10,909
Caregiver Amount	$4,101	$4,198
Infirm Dependent >18 years	$4,101	$4,198

	Northwest Terr.	Nunavut
Range of 1st bracket	$0 to $36,885	$0 to $40,726
Rate	5.90%	4.00%
Range of 2nd bracket	$36,886 to $73,772	$40,727 to $81,452
Rate	8.60%	7.00%
Range of 3rd bracket	$73,773 to $119,936	$81,453 to $126,264
Rate	12.20%	9.00%
Range of 4th bracket	$119,937 and over	$126,265 and over
Rate	14.05%	11.50%
Range of 5th bracket	N/A	N/A
Rate	N/A	N/A
1st Tier Surtax criteria	N/A	N/A
Rate	N/A	N/A
2nd Tier Surtax criteria	N/A	N/A
Rate		
Basic Personal Amount	$12,664	$11,644
Age Amount	$6,195	$8,733
Pension Income Amount	$1,000	$2,000
Education full time/month	$400	$400
Education part time/month	$120	$120
Textbook full time/month	N/A	$65
Textbook part time/month	N/A	$20
Disability Amount	$10,270	$11,644

	Northwest Terr.	Nunavut
Spouse Amount	$12,664	$11,644
Eligible Dependent Amount	$12,664	$11,644
Child Amount <18 years	N/A	N/A
Child Amount <6 years	N/A	$1,200
Adoption Amount	N/A	N/A
Caregiver Amount	$4,198	$4,198
Infirm Dependent >18 years	$4,198	$4,198

Table 2/2009 Top Marginal Rates of Tax (Federal and provincial combined)

Province	Interest & foreign dividends (%)	Capital gains (%)	Eligible dividends (%)	Other Canadian dividends (%)
British Columbia	43.70	21.85	19.92	32.71
Alberta	39.00	19.50	14.56	27.71
Saskatchewan	44.00	22.00	20.35	30.83
Manitoba	46.40	23.20	23.83	38.21
Ontario	46.41	23.21	23.06	31.34
Quebec	48.22	24.11	29.69	36.35
New Brunswick	46.00	23.00	21.80	34.21
Prince Edward Island	47.37	23.69	24.44	38.15
Nova Scotia	48.25	24.13	28.35	33.06
Newfoundland and Labrador	44.50	22.25	22.89	32.71
Yukon	42.40	21.20	17.23	30.49
Northwest Territories	43.05	21.53	18.25	29.65
Nunavut	40.50	20.25	22.23	28.96

Table 3/2009 Tax Payable at Various Levels of Taxable Income[a]

Taxable Income ($)	British Columbia[b]	Alberta
$20,000	$1,688	$1,775
$25,000	$2,851	$3,025
$30,000	$3,996	$4,275
$35,000	$4,999	$5,525
$40,000	$6,115	$6,775
$45,000	$7,549	$8,324
$50,000	$9,034	$9,924
$55,000	$10,519	$11,524
$60,000	$12,004	$13,124
$65,000	$13,489	$14,724
$70,000	$14,974	$16,324
$75,000	$16,559	$17,924
$80,000	$18,184	$19,524
$85,000	$20,004	$21,266
$90,000	$21,919	$23,066
$95,000	$23,833	$24,866
$100,000	$25,758	$26,666
$105,000	$27,793	$28,466
$115,000	$31,863	$32,066
$125,000	$35,933	$35,666
$150,000	$46,820	$45,378
$200,000	$68,670	$64,878
$250,000	$90,520	$84,378
$500,000	$199,770	$181,878

Taxable Income ($)	Saskatchewan	Manitoba[c]
$20,000	$2,192	$2,705
$25,000	$3,492	$4,024
$30,000	$4,792	$5,314
$35,000	$6,092	$6,682
$40,000	$7,392	$8,069
$45,000	$9,089	$9,756
$50,000	$10,839	$11,493
$55,000	$12,589	$13,231
$60,000	$14,339	$14,968
$65,000	$16,089	$16,706
$70,000	$17,839	$18,583
$75,000	$19,589	$20,553

Taxable Income ($)	Saskatchewan	Manitoba[c]
$80,000	$21,339	$22,523
$85,000	$23,231	$24,635
$90,000	$25,181	$26,805
$95,000	$27,131	$28,975
$100,000	$29,081	$31,145
$105,000	$31,031	$33,315
$115,000	$34,939	$37,655
$125,000	$39,039	$41,995
$150,000	$50,001	$53,557
$200,000	$72,001	$76,757
$250,000	$94,001	$99,957
$500,000	$204,001	$215,957

Taxable Income ($)	Ontario[d]	Quebec[e]
$20,000	$2,125	$2,321
$25,000	$3,477	$3,748
$30,000	$4,530	$5,174
$35,000	$5,582	$6,600
$40,000	$6,882	$8,091
$45,000	$8,389	$9,967
$50,000	$10,097	$11,886
$55,000	$11,654	$13,804
$60,000	$13,212	$15,723
$65,000	$14,771	$17,641
$70,000	$16,420	$19,560
$75,000	$18,251	$21,478
$80,000	$20,163	$23,526
$85,000	$22,276	$25,763
$90,000	$24,446	$28,048
$95,000	$26,617	$30,334
$100,000	$28,787	$32,619
$105,000	$30,958	$34,905
$115,000	$35,299	$39,476
$125,000	$39,639	$44,047
$150,000	$51,204	$56,069
$200,000	$74,409	$80,177
$250,000	$97,764	$104,284
$500,000	$213,788	$224,822

Taxable Income ($)	New Brunswick[f]	PEI
$20,000	$2,222	$2,657
$25,000	$3,655	$3,897
$30,000	$5,017	$5,137
$35,000	$6,249	$6,497
$40,000	$7,690	$7,937
$45,000	$9,464	$9,676
$50,000	$11,289	$11,466
$55,000	$13,114	$13,256
$60,000	$14,939	$15,046
$65,000	$16,764	$16,866
$70,000	$18,589	$18,801
$75,000	$20,468	$20,736
$80,000	$22,368	$22,671
$85,000	$24,410	$24,748
$90,000	$26,510	$26,883
$95,000	$28,610	$29,018
$100,000	$30,710	$31,184
$105,000	$32,810	$33,403
$115,000	$37,010	$37,840
$125,000	$41,299	$42,277
$150,000	$52,761	$54,081
$200,000	$75,761	$77,766
$250,000	$98,761	$101,451
$500,000	$213,761	$219,876

Taxable Income ($)	Nova Scotia[g]	Newfoundland
$20,000	$2,458	$2,393
$25,000	$3,698	$3,528
$30,000	$4,913	$4,663
$35,000	$6,410	$5,999
$40,000	$7,908	$7,389
$45,000	$9,704	$9,078
$50,000	$11,552	$10,818
$55,000	$13,399	$12,558
$60,000	$15,261	$14,298
$65,000	$17,195	$16,116
$70,000	$19,128	$17,991
$75,000	$21,062	$19,866
$80,000	$22,995	$21,741
$85,000	$25,133	$23,758
$90,000	$27,350	$25,833

Taxable Income ($)	Nova Scotia[g]	Newfoundland
$95,000	$29,585	$27,908
$100,000	$31,848	$29,983
$105,000	$34,110	$32,058
$115,000	$38,635	$36,208
$125,000	$43,160	$40,358
$150,000	$55,185	$51,445
$200,000	$79,310	$73,695
$250,000	$103,435	$95,945
$500,000	$224,060	$207,195

Taxable Income ($)	Yukon	Northwest Terr.[h]
$20,000	$2,133	$1,473
$25,000	$3,235	$2,455
$30,000	$4,337	$3,438
$35,000	$5,439	$4,420
$40,000	$6,541	$5,487
$45,000	$8,055	$6,903
$50,000	$9,639	$8,376
$55,000	$11,223	$9,856
$60,000	$12,807	$11,336
$65,000	$14,391	$12,816
$70,000	$15,975	$14,336
$75,000	$17,559	$15,910
$80,000	$19,143	$17,620
$85,000	$20,956	$19,472
$90,000	$22,857	$21,382
$95,000	$24,757	$23,292
$100,000	$26,658	$25,202
$105,000	$28,559	$27,112
$115,000	$32,360	$30,932
$125,000	$36,161	$34,846
$150,000	$46,705	$45,571
$200,000	$67,904	$67,096
$250,000	$89,103	$88,621
$500,000	$195,098	$196,246

Taxable Income ($)	Nunavut[i]
$20,000	$1,386
$25,000	$2,236
$30,000	$3,086
$35,000	$3,936

Taxable Income ($)	Nunavut[i]
$40,000	$4,786
$45,000	$6,064
$50,000	$7,414
$55,000	$8,764
$60,000	$10,114
$65,000	$11,564
$70,000	$13,014
$75,000	$14,464
$80,000	$15,914
$85,000	$17,577
$90,000	$19,327
$95,000	$21,077
$100,000	$22,827
$105,000	$24,577
$115,000	$28,077
$125,000	$31,577
$150,000	$41,632
$200,000	$61,882
$250,000	$82,132
$500,000	$183,382

Notes

(a) This table shows the amount of tax payable for a given taxable income by a person whose only tax credit is the basic non-refundable personal credit and who has no income from taxable Canadian dividends. Taxable income is assumed to be equal to net income.

(b) Considers the BC low-income tax reduction.

(c) Considers the Manitoba low-income family tax benefit.

(d) Considers the Ontario Health Premium Tax.

(e) Quebec's tax system is significantly different from those of the other provinces, and the amounts listed are illustrative rather than exact calculations. Allowable deductions will generally make taxable income somewhat lower for a resident of Quebec than for a resident elsewhere in Canada with the same total income.

(f) Considers the New Brunswick low-income tax reduction.

(g) Considers the Nova Scotia low-income tax reduction.

(h) Considers the cost-of-living tax credit.

(i) Considers the cost-of-living tax credit.

Table 4/Canada Pension Plan Contributions and Benefits (2009)

Contributions	
Pensionable earnings	$46,300
Year's basic exemption	$3,500
Maximum contributory earnings	$42,800
Employee and employer rate	4.95%
Maximum annual employee/employer contribution	$2,118.60
Maximum annual self-employed contribution	$4,237.20

Benefits	
Maximum monthly pension	
if starting at age 60	$636.13
if starting at age 65	$908.75
if starting at age 70	$1,181.38
Maximum single payment on death	$2,500.00
Maximum monthly pension for surviving spouse or common-law partner	
under 65 years of age	$506.38
65 years of age and older	$545.25
Maximum monthly disability pension	$1,105.99

There are also benefits for children of deceased or disabled contributors.

Notes

1. Persons over 60 years of age are eligible to receive pension benefits. The pension amount is reduced before age 65 or increased after age 65 by 0.5% (or 6% per year) for each month between the beneficiary's 65th birthday and the month the pension becomes payable. The contributor has the option of drawing retirement benefits as early as age 60 or as late as age 70. (See article 13 for proposed changes to the adjustment factors.)
2. When the surviving spouse or common-law partner reaches 65, the pension is equal to 60% of the retirement pension.
3. An individual who is married or living common law can apply to have up to 50% of his or her CPP retirement benefits assigned to his or her spouse or common-law partner, provided that both are at least 60 years old and that both have either applied for, or are

already in receipt of, CPP retirement benefits. CPP credits may also be divided on application by a legal spouse or common-law partner after a separation of at least one year, provided that both spouses or common-law partners had previously lived together continuously for at least one year.

4. CPP disability benefits can be reinstated if a former recipient is required to cease working for reasons relating to his or her disability within two years of returning to work.

Table 5/Employment Insurance (2009)

Maximum insurable earnings	$42,300
Employee rate	1.73%
Maximum employee premiums	$731.79
Employer rate	2.42%
Maximum employer premiums	$1,024.51
Regular benefits—maximum weekly amount	$447*

* Could be higher for low-income families with children.

Repayment of Employment Insurance (EI) benefits

You must repay a percentage of your EI benefits if your net income for the year exceeds the threshold. The repayment is equal to 30% of the lesser of (1) total benefits paid to you in the tax year or (2) the amount by which your net income exceeds $52,875 ($51,375 for 2008). All first-time claimants and EI special benefits for illness, maternity, compassionate care or parental reasons are exempt from this benefit repayment.

The repayment must be included in your income tax return as taxes payable. The amount of the repayment is deductible in calculating net income for the year.

Non-insurable employment

No EI is collected in the case of:

- employment by a corporation of a person who owns more than 40% of the issued voting shares;
- certain non-arm's-length employment; or
- casual employment, if it is not for your usual trade or business.

Compassionate care program

You can receive up to a maximum of six weeks of benefits if you have to be away from work temporarily to provide care or support to a member of your family who is gravely ill, with a significant risk of death within the next six months. A medical certificate will be required to obtain benefits under this program. For purposes of this program, a family member includes a child or the child of a spouse or common-law partner, a spouse or common-law partner, or a parent (including a step-parent or common-law partner of one parent).

Table 6/2009 Federal Corporate Income Tax Rates

Income eligible for the small-business deduction	11%[1,2]
Active business income not eligible for the small-business deduction—manufacturing and processing profits earned in Canada and other business income	19%[3]
Income not from an active business (CCPC)	28%[4]

Notes

1. The corporate surtax was eliminated for all corporations effective January 1, 2008, prorated for taxation years that include that date (the surtax added 1.12% to the corporate tax rate).
2. The amount of annual active business income that qualifies for this low rate of tax increased from $400,000 to $500,000 effective January 1, 2009. Larger corporations' access to this rate is restricted. The restriction applies to CCPCs whose taxable capital exceeds $10 million for the preceding year. If the taxable capital is between $10 million and $15 million, the amount eligible for the low rate is reduced, and any eligibility ceases if taxable capital surpasses $15 million.
3. For 2008 and 2009, the general corporate rate is 28% (29.12% prior to 2008, as the rate included the corporate surtax). There is a 9% rate reduction to 19% for 2009 for most active business income in excess of the small-business limit. This rate reduction does not apply to corporations that are investment corporations, mortgage investment corporations, mutual fund corporations or non-resident-owned investment corporations. This rate is further reduced to 18% (effective January 1, 2010), 16.5% (effective January 1, 2011), and then 15% (effective January 1, 2012).
4. A refundable tax of 6.67% is imposed on the investment income of a CCPC. This tax is in addition to the taxes outlined above and will be included as a portion of the taxes that may be refunded to a corporation on the payment of a taxable dividend. This results in a federal tax rate of 34.67%.
5. Although the federal Large Corporations Tax was eliminated as at January 1, 2006, the federal capital tax levied on large financial institutions continues to apply. This tax is currently calculated as 1.25% of taxable capital in excess of $1 billion.

Table 7/2009 Provincial Corporate Tax Rates

Province/ territory	Small-business deduction only	Manufacturing & processing only	Other income
British Columbia	2.5%[1]	11%[1]	11%[1]
Alberta	3%[2]	10%	10%
Saskatchewan	4.5%[3]	10%	12%[4]
Manitoba	1%[5]	13% or 12%[6]	13% or 12%[6]
Ontario	5.5%[7,8]	12%[9]	14%[9]
Quebec	8%[10]	11.9%[11]	11.9%[11]
New Brunswick	5%[12]	13% or 12%[13]	13% or 12%[13]
Prince Edward Island	3.2% or 2.1%[14]	16%	16%
Nova Scotia	0% or 5%[15]	16%	16%
Newfoundland and Labrador	5%[16]	5%	14%
Yukon	2.5% or 4%[17]	2.5%	15%
Northwest Territories	4%[18]	11.5%	11.5%
Nunavut	4%[19]	12%	12%

Notes

1. The rate for manufacturing and processing, and other income decreased from 12% to 11%, effective July 1, 2008. This rate will be further reduced to 10.5% effective Jan. 1, 2010 and then to 10% effective Jan. 1, 2011. The small-business rate decreased from 3.5% to 2.5%, effective Dec. 1, 2008. The small-business rate applies to the first $400,000 of active business income. It is proposed that the small-business threshold will increase to $500,000 on January 1, 2010.
2. In September 2006, the province announced a phased-in increase in the small-business limit from $400,000 to $500,000 by 2009. The threshold increased to $430,000 on April 1, 2007, $460,000 on April 1, 2008, and to $500,000 on April 1, 2009.
3. The small-business limit increased from $450,000 to $500,000, effective July 1, 2008.
4. The general corporate income tax rate was reduced from 13% to 12%, effective July 1, 2008.
5. The small-business rate was reduced from 2% to 1% effective Jan. 1,

2009. The small-business income tax rate will be reduced from 1% to zero, effective December 1, 2010. The small-business rate applies to the first $400,000 of active business income.

6. The general corporate rate was reduced from 13% to 12%, effective July 1, 2009.
7. Effective January 1, 2007, the small-business limit increased from $400,000 to $500,000. It is also proposed that the small-business rate will be reduced from 5.5% to 4.5%, effective July 1, 2010.
8. Ontario claws back the benefit of the small-business tax rate (in the form of a surtax) if taxable income (on an associated group basis) falls within a specified range. This surtax "claws back" the provincial small-business deduction, on a graduated basis, when the taxable income falls between $500,000 and $1,500,000. The effect is to recover the entire small-business deduction once taxable income of an associated group reaches $1,500,000. Effective July 1, 2010, it is proposed that this clawback will be eliminated. As a result, all CCPCs will be taxed at the small-business rate on the first $500,000 of active business income regardless of income level.
9. It is proposed that the general income tax rate will be reduced from 14% to 12% effective July 1, 2010 with further reductions to 11.5% on July 1, 2011, 11% on July 1, 2012, and 10% on July 1, 2013. It is also proposed that the rate applicable to manufacturing and processing companies will be reduced from 12% to 10%, effective July 1, 2010.
10. It is proposed that the small-business limit will increase from $400,000 to $500,000 of active business income, effective March 20, 2009. The small-business limit is gradually reduced for corporations with paid-up capital between $10 million and $15 million, and is totally eliminated for corporations with paid-up capital in excess of $15 million.
11. This rate was increased from 11.4% to 11.9%, effective January 1, 2009.
12. The small-business limit was increased from $400,000 to $500,000, effective Jan. 1, 2009.
13. The general corporate tax rate is reduced from 13% to 12%, effective July 1, 2009. This rate will be further reduced to 11% on July 1, 2010, 10% on July 1, 2011 and to 8% on July 1, 2012.
14. The small-business limit was increased from $400,000 to $500,000 effective Jan. 1, 2009. The small-business rate is being reduced by

1.1% each year, effective April 1 of each year. Therefore, the rate is reduced to 3.2% (effective April 1, 2008), to 2.1% (effective April 1, 2009), and to 1.0% (effective April 1, 2010).

15. Applies to the first $400,000 of active business income. Certain newly incorporated small businesses are not subject to any tax on income qualifying for the small-business deduction for their first three taxation years. Although it was proposed that the current small-business rate of 5% would be reduced to 2.5% (over a three-year period from 2011 to 2013) the government was defeated in a vote of non-confidence immediately following the 2009 Nova Scotia budget announcement.
16. The small-business limit increased from $400,000 to $500,000, effective January 1, 2009.
17. The rate for manufacturing income is 2.5% and the rate for non-manufacturing income is 4%. The non-manufacturing rate applies to the first $400,000 of active business income.
18. Applies to the first $500,000 of active business income.
19. Applies to the first $500,000 of active business income.

GRANT THORNTON LLP OFFICES

NATIONAL OFFICES

Toronto Office
12th Floor
50 Bay Street
Toronto, ON
M5J 2Z8
Tel: (416) 366-4240
Fax: (416) 360-4944

Halifax Office
Suite 1100
2000 Barrington Street
Halifax, NS
B3J 3K1
Tel: (902) 421-1734
Fax: (902) 421-1677

LOCAL OFFICES

Antigonish, NS
257 Main Street, PO Box 1480
Antigonish, NS
B2G 2L7
Tel: (902) 863-4587
Fax: (902) 863-0917

Barrie, ON
Unit 201
85 Bayfield Street
Barrie, ON
L4M 3A7
Tel: (705) 730-6574
Fax: (705) 730-6575

Bathurst, NB
Suite 500, Harbourview Place
275 rue Main Street, PO Box 220
Bathurst, NB
E2A 3Z2
Tel: (506) 546-6616
Fax: (506) 548-5622

Bridgewater, NS
4th Floor, Dawson Centre
197 Dufferin Street, PO Box 220
Bridgewater, NS
B4V 2W8
Tel: (902) 543-8115
Fax: (902) 543-7707

Calgary, AB
Suite 900
833 – 4th Avenue SW
Calgary, AB
T2P 3T5
Tel: (403) 260-2500
Fax: (403) 260-2571

Charlottetown, PE
Suite 501
199 Grafton Street, PO Box 187
Charlottetown, PE
C1A 7K4
Tel: (902) 892-6547
Fax: (902) 566-5358

Corner Brook, NL
49-51 Park Street
Corner Brook, NL
A2H 2X1
Tel: (709) 634-4382
Fax: (709) 634-9158

Digby, NS
Basin Place
68 Water Street, PO Box 848
Digby, NS
B0V 1A0
Tel: (902) 245-2553
Fax: (902) 245-6161

Edmonton, AB
1401 Scotia Place 2
10060 Jasper Avenue NW
Edmonton, AB
T5J 3R8
Tel: (780) 422-7114
Fax: (780) 426-3208

Fredericton, NB
4th Floor
570 Queen Street, PO Box 1054
Fredericton, NB
E3B 5C2
Tel: (506) 458-8200
Fax: (506) 453-7029

Grand Falls, NL
9 High Street, PO Box 83
Grand Falls, NL
A2A 2J3
Tel: (709) 489-6622
Fax: (709) 489-6625

Halifax, NS
Suite 1100
2000 Barrington Street
Halifax, NS
B3J 3K1
Tel: (902) 421-1734
Fax: (902) 420-1068

Hamilton, ON
Standard Life Centre
1040 – 120 King Street W
Hamilton, ON
L8P 4V2
Tel: (905) 525-1930
Fax: (905) 527-4413

Kelowna, BC
200-1633 Ellis Street
Kelowna, BC
V1Y 2A8
Tel: (250) 712-6800
Fax: (250) 712-6850

Kentville, NS
15 Webster Street, PO Box 68
Kentville, NS
B4N 3V9
Tel: (902) 678-7307
Fax: (902) 679-1870

Langley, BC
Suite 320
8700 – 200th Street
Langley, BC
V2Y 0G4
Tel: (604) 455-2600
Fax: (604) 455-2609

London, ON
Suite 406
140 Fullarton Street
London, ON
N6A 5P2
Tel: (519) 672-2930
Fax: (519) 672-6455

Markham, ON
Suite 200
15 Allstate Parkway
Markham, ON
L3R 5B4
Tel: (416) 366-0100
Fax: (905) 475-8906

Marystown, NL
2 Queen Street, PO Box 518
Marystown, NL
A0E 2M0
Tel: (709) 279-2300
Fax: (709) 279-2340

Miramichi, NB
135 Henry Street
Miramichi, NB
E1V 2N5
Tel: (506) 622-0637
Fax: (506) 622-5174

Mississauga, ON
Suite 401
350 Burnhamthorpe Road W
Mississauga, ON
L5B 3J1
Tel: (416) 366-0100
Fax: (905) 804-0509

Moncton, NB
Suite 500
633 rue Main Street, PO Box 1005
Moncton, NB
E1C 8P2
Tel: (506) 857-0100
Fax: (506) 857-0105

Montague, PE
1 Bailey Drive, PO Box 70
Montague, PE
C0A 1R0
Tel: (902) 838-4121
Fax: (902) 838-4802

New Glasgow, NS
Suite 270, Aberdeen Business Centre
610 East River Road, PO Box 427
New Glasgow, NS
B2H 5E5
Tel: (902) 752-8393
Fax: (902) 752-4009

New Liskeard, ON
17 Wellington Street, PO Box 2170
New Liskeard, ON
P0J 1P0
Tel: (705) 647-8100
Fax: (705) 647-7026

North Bay, ON
Suite 200
222 McIntyre Street W
North Bay, ON
P1B 2Y8
Tel: (705) 472-6500
Fax: (705) 472-7760

Orillia, ON
Suite 300
6 West Street N
Orillia, ON
L3V 5B8
Tel: (705) 326-7605
Fax: (705) 326-0837

Port Colborne, ON
Suite B
222 Catharine Street, PO Box 336
Port Colborne, ON
L3K 5W1
Tel: (905) 834-3651
Fax: (905) 834-5095

Saint John, NB
4th Floor, Brunswick House
44 Chipman Hill
Saint John, NB
E2L 2A9
Tel: (506) 634-2900
Fax: (506) 634-4569

Sault Ste. Marie, ON
5th Floor, Station Tower
421 Bay Street
Sault Ste. Marie, ON
P6A 1X3
Tel: (705) 945-9700
Fax: (705) 945-9705

St. John's, NL
187 Kenmount Road
St. John's, NL
A1B 3P9
Tel: (709) 722-5960
Fax: (709) 722-7892

Summerside, PE
Holman Technology Centre
250 Water Street, Suite 301
Summerside, PE
C1N 1B6
Tel: (902) 436-9155
Fax: (902) 436-6913

Sydney, NS
Suite 200, George Place
500 George Street
Sydney, NS
B1P 1K6
Tel: (902) 562-5581
Fax: (902) 562-0073

Thunder Bay, ON
979 Alloy Drive
Thunder Bay, ON
P7B 5Z8
Tel: (807) 345-6571
Fax: (807) 345-0032

Toronto, ON
19th Floor, Royal Bank Plaza South Tower
200 Bay Street, PO Box 55
Toronto, ON
M5J 2P9
Tel: (416) 366-0100
Fax: (416) 360-4949

Truro, NS
Suite 400
35 Commercial Street, PO Box 725
Truro, NS
B2N 5E8
Tel: (902) 893-1150
Fax: (902) 893-9757

Vancouver, BC
Suite 1600, Grant Thornton Place
333 Seymour Street
Vancouver, BC
V6B 0A4
Tel: (604) 687-2711
Fax: (604) 685-6569

Victoria, BC
3rd Floor
888 Fort Street
Victoria, BC
V8W 1H8
Tel: (250) 383-4191
Fax: (250) 381-4623

Wetaskiwin, AB
5108 – 51st Avenue
Wetaskiwin, AB
T9A 0V2
Tel: (780) 352-1679
Fax: (780) 352-2451

Winnipeg, MB
94 Commerce Drive
Winnipeg, MB
R3P 0Z3
Tel: (204) 944-0100
Fax: (204) 957-5442

Yarmouth, NS
328 Main Street, PO Box 297
Yarmouth, NS
B5A 4B2
Tel: (902) 742-7842
Fax: (902) 742-0224

Grant Thornton is affiliated with Raymond Chabot Grant Thornton, which offers services within Quebec and in a few select locations in other provinces.

Montréal, QC
National Bank Tower
600 de la Gauchetière Street West, Suite 2300
Montréal, QC
H3B 4L8
Tel: (514) 878-2691
Fax: (514) 878-2127

Ottawa, ON
2505 St.-Laurent Boulevard
Ottawa, ON
K1H 1E4
Tel: (613) 236-2211
Fax: (613) 236-6104

WEBSITES
Grant Thornton LLP:
www.GrantThornton.ca
Raymond Chabot Grant Thornton:
www.rcgt.com
Canada Revenue Agency (CRA):
www.cra-arc.gc.ca

ABBREVIATIONS

ABI	active business income
ABIL	allowable business investment loss
ACB	adjusted cost base
AMT	alternative minimum tax
CCA	capital cost allowance
CCPC	Canadian-controlled private corporation
CLB	Canada Learning Bond
CRA	Canada Revenue Agency
CCTB	Canada Child Tax Benefit
CESG	Canada Education Savings Grant
CNIL	cumulative net investment loss
CPP	Canada Pension Plan
DPSP	deferred profit sharing plan
EI	Employment Insurance
GRIP	general rate income pool
GST	Goods and Services Tax
HBP	Home Buyers' Plan
HST	Harmonized Sales Tax
IPP	individual pension plan
ITC	investment tax credit or input tax credit (GST/HST)
LRIP	low rate income pool
NCB	National Child Benefit
OAS	Old Age Security
PA	pension adjustment
PAR	pension adjustment reversal
PSPA	past service pension adjustment
QSBC	qualified small-business corporation
RDSP	Registered Disability Savings Plan
RESP	Registered Education Savings Plan
RPP	registered pension plan
RRIF	Registered Retirement Income Fund
RRSP	Registered Retirement Savings Plan
SBC	small-business corporation
SR&ED	scientific research and experimental development
TFSA	Tax-Free Savings Account
UCC	undepreciated capital cost
UCCB	Universal Child Care Benefit

GLOSSARY

Active business

Includes any business, as well as an adventure or concern in the nature of trade, but excludes (1) a business that derives its income from property (including interest, dividends, royalties and rent) and has fewer than six full-time employees; and (2) a business that provides personal services through a corporation, has fewer than six full-time employees and where, were it not for the presence of the corporation, the individuals providing the services would be considered employees or officers of the entity using those services.

Active business income (ABI)

Uses corporate income as the benchmark for calculating certain tax credits. It includes income derived from an active business (including incidental income from its active business, such as interest earned on customers' delinquent receivables) and specifically excludes income derived from property such as capital gains, interest, dividends, royalties and rent.

Affiliated

A relationship that exists between persons for purposes of determining whether certain stop-loss rules apply. For example, individuals are affiliated with themselves and their spouse or common-law partner (but not with their children). They are also affiliated with a corporation that they and/or another affiliated person control.

Amortization

See **Depreciation**. The term "amortization" is also used to describe the systematic repayment of a debt's principal and interest.

Annuity

A form of investment that yields a sequence of periodic, usually equal, payments made at equal intervals of time (e.g., $1,200 every month). In return for a single payment to the provider, the annuitant receives a series of payments for a specific term that can begin immediately or be deferred into the future. Annuities can have a variety of options associated with them.

Arm's length

"At arm's length" indicates that the parties to a transaction are unrelated and have separate interests in entering the transaction. A "non-arm's-length" transaction would be one between related parties or between parties with a common interest acting in concert.

Calendar year

The period between January 1 and December 31 of any given year.

Capital asset

An asset intended to be used on a continuing basis by a business in its daily operations for production or supply of goods and services, for rental to others or for administrative purposes. It is not an asset intended for sale in the ordinary course of business, such as an inventory item. A depreciable asset is an example of a capital asset.

Carry-forward

A carry-forward arises when a loss or tax credit is not fully utilized in the current period and, as a result, the unused portion may be used in a future period. For example, a loss carry-forward arises when a taxpayer has incurred a loss in the current period and cannot use it to offset income from a previous period. The loss can be carried forward to offset future income.

Common-law partner

A person of the opposite or the same sex who has either cohabited with you for at least one year in a conjugal relationship or is the parent of your child.

Depreciation

An accounting procedure that aims to distribute the cost of tangible capital assets, less any expected salvage value, over the estimated useful life of the asset in a rational and systematic manner. The depreciation for a period is the portion of the total cost allocated to that period.

Fair market value

The highest price that can be obtained for the sale of an asset between informed parties who deal at arm's length and are under no compulsion to act.

Fiscal year-end

The point in time that a business has chosen to account for its profits and losses. Generally, a corporation may choose any date in the year, but special rules exist for individuals and partnerships (see article 2). Once a business establishes a fiscal year-end date, it cannot be changed for tax purposes without the CRA's approval.

Flow-through share

A form of investment specifically related to the resource industry. Unlike a typical share, certain expenditures incurred by the corporation can be renounced by the corporation and "flowed through" to the shareholders. The shareholders can then deduct these items on their own tax returns.

Goodwill

An intangible asset that represents the superior earning power of a business. Generally, the value assigned to the goodwill of a business is the fair market value of the business as a whole, less the fair market value of the net tangible assets and identifiable intangible assets that comprise the business.

Holding company

A corporation whose principal purpose is to hold investment assets, such as shares in other companies and portfolio investments.

Information returns

Forms or documents containing tax-related information about individuals, corporations, trusts or other entities that the CRA requires them to file so it can administer the provisions of the Income Tax Act.

Joint venture

An economic activity resulting from a contractual arrangement whereby two or more entities jointly control an economic activity. Unlike other investments, none of the venturers can exercise unilateral control over the joint venture, regardless of the ownership interest any of them might hold. A joint venture has no legal status itself. The venturers may own property in common, but each has a direct share in the property.

Limited partnership

In a limited partnership, the limited partners have limited liability. This is a similar responsibility to that of shareholders of a corporation and means that liability is restricted to the amount invested in the partnership. There must be at least one general partner who is fully liable for the debts of the partnership. The general and limited partners share the profits of the partnership in accordance with the terms of a partnership agreement.

Marginal tax rate

The income tax rates that apply to each dollar of additional income at different levels of taxable income. As an individual's income level rises, his or her marginal tax rate also rises.

Non-refundable tax credit

A tax credit earned during the year that is applied to reduce income tax payable for that year but is limited to reducing taxes to a nil balance. If there is an unused portion of the tax credit after reducing taxes to a nil balance, it cannot be used to create a refund. The basic personal credit is an example of a non-refundable tax credit.

Non-resident

The determination of whether a person is a non-resident is a question of fact based on residential ties with another country or the amount of time away from Canada.

Partnership

An arrangement between persons carrying on a common business to earn a profit. It can be formed by a group of individuals, by corporations or by a combination thereof. The partners share the net profits and not the gross returns of a business. A partnership can be formed by verbal or written agreement and is governed by provincial law.

Probate

A fee that has to be paid to probate a will. The fee varies from province to province, but it is essentially levied on the fair market value of an individual's estate that passes through his or her will on death. Assets passing outside the will—for example, by right of survivorship or direct beneficiary designation—are not subject to probate.

Recapture

An income item created when the balance of the undepreciated capital cost (UCC) of a class of depreciable assets becomes negative. This can occur when the proceeds of the disposition of a capital asset (which is limited to the original cost of the asset) is applied to reduce the UCC of the class and results in a negative balance. In essence, a capital cost allowance (CCA) had been recorded in excess of the asset's remaining economic value. On the sale of the assets of that class, a portion of the previous CCA is recovered.

Renunciation

The process of foregoing, or giving up, a particular benefit in a formal manner. Certain tax credits or deductions can be renounced in favour of an alternative treatment.

Reserve

Generally, an income amount that relates to a future period and therefore can be set aside and included in income for that period. A reserve is excluded from the current period's income and included in the next period's income. A new reserve would be established in the next period, if applicable.

Resident

The determination of whether a person is a resident of Canada is a question of fact. The factors considered are residential ties with Canada, length of time in Canada, object, intention and continuity with respect to stays in Canada.

Retained earnings

The total net after-tax income of a corporation, minus distributions of dividends to shareholders that have accumulated since incorporation.

Share capital

Basically, the owner's investment in a corporation, represented by common and preferred shares. A monetary value is assigned to shares when they are first issued from a corporation's treasury.

Small-business limit

The amount of corporate income that qualifies for the low rate of tax. The federal small-business limit is currently $500,000. This limit is shared between associated corporations.

Spouse

The person to whom you are legally married.

Superannuation

The term "superannuation" is synonymous with a pension benefit and includes any amount received out of a pension fund or pension plan. Some examples of items that would be considered a superannuation would be Old Age Security payments, Canada Pension Plan payments and payments from a privately established pension plan.

Testamentary trust

A trust created as a consequence of the death of an individual.

Trust

An entity in which a person (a trustee) acting on behalf of a trust holds property for the benefit of one or more other people (beneficiaries). A trust can be created at any time (inter vivos or testamentary) and is taxed as a separate taxpayer.

Trustee

A person who, alone or with other trustees, administers the operation of a trust and makes various decisions with respect to the trust—for example, when and how much trust income and/or capital to distribute to the trust's beneficiaries—based on the terms of the trust document.

Write-off

A deduction used to reduce net income for tax purposes.

INDEX

A
abbreviations, list of, 304
accrual method, 78
active business, 305
active business income (ABI), 305
active income, 43
actors, 84
administrator, 207
adoption expense credit, 151–152
affiliated, 305
affiliated person, 232
age credit, 157, 195
airline employees, 56–57
Alberta, 285*t*, 288*t*
alimony, 126–128
allowable business investment loss (ABIL), 227, 228, 229, 234
alter-ego trusts, 201–202
alternative minimum tax (AMT), 231, 237, 252, 258
amortization, 305
anniversary award, 54
annual membership dues, 30–31
annuity, 106, 116–117, 203–204, 305
apprentice mechanic deduction for tools, 165–166
apprenticeship job creation tax credit, 40–41
arm's length, 306
arm's length principle, 81
art, donations of, 141–142
artists, 164–165
asset transfers, 200–201
associated-company rules, 46–47
attendant care
  as eligible medical expense, 146, 147
  in retirement home, 151
attendant care/disability supports deduction, 150–151
attribution rules, 174, 180, 240
automobiles
  business use, 59, 60, 61
  employee or partner expenses GST rebate, 92–93
  expenses, 61–63
  GST/HST, 90–93
  interest deduction, maximum, 62
  lease amount, maximum, 62
  moving expenses related to, 131–132
  operating costs, 60–61
  personal use, 58–61
  Quebec requirements, 59
  recapture, 62–63
  standby charge, 58–60, 61
  terminal loss, 62–63
  travel allowances, 63–64, 92, 93
  travel between workplace and home, 62
available-for-use rules, 25
awards, 54–55

B
babysitting costs, 125
blind employees, 57
boarding school, 125
bonuses to shareholders, 47–48
books, 274–275
British Columbia, 285–286*t*, 288*t*
buildings, 22
bulk donations, 142–143
bursary income, 132
business assets, sale of, 47–48
business income
  active income, 43
  First Nations individuals, 214–215
  province of taxation, 19–20
business investment losses, 233–234
business reorganization, 27
buying a business, 94

C
calendar year, 306
Canada Child Tax Benefit (CCTB), 162–163, 208
Canada Disability Savings Grant (CDSG), 178–180
Canada Education Savings Grant (CESG), 176–177
Canada Employment Credit, 158, 166
Canada Learning Bond (CLB) program, 178
Canada Pension Plan (CPP), 34–36, 99, 123, 180, 208, 293*t*
Canada Revenue Agency (CRA), 9, 70, 252–253, 261–262, 262, 265, 266, 269–270
Canada Savings Bonds (CSBs), 240
Canada-United States Tax Convention, 190
Canadian Armed Forces, 184
Canadian-controlled private corporation (CCPC)
  eligible dividends, 236–237
  employee stock options, 64–65
  general rate income pool (GRIP), 232
  optimal compensation, 7
  scientific research and experimental development (SR&ED), 71
  small-business deduction, 43–45
  tax instalments, 273
Canadian residence
  Canadian residents working in U.S., 190
  Closer Connection Exemption Statement, 198–199
  giving up Canadian residence, 187–189
  residency, defined, 189
  resident, defined, 309
  taking up residence, 185–187
  U.S. citizens resident in Canada, 193–195
  U.S. real estate, ownership of, 195–196
capital assets
  capital cost allowance, 21–25
  defined, 306
  non-deductibility, as expense, 21
capital cost allowance (CCA)
  automobiles, 62–63
  available-for-use rules, 25
  calculation of, 23–24
  classes and rates, 23*t*
  declining-balance basis, 22
  generally, 21–22
  half-year rule, 24
  home used for business purposes, 28
  maximum depreciation claim, 25
  rental property, 25, 222, 223
  special rules and restrictions, 25
  undepreciated capital cost (UCC), 24, 223
  useful life of assets, 21–22
capital dividend account, 45
capital gains
  deferral for small business investments, 230
  election, implications of, 225
  election on residential property, 170
  exempt capital gains balance, 241
  generally, 224

going public election, 228
identical properties, 225
lifetime capital gains deduction, 226
losses, offsetting with, 7
mutual funds, 241–242
non-residents, 188
personal-use capital property, sale of, 171–172
qualified farm property, 79–80, 228–229
qualified fishing property, 81, 229
qualified small-business corporations, 227–228
reserves, 98, 230–231
stock option shares, 225–226
treatment as, 224–225
capital gains dividends, 240
capital losses, 231–233
capital property
death of taxpayer, 211
deemed disposition rules, 187
depreciation, 21–25
donation, 139–140
donation of, 139–140
eligible capital property, 25–27
freeze or refreeze, 201
gifts of, 181
giving up Canadian residence, 187–189
intangible capital property, 25–27
personal-use capital property, sale of, 171–172
sale or disposal of, 98
caregiver tax credit, 135
carry-forward, 306
cars. *See* automobiles
cash awards, 55
cash gifts, 181
cash method, 78
change of control, 52–53
charitable annuities, 203–204
charitable donations
art, 141–142
bulk donations, 142–143
charitable annuities, 203–204
charitable remainder trusts, 204
donations in kind, 141–142
as estate planning, 202–205
life insurance policy, 140–141, 203
official receipts, 138
private foundations, 204
property, donation of, 139–140
receipting guidelines, 143–144
RRSP, RRIF and life insurance proceeds, 141
tax credits for, 138–144
tax shelter arrangements, 252–253
charitable remainder trusts, 204
Child Disability Benefit, 162, 163
child support, 126–128
child tax benefit, 99
child tax credit, 135
childcare expenses, 57, 125–126
childcare spaces, 41
children
birth of child, 101
eligible dependant tax credit, 134
filing tax returns, 100
financially dependant child or grandchild, 114–115
gifts, 181
gifts to, 175, 181
GST credit, 102
income splitting, 6–7
intergenerational transfers of farm property, 80–81
intergenerational transfers of fishing property, 81
"kiddie tax," 182–183
medical expenses, 149–150
physical activity programs, 7, 160–162
salaries paid to, 20
and share ownership, 46–47
children's fitness credit, 7, 160–162
Christmas parties, 53–54
Christmas trees, 77
clawback, 124, 195
clearance certificate, 192
clergy residence deduction, 168–169
Closer Connection Exemption Statement, 198–199
club dues, 30–31
collection procedures, 269–270
common-law couples, 164
common-law partner
capital properties left to, 211
defined, 164, 306
income splitting, 6–7
pension income, 6
salaries paid to, 20
sale of transferred property, 173–174
same-sex partners, 164
splitting CPP benefits, 180
tax credit, 134
transfer of capital property, 172–174
transfer of dividend income, 124, 239
unused tax credits, 155–156
computer hardware, 22
construction business, 75–76
contractors, 75–76
control, 47, 52–53
convention expenses, 33–34
corporate tax rate, 44–45, 296*t*
corporations
see also business income; deductible expenses (businesses)
associated-company rules, 46–47
Canadian-controlled private corporation. *See* Canadian-controlled private corporation (CCPC)
capital dividend account, 45
change of control, 52–53
control, 47
eligible dividend rules, 236–237
and First Nations individuals, 214–215, 215
foreign affiliates, investments in, 83
going public, 228
incorporation decision, 41–42
Internet filing, 265
Large Corporations Tax, 45–46
loans from, 51–52
losses, 52–53
low rate income pool (LRIP), 236
mineral exploration tax credit, 250–251
operating losses, 53
qualified small-business corporation (QSBC), 227–228
reorganization, 274
salary *vs.* dividends, 48–49
shareholders. *See* shareholders
small-business deduction, 43–45
succession planning, 206–207
tax information online, 267
tax instalments, 272–274
thin capitalization rules, 82–83
transfer of business assets, 42
transfer pricing, 81–82
cost base adjustment, 238–239
cottages, 170
counselling services, 57, 58
cumulative eligible capital (CEC) pool, 26

cumulative net investment loss (CNIL), 80, 227, 228, 229, 231, 245–246, 252

D

damage awards, 184
daycare, 125
death of taxpayer. *See* deceased taxpayer
debt
  investment or business purposes, 250
  payment of, *vs.* RRSP contribution, 108
  payment of, *vs.* TFSA contributions, 122
  personal purposes, 250
deceased taxpayer
  Canada Child Tax Benefit (CCTB), 208
  Canada Pension Plan payments, 208
  capital property, 211
  deemed disposition on death, 200
  disability tax credit, 138
  estate administration expenses, 211
  executor's responsibilities, 207
  funeral expenses, 211
  GST/HST credit, 208
  income, 210–211
  instalments, 208
  medical expenses, 148
  Old Age Security payments, 208
  "rights or things" return, 209, 210–211
  RRSPs, 114–116
  spousal RRSP contribution, 106
  stock options held at death, 68
  tax return, 209–210
  transfer of farm property, 80–81
deductible expenses (businesses)
  automobile expenses, 61–63
  convention expenses, 33–34
  health/dental insurance premiums, 36
  home office. *See* home office
  life insurance premiums, 36–37
  meals and entertainment expenses, 31–33
  partnerships, 18
  salaries and bonuses, 47–48
  scientific research and experimental development (SR&ED), 68–74
  wage-loss replacement plans, 36
deductible expenses (individuals)
  alimony and maintenance payments, 126–128
  apprentice mechanic deduction for tools, 165–166
  artists and entertainers, 164–165
  attendant care/disability supports, 150–151
  child support, 126–128
  childcare expenses, 125–126
  legal fees, 128–129, 152
  moving expenses, 129–132
  tradespeople's tool expenses, 166
  travel allowances, 63–64
deductible expenses (investments)
  interest expense, 246–250
  rental property expenses, 221
deemed disposition on death, 200
deemed disposition rules, 187
deferred profit sharing plan (DPSP), 56, 58, 104–105, 112, 117, 119
defined benefit plans, 117–118
dental insurance premiums, 36
dependants
  eligible dependent tax credit, 134
  financially dependant child or grandchild, 114–115
  medical expenses, 149–150
depreciation, 306
  see also capital cost allowance (CCA)
designation of principal residence, 170
directors' fees, 50
disabilities
  attendant care/disability supports deduction, 150–151
  disability supplement, 159
  disability tax credit, 135–138, 178, 179
  Henson trust, 179–180
  Home Buyers' Plan withdrawals, 114
  infirm-dependant tax credit, 134
  Registered Disability Savings Plan (RDSP), 6, 178–180
  RESPs, 176
  "support" for tax credit purposes, 137
  and textbook tax credit, 152
  trust to hold investments, 254
disability tax credit, 135–138, 178, 179
discounts, 56
dividends
  capital gains dividends, 240
  dividend gross-up, 235, 236
  eligible dividends, 48–49, 200, 234–238
  from foreign corporation, 235–236, 238–239
  foreign spinoffs, 238–239
  general rate income pool (GRIP), 236–237
  low rate income pool (LRIP), 236
  vs. salary, 48–49
  tax credit mechanism, 235, 236
  transfer between spouses, 124, 239
donations
  charitable donations. *See* charitable donations
  political donations, 144
donations in kind, 141–142
DPSP. *See* deferred profit sharing plan (DPSP)

E

earned income, 100, 109
education credit, 152–154
EFILE, 262–263
elder care, 135
eligible capital property, 25–27
eligible dependant tax credit, 134
eligible dividends, 48–49, 200, 234–238
eligible employees, 66
eligible medical expenses, 144–148
eligible pension income, 123
eligible property, 139
emergency medical service vehicles, 60
emergency volunteers, 169
employees
  see also employment income
  discounts to, 56
  eligible employees, and stock options, 66
  GST/HST employee or partner automobile expenses rebate, 92–93
  loans to, 52, 58
  non-taxable benefits, 55–58
  part-time employees, 57
  vs. self-employment, 16
  stock options, 64–68
employers
  childcare spaces, creation of, 41
  CPP remittances, 35–36
  recreational facilities, use of, 56

employment income
  Christmas parties, 53–54
  CPP contributions, 34–36
  directors' fees, 50
  First Nations individuals, 212–213
  gifts and awards, 54–55
  home office expenses, 29–30
  membership dues, 30–31, 55
  non-taxable benefits, 55–57
  taxable benefits, 53–58
Employment Insurance (EI), 21–22, 35, 98, 295*t*
entertainers, 164–165
entertainment expenses, 31–33
epass, 266, 267
equipment for SR&ED, 72
estate administration expenses, 211
estate freezing, 6, 201
estate planning
  alter-ego trusts, 201–202
  asset transfers, 200–201
  deemed disposition on death, 200
  eligible dividends, 200
  estate freezing, 201
  generally, 199–200
  joint-partner trusts, 201–202
  life insurance, 205–206
  planned giving, 202–205
  succession planning, 206–207
  wills, 205
estate tax, U.S., 197–198
executors, 207
exempt capital gains balance, 241
exempt life insurance policies, 205–206
expenses
  apprentice mechanic deduction for tools, 165–166
  attendant care/disability supports deduction, 150–151
  automobile expenses, 61–63
  capital assets, 21
  childcare expenses, 125–126
  convention expenses, 33–34
  estate administration expenses, 211
  fines and penalties, 37
  funeral expenses, 211
  health/dental insurance premiums, 36
  home office. *See* home office
  interest expense, deductibility of, 246–250
  legal fees, 128–129, 152
  life insurance premiums, 36–37
  meals and entertainment expenses, 31–33, 131–132
  medical expenses, 57, 137, 144–150, 151
  moving expenses, 129–132
  partnerships, 18
  rental property expenses, 221
  scientific research and experimental development (SR&ED), 68–74
  tradespeople's tool expenses, 166
  travel allowances, 63–64
  wage-loss replacement plans, 36
extended-cab pickup trucks, 60

F
fair market value, 306
false statements, 277
family members
  and Employment Insurance (EI), 20–21
  income splitting, 6–7, 180–182
  interest-free loans, 175
  salaries paid to, 20
  transfer of capital property, 174
  transportation passes, 57
family trusts, 182–183
farming businesses
  generally, 76–77
  intergenerational transfers, 80–81
  losses, 79
  qualification as business, 76–77
  qualified farm property, 27, 79–80
  related businesses, 77–78
  reporting methods, 78
  restricted farm losses, 79
federal capital tax, 45–46
federal corporate income tax rates, 296*t*
federal personal tax credits
  basic personal credit, 133
  eligible dependant credit, 134
  generally, 133
  spouse or common-law partner credit, 134
federal tax rates and credits, 282*t*
fellowship income, 132
filing and reporting
  see also tax returns
  deceased taxpayer, 209–210
  due dates, 279*t*–281
  EFILE, 262–263
  foreign reporting requirements, 255–258
  GST/HST, 87
  late filing penalty, 275–276
  NETFILE, 263–264
  Notice of Assessment, 266
  Notice of Objection, 266
  request to file, receipt of, 99
  SR&ED expenditures, 69–71, 72, 73
  tax return, 98–100
  TELEFILE, 263–264
financial institutions, 46, 89
financially dependant child or grandchild, 114–115
financing leases, 39
fines, 37
fire vehicles, 60
First Nations individuals
  band management activity, 217
  bands, and share ownership, 215
  business income, 213–214
  and corporate form of ownership, 214–215
  employment income, 212–213
  exemption, 212–215
  GST/HST, 216–217
  investment income, 213–214
  limited partnership (LP) structures, 216
  trusts, 216
first-time home buyers' tax credit, 157
fiscal year-end, 307
fishing businesses
  intergenerational transfers, 81
  qualified fishing property, 27, 81
"flipping" property, 224
flow-through shares, 250–251, 307
foreign affiliates, 83, 256
foreign educational institutes, 153
foreign investment entities (FIEs), 257
foreign pension plans, 186–187
foreign property holdings, 256–257
foreign-source dividend income, 238–239
foreign tax credit, 255
foreign trusts, 256
Form T661 (SR&ED expenses), 69–71, 73
freezing your estate, 6, 201
funeral expenses, 211

G
gambling, 184
general rate income pool (GRIP), 236–237
gifts, 54–55, 175, 181, 201
  see also charitable donations

glossary of terms, 305–310
going public, 228
golf club dues, 30–31
goodwill, 25–26, 307
Grant Thornton LLP, 9, 11, 300–303
gravel, sale of, 78
GST/HST
  allocation of tax between taxable and exempt supplies, 89–90
  and automobiles, 90–93
  buying and selling a business, 94
  collection, 86–87
  credit, 99, 101–102
  death of taxpayer, 208
  directors' liability, 50
  employee or partner expenses rebate, 92–93
  exempt supplies, 86, 89–90
  First Nations individuals, 216–217
  generally, 85–86
  home office expenses, 28–29, 30
  input tax credits, 88–90
  meals and entertainment expenses, 32–33
  NETFILE/TELEFILE, 87, 264
  new businesses, 87
  real property sales, 93–94
  registration, 86–87
  remittances, 87
  reporting period, 87
  travel allowances, 64, 92, 93
  zero-rated goods, 86, 87, 88
Guaranteed Income Supplement, 99, 135
guaranteed investment certificates (GICs), 111

H
half-year rule, 24
health care spending account (HCSA) credits, 57
health insurance premiums, 36
Henson trust, 179–180
high-risk international missions, 184
higher education financing, 114
holding company, 183, 240, 244–245, 307
Home Buyers' Plan, 99, 112–114
home office
  deduction limits, 27–28
  depreciation on portion of home, 28
  employees, 29–30
  GST/HST, 28–29, 30
  self-employment income, 27–29
home purchase loan, 58
home renovation tax credit (HRTC), 157–158
HST. *See* GST/HST

I
identical properties, 225
immigration trust, 186
income
  active business income (ABI), 305
  active income, 43
  business income. *See* business income
  deceased taxpayer, 210–211
  earned income, 109
  earned on income, 181
  employment income. *See* employment income
  interest income, 239–240
  investment income. *See* investment income
  pension income. *See* pension income
  rental income. *See* rental property
  scholarship income, 131, 132
  tax-free income, 184
  from U.S. sources, 196–197
income splitting
  CPP benefits, 180
  family members, 6–7, 180–182
  family trusts, 182–183
  loan to spouse, 6, 174
  pension income, 6, 99, 122–123
income tax instalments, 271–274
income tax overpayments, 272
income tax rates
  corporate tax rates, 44–45, 296*t*
  federal and provincial, table, 282–287*t*
  federal corporate income tax rates, 296*t*
  provincial corporate tax rates, 297*t*
  tax payable at various income levels, 288–292*t*
  top marginal tax rates, 287*t*
income tax refunds, 99, 100, 268, 270–271
income tax returns. *See* filing and reporting; tax returns
income trusts, 242–244
incorporation decision, 41–42
individual pension plans (IPP), 119–120
individual retirement account (IRA), 112
individual tax number (ITN), 191
infirm-dependant tax credit, 134–135
information return, 18–19, 264–265, 307
information slips, 262
input tax credits, 88–90
instalment sales, 37–38
insurance corporations, 46
intangible capital property, 25–27
integration, 42–43
interest
  cross-border interest payments, 83–84, 191–192
  deductibility of, 240, 246–250
  foreign affiliates, investments in, 83
  interest income, 239–240
  recent court cases, 247–249
  on refund amounts, 271
  on tax overpayments, 272
  on tax owing, 276
  waiver of, 268, 276
  withholding tax, 83–84
interest on student loan tax credit, 154
intergenerational transfers. *See* transfers
Internal Revenue Service (IRS), 194
Internet
  corporate tax information, 267
  filing, for corporations, 265
  NETFILE, 263–264, 264
  personal tax information, 266–267
Internet services, 57
inventory valuation, 37
investment holding company. *See* holding company
investment income
  allowable business investment loss (ABIL), 234
  alternative minimum tax (AMT), 258
  business investment losses, 233–234
  capital gains. *See* capital gains
  capital losses, 231–233
  cumulative net investment loss (CNIL), 245–246
  dividend income. *See* dividends

  exempt life insurance policies, 205–206
  First Nations individuals, 213–214
  foreign investment entities (FIEs), 257
  foreign reporting requirements, 255–258
  foreign taxes, 254–255
  holding company, 244–245
  income trusts, 242–244
  interest expense, deductibility of, 246–250
  interest income, 239–240
  limited partnerships, 251–252
  mineral exploration tax credit, 250–251
  mutual funds, 240–242
  non-resident trusts, 252–253
  personal trusts, taxation of, 253–254
  real estate investment trusts (REITs), 242–244
  rental property. *See* rental property
  resource sector, 250
  segregated funds, 242
  tax shelters, 252–253
investment loans, 18
investment tax credit
  childcare spaces, 41
  mineral exploration tax credit, 250–251
  scientific research and experimental development (SR&ED), 71–72, 73
investment transfers, 110–111

J
joint-partner trusts, 201–202
joint venture, 222, 307

K
"kiddie tax," 182–183

L
Large Corporations Tax, 45–46
lease (automobile), 62
lease-option arrangements, 38–39
legal fees
  adoption expense credit, 152
  business reorganization, 27
  deductibility, 129
  separation or divorce, 128–129
legal representatives, 207, 208
Life Income Fund (LIF), 118–119
life insurance, 205–206
life insurance policy, 140–141, 203
life insurance premiums, 36–37
life insurance proceeds, 74
Lifelong Learning Plan, 99
lifetime capital gains deduction, 226
limitation period, 269–270
limited partnerships, 216, 243, 251–252, 308
limited recourse financing, 251
listed personal property, 172
loans
  deemed interest benefit, 52
  to employees, 52, 58
  to family members, 175
  foreign trusts, 256
  home purchase loan, 58
  income-splitting loan to spouse, 6, 174
  payroll deduction plan, 240
  RRSP loans, 112
  student loans, 154
  10% rule, 52
  from your corporation, 51–52
lodging, 56
long-haul truckers, 32
long-service/anniversary award, 54
losses
  allowable business investment loss (ABIL), 234
  business investment losses, 233–234
  capital losses, 231–233
  carry back of, 40, 232
  corporate losses, 52–53
  cumulative net investment loss (CNIL), 245–246
  disposal of employee's residence, 56
  farming losses, 79
  and home office expenses, 28
  operating losses, 39–40, 53
  property held in inventory, 37
  realization of, 7
  sale of personal property, 171, 172
  terminal loss, 223–224
lottery winnings, 184
low rate income pool (LRIP), 236
loyalty points, 57
lump-sum payments, 183–184
lump-sum transfers to RRSPs, 112, 271

M
maintenance payments, 126–128
management company, 181
Manitoba, 284*t*, 288–289*t*
manufacturing and processing (M&P) machinery and equipment, 22
marginal tax rates, 287*t*, 308
marijuana (medical), 147
marketing quotas, 77
meals, subsidized, 56
meals and entertainment expenses, 31–33, 56, 131–132
medical devices, 147–148
medical expense tax credit, 144–150, 151
medical expenses, 57, 137, 144–150, 151
Medical Marijuana Access Regulations, 147
membership fees, 30–31, 55, 57
mineral exploration tax credit, 250–251
minors. *See* children
misrepresentation, 277
money purchase plans, 117, 118–119
motor-impaired employees, 57
moving expenses, 55–56, 129–132
municipal organizations, 56
musicians, 164
mutual funds, 240–242
My Account service, 266–267

N
National Child Benefit (NCB), 162–163, 178
near-cash awards, 55
NETFILE, 263–264, 264
NETFILE (GST/HST), 87, 264
New Brunswick, 283–284*t*, 290*t*
Newfoundland, 282*t*, 290–291*t*
non-arm's length
  associated-company rules, 46–47
  gifts and awards to employees, 54–55
  withholding tax on interest payments, 83–84
non-calendar year-end, 17
non-cash gifts and rewards, 54–55
non-competition payments, 184–185
non-prescription drugs and medications, 148
non-refundable tax credit
  see also tax credits
  adoption expense credit, 151–152
  apprenticeship job creation tax credit, 40–41
  child tax credit, 135

  defined, 308
  first-time home buyers' tax credit, 157
  home renovation tax credit (HRTC), 157–158
  pension credit, 156
  public transit credit, 159–160
non-resident trusts, 186, 257–258
non-residents
  actors, 84
  Canadian tax obligations, 190–192
  capital gains deduction and, 188
  capital property in Canada, 99
  defined, 308
  disposition of taxable Canadian property, 192–193
  giving up Canadian residence, 187–189
  individual tax number (ITN), 191
  payments for services rendered in Canada, 84–85
  residency, 189
  tax returns, 99, 192
  thin capitalization rules, 82–83
  treaty-protected property, 193
  withholding tax, 191–192
non-taxable benefits, 55–57
northern residents deduction, 166–168
Northwest Territories, 286–287*t*, 291*t*
Notice of Assessment, 266, 269
Notice of Objection, 266
Nova Scotia, 282–283*t*, 290–291*t*
Nunavut, 286–287*t*, 291–292*t*
nursing home care, 146–147

O
Old Age Security, 98, 103, 123, 135, 208
Old Age Security clawback, 124, 195
Ontario, 284*t*, 289*t*
operating costs (car), 60–61
operating losses, 39–40, 53
overcontributions, 108
overhead expenses, SR&ED, 72–73

P
parking expenses, 57, 62
part-time employees, 57
partnerships
  allocation of income, 17–18
  death of taxpayer, 211
  deductible expenses, 18
  defined, 308
  eligible depreciation claim for vehicles, 62
  GST/HST and automobiles, 90
  GST/HST employee or partner automobile expenses rebate, 92–93
  information return, 18–19
  limited partnerships, 216, 243, 251–252
  money borrowed for investment in, 18
  operating losses, 39–40
  rental property, 222
  taxation of income, 17–19
  year-end, 17
past service pension adjustment (PSPA), 104–105
payroll deduction plan, 240
payroll remittances, 277–278
penalties
  deduction of, 37
  generally, 275–276
  late filing, 275–276
  late payroll remittances, 277–278
  misrepresentation by third parties, 277
  preparer penalty, 277
  waiver of, 268, 276
pension adjustment (PA), 104–105, 117
pension adjustment reversals (PAR), 105, 118
pension credit, 156
pension income
  election form for splitting income, 123
  eligible pension income, 123
  from foreign country, 184
  qualifying pension income, 156
  splitting, 6–7, 99, 122–123
  transfer to RRSP, 112
pension income tax credit, 122
pension plans
  defined benefit plans, 117–118
  foreign pension plans, 186–187
  individual pension plans (IPP), 119–120
  money purchase plans, 118–119
  pension income splitting, 6, 122–123
  registered pension plans, 56, 104–105, 112, 117–119
performance-related awards, 55
personal services business income, 43
personal-use capital property, 171–172
personal-use property rules, 141
persons with disabilities. *See* disabilities
physical activity programs, 7, 160–162
planned giving, 202–205
police, 184
police vehicles, 60
political donations, 144
post-secondary institution, 153
pre-authorized payment plan, 272
preparer penalty, 277
prescribed intermediate zone, 166
prescribed northern zone, 166
Prince Edward Island, 282–283*t*, 290*t*
principal residence, 157, 169–171
private foundations, 204
private health services plan, 56, 57
probate, 308
professional corporations
  incorporation, 42
  year-end, 17
professional membership fees, 55
property
  capital property. *See* capital property
  eligible property, 139
  for "flipping," 224
  foreign property holdings, 256–257
  held in inventory, 37
  identical properties, 225
  listed personal property, 172
  qualified farm or fishing property, 27, 79–80, 81
  rental properties. *See* rental property
  reportable property, 188
  sale of. *See* sale
  taxable Canadian property, 192–193
  transfers. *See* transfers
  treaty-protected property, 193
  U.S. real estate, ownership of, 195–196
provincial corporate tax rates, 297*t*
provincial sales taxes, 85
provincial SR&ED incentives, 73
provincial tax credits, 99
provincial tax systems, 133
public company stock options, 66–67
public transit credit, 159–160

Q

qualified farm property, 27, 79–80, 228–229
qualified farm property capital gains deduction, 228–229
qualified fishing property, 27, 81
qualified fishing property capital gains deduction, 81, 229
qualified scientific research expenditures, 68–74
qualified small-business corporation (QSBC), 188, 227–228
qualified small-business corporations capital gains deduction, 227–228
qualified small-business investment, 230
qualifying pension income, 156
qualifying spouse trust, 211
Quebec, 59, 85, 283–284*t*, 289*t*

R

racehorses, 77
reader's guide, 11
real estate investment trusts (REITs), 242–244
real property sales, 93–94
reasonable expectation of profit (REOP), 223
reassessments, 266
recapture, 62–63, 309
records, 274–275
reforestation, 78
refreezing your estate, 6, 201
refund of tax. *See* income tax refunds
refundable medical expense supplement, 149
Registered Disability Savings Plan (RDSP), 6, 178–180
Registered Education Savings Plan (RESP), 175–178
registered pension plans (RPPs), 56, 58, 104–105, 112, 117–119
Registered Retirement Income Fund (RRIF), 106, 115, 116, 118–119, 141, 195
Registered Retirement Savings Plans. *See* RRSPs
relief provisions, 268
religious orders, 168–169
relocation for employment, 130–131
rental property
  deductions, 221
  depreciation restrictions, 25, 222
  joint venture *vs.* partnership, 222
  reasonable expectation of profit (REOP), 223
  rental of home, 171
  sale of, 222–223
  terminal loss, 223–224
  U.S. real property, 196
renunciation, 309
reportable property, 188
representatives, 267–268
research grant income, 131
reserve, 309
reserves, capital gains, 230–231
residency, 189
residency deduction, 167
resident, 309
  see also Canadian residence
resource sector, 250
RESP. *See* Registered Education Savings Plan (RESP)
restricted farm losses, 79
Restricted Life Income Fund (RLIF), 119
restrictive covenant, 185
retained earnings, 309
retirement home, 151
retiring allowances, 111–112
retroactive lump-sum payments, 183–184
returns. *See* tax returns
"rights or things" return, 209, 210–211
RPP. *See* registered pension plans (RPPs)
RRSPs
  age limits, 105–106
  beneficiary, 114–115
  carry-forward rules, 109
  charitable donations, 141
  contribution limit, 103–106, 107
  contributions, 6
  conversion, 106–107
  and death, 114–116
  debt payment *vs.* RRSP contribution, 108
  earned income, 100, 109
  effective use of, 107
  foreign investments, no restrictions on, 110
  higher education financing, 114
  Home Buyers' Plan, 99, 112–114
  Lifelong Learning Plan, 99
  loans, 112
  lump-sum transfers, 112, 271
  non-qualified investments, 110
  overcontributions, 108
  ownership by U.S. persons, 195
  pension adjustment reversals (PAR), 105, 118
  persons with disabilities, 114
  reasons for buying, 102–103
  and retirement, 116–117
  and retiring allowances, 111–112
  RPP and DPSP members, 104–105
  self-directed RRSPs, 109–111
  shares in, 111
  spousal RRSPs, 6, 102–103, 107
  stop-loss rules, 233
  transfer of pension income, 112
  and your mortgage, 110

S

salary
  vs. dividends, 48–49
  to family members, 20
  to shareholders, 47–48
salary deferral arrangements, 49–50
sale
  of business, 94
  of business assets, 47–48
  personal-use capital property, 171–172
  real property, 91–92
  of rental property, 222–223
  of sand, gravel and topsoil, 78
  stock option shares, 225–226
  of taxable Canadian property by non-residents, 192–193
  of transferred property, subsequent, 173–174
  of U.S. property, 196
same-sex partners, 164
sand, sale of, 78
Saskatchewan, 285*t*, 288–289*t*
scholarship income, 131, 132
scientific research and experimental development (SR&ED), 68–74
securities, 139, 233
segregated funds, 242
self-directed RRSPs, 109–111
self-employment
  see also business income
  CPP contributions, 34, 99
  death of taxpayer, 211
  determination of status, 16
  eligible depreciation claim for vehicles, 62
  GST/HST and automobiles, 90
  health/dental insurance premiums, 36

home office expenses, 27–29
operating losses, 39–40
U.S.-source self-employment income, 190
wage-loss replacement plans, 36
year-end, 17
settlement trusts, 216
share capital, 309
share restructuring, 239
sharecropping, 77
shareholder agreements, 74
shareholders
bonuses to, 47–48
loans from corporation, 51
salaries paid to, 47–48
share ownership, 46–47
shareholder agreements, 74
specified shareholder, 82
shares
decline in stock value, 67–68
donation of, 139
flow-through shares, 250–251
foreign corporation, 239
ownership of, 46–47
repurchase, and life insurance proceeds, 74
in RRSP, 111
of a specified class, 47
stock option shares, 225–226
stock options, 64–68
SIFT trust, 243, 244
small-business deduction, 43–45
small business investments, 230
small-business limit, 310
social events, 53–54
social security benefits, 195
sole proprietors. *See* self-employment
source withholdings. *See* withholding tax
Special Access Program, 147
special clothing, 56
specified investment business, 43
specified investment flow-through (SIFT) trusts, 243, 244
specified shareholder, 82
spinoff transaction, 238–239
spousal RRSPs, 6, 102–103, 107
spousal support, 126–128
spouse
capital properties left to, 211
convention expenses, 34
defined, 310
income splitting, 6–7
income-splitting loan to, 6, 174
pension income, 6
RRSPs. *See* spousal RRSPs
salaries paid to, 20
sale of transferred property, 173–174
splitting CPP benefits, 180
tax credit, 134
TFSA contributions, 122
transfer of capital property, 172–174
transfer of dividend income, 124, 239
travel expenses, 57
unused tax credits, 155–156
standby charge, 58–60, 61
stock option shares, 225–226
stock options, 64–68, 73
stop-loss rules, 233
student loans, 154
student moving expenses, 131
subcontractors, 75
subsidized meals, 56
succession planning, 206–207
superannuation, 310
supplementary employment benefit plan, 56
systems software, 22

T

tax credits
adoption expense credit, 151–152
age credit, 157
apprenticeship job creation tax credit, 40–41
Canada Employment Credit, 158
charitable donations, 138–144
child tax credit, 135
children's fitness credit, 7, 160–162
disability credit, 135–138
disability tax credit, 178, 179
education credit, 152–154
federal personal tax credits, 133–135
filing return to claim, 99
first-time home buyers' tax credit, 157
foreign tax credit, 255
generally, 132–133
home renovation tax credit (HRTC), 157–158
interest on student loan, 154
medical expenses, 144–150, 151
mineral exploration tax credit, 250–251
pension credit, 156
political donations, 144
public transit credit, 159–160
spouse's unused credits, 155–156
vs. tax deduction, 132
textbook credit, 152–154
tuition fee credit, 152–154
working income tax benefit (WITB), 158–159
tax-free income, 184
Tax-Free Savings Account (TFSA), 7, 120–122, 255
tax instalments, 271–274
tax payment, preauthorized, 272
tax payment due dates, 279*t*–281
tax payment schedule, 269
tax rates. *See* income tax rates
tax records, 274–275
tax returns
see also filing and reporting
deceased taxpayer, 209–210
due date, 100
filing, 98–100
GST credit claim, 102
late filing penalty, 275
non-residents, 99, 192
request to file, receipt of, 99
"rights or things" return, 210–211
U.S. citizens resident in Canada, 193–195
tax shelters, 25, 250, 252–253
taxable benefits
Christmas parties, 53–54
gifts and awards, 54–55
professional membership fees, 55
social events, 53–54
stock options, 64–68
taxable Canadian property, 192–193
taxpayer relief provisions, 268
TELEFILE, 263–264, 264
TELEFILE (GST/HST), 87, 264
temporary assignments outside Canada, 189
terminal loss, 62–63, 223–224
testamentary trusts, 181, 202, 209, 211, 254, 266, 310
textbook credit, 152–154
thin capitalization rules, 82–83
third-party access to client information, 267–268
TONI (Tax ON Income) system, 133
topsoil, sale of, 78
tradespeople's tool expenses, 166
transfer pricing, 81–82
transfers

asset transfers, 200–201
business assets to corporation, 42
dividend income, 239
to family members, 172–174
foreign trusts, 256
intergenerational transfers of farm property, 80–81
intergenerational transfers of fishing property, 81
investments, to self-directed RRSP, 110–111
sale of transferred property, subsequent, 173–174
of tuition, education and textbook credits, 154
transit employees, 56–57
transportation, 56, 57
transportation passes, 56–57
travel allowances, 63–64, 92, 93
travel deduction, 167–168
travel expenses, 57, 152
Treasury bills, 240
treaty-protected property, 193
trustee, 310
trusts
alter-ego trusts, 201–202
charitable remainder trusts, 204
for child or parent with disability, 254
defined, 310
family trusts, 182–183
First Nations individuals and, 216
foreign trusts, 256
generally, 253
gifting trust arrangements, 252
Henson trust, 179–180
immigration trust, 186
income trusts, 242–244
joint-partner trusts, 201–202
"kiddie tax," 182–183
non-resident trusts, 186, 257–258
preferred-beneficiary election, 254
qualifying spouse trust, 211
real estate investment trusts (REITs), 242–244
settlement trusts, 216
specified investment flow-through (SIFT) trusts, 243, 244
taxation of, 253–254
testamentary trusts, 181, 202, 209, 211, 254, 266
21-year rule, 254
T4s, 262, 264–265
T5s, 262, 264–265
tuition fees, 58, 152–154
21-year rule, 254

U
undepreciated capital cost (UCC), 24, 223
uniforms, 56
United States
Canadian residents working in, 190
child support payments from, 127
Closer Connection Exemption Statement, 198–199
estate tax, 197–198
income from U.S. sources, 196–197
non-filer program, 194
ownership of registered savings plans, 195
real estate owned by Canadian residents, 195–196
residency regulations, 198–199
social security benefits, 195
spinoff transactions, 238
TFSA investments, 122
U.S. citizens resident in Canada, 193–195
U.S.-source self-employment income, 190
Universal Child Care Benefit (UCCB), 163
unreasonable allowance, 64
unused tax credits, 155–156

V
vehicles. *See* automobiles
voluntary disclosures, 276
volunteers, emergency, 169

W
wage-loss replacement plans, 36
wages. *See* salary
war veterans, 184
welfare payments, 184
wills, 205
withholding tax
directors and, 50
foreign tax credit, 255
income from U.S. sources, 197
interest payments, 83–84
investment income, 254–255
non-resident actors, 84
non-residents, 191–192
reduction of source withholdings, 270
RRSP withdrawals, 117
woodlot operation, 77
Workers' Compensation benefits, 184
Working Income Tax Benefit advance payments, 99
working income tax benefit (WITB), 158–159
write-off, 310

Y
year-end, 17, 307
Year's Maximum Pensionable Earnings, 119
Yukon, 285–286*t*, 291*t*